WHY I AM A SALAFI

WHY I AM A SALAFI

MICHAEL MUHAMMAD KNIGHT

SOFT SKULL PRESS
BERKELEY

Library of Congress Cataloging-in-Publication Data is available

ISBN 978-1-59376-606-1

Cover art by Rob Regis
Interior design by Megan Jones Design

SOFT SKULL PRESS
An imprint of COUNTERPOINT
2560 Ninth Street, Suite 318
Berkeley, CA 94710
www.softskull.com

Printed in the United States of America
Distributed by Publishers Group West

10 9 8 7 6 5 4 3 2 1

With love and peace to Azreal, pious predecessor

1948–2013

1

ISLAM FOR THE POST-APOCALYPSE

>>> What are you doing after the orgy? <<< —Jean Baudrillard[1]

I WAS ON THE edge of the desert when the drugs wore off, good-bye Muslim Gonzo. After several hours of dimethyltryptamine-powered inward pilgrimage, the crazy was gone by sunrise. The Mother Wheel had beamed me up screaming, but the beaming back to Earth came slow and easy, leaving me in happy dumb peace. Eyad and I rolled up our sleeping bags, shared good-byes with the people who had provided the medicine, and drove off their land, back to Los Angeles.

The medicine was ayahuasca, a hallucinogenic tea from the Amazon that had found its way into white New Age scenes and spiritual therapy culture. Ayahuasca's main ingredients consisted of a sacred vine that opened my body up to the dimethyltryptamine, and another plant that provided the dimethyltryptamine itself. Many Muslims would insist that drinking ayahuasca is not Islamically permissible, that its physical effects amount to either a state of prohibited intoxication or something like black magic. The concern from my sisters and brothers is reasonable: In ayahuasca world, the sublime devotions came with unspeakable transgressions that simultaneously denied and affirmed the words on Allāh's pages. Whether this pushed me out of Islam or drilled me straight into its deepest guts, I can't say, but that is an old problem of mystical experience.

Whether ḥalāl or ḥarām, I couldn't have experienced ayahuasca as anything other than a Muslim, embarking on an entirely Muslim trip. The chemical purging and healing found their expression through the symbolic language of Islam, or at least an archive of stories and reference points in my brain that I have catalogued as "Islam." In the car I told Eyad about some of the visions, not sure how it might strike his own Muslim sensibilities or if it was even the kind of thing that I should share with others. Within Islamic tradition, sages have often advised that we lock this kind of experience in our hearts, as the disclosure could harm our communities or even ourselves. I didn't mention every detail of the trip to Eyad; some of the visions were so far off the map that I needed time alone with them first, if only to ask what in my head could have made those visions possible.

It would have to come out sooner or later, because writing is my religion as much as anything. The full story went into *Tripping with Allah*, my Great American Muslim Drug Adventure. After the book came out, the *American Journal of Islamic Social Sciences* described my ayahuasca vision as a "frankly disturbing blending of erotic and religious imagery."[2] This pretty much fits.

Reclining the passenger seat all the way back, carried by Eyad's machine back to civilization, I not only felt gratitude for what had transpired (whether it had been a genuine mystical penetration or just an explosion of the right chemicals), but also had to smile at what seemed like a private joke between Creator and created. It was at the edge of the desert, far beyond the limits of proper Muslims, that my Islam looked anything like the Ḥaqq, the Absolute Reality. It was Out There, viewing the center from the outermost edge, that I found my sweetness for the center. For all the erotic disturbances and throw-stones-at-his-head levels of blasphemy, ayahuasca had put me in the right condition for visiting a mosque.

Fynd drove us to one of the big ones in the city. We made slow steps in, still feeling clumsy from what we had been through, and found the restrooms. Sitting on the wudhū bench in front of a faucet, I pulled off my socks and rolled up my pant legs and my sleeves and formalized the intention to myself. My mind wasn't exactly running at full capacity, but I wasn't "intoxicated" on any level that could have invalidated my prayers. Moving at about a third of my normal speed, I turned on the water and put my right hand under it, washing the hand up to the wrist three times. Then I washed my left hand three times. I scooped up water in my right hand, pushed it into my mouth, and immediately spit it out, three times. Then I brought a handful of water to my nose, sniffed the water in and then snorted it out, three times. Using both hands, I splashed water into my face and made sure that my entire face had been touched. Three times. Then I washed my arms up to the elbows, each three times, starting with the right arm, and wiped my wet hands once over my head. Three times, I wiped the inner and outer parts of my ears with my wet index fingers and thumbs. I wiped my wet hands over the back of my neck. The final act was to wash my feet up to the ankles, three times each, starting with the right.

I had no decoder ring that could tell me what secret messages were hiding within this performance. I washed for the immediacy of my washing itself, the secret knowledge that my arms and feet expressed no secret at all, being symbols of nothing beyond themselves. Even if the visions had expired hours ago, my brain remained wary of having to exert much effort. *Being* Muslim, *doing* Islam, worked in moments like this as procedural memory, like riding a bike. I didn't have to think about it. After washing, I sat, lingering on empty details such as the color of the tiles, the sensation of my arms dripping wet, my face still wet, my bare feet wet, the feeling of the floor. I could at least register the fact that I was now in a state of ritual purity, my body ready for prayer, and that I should guard myself against farting. Did I need to urinate? Briefly focusing attention on my anus and penis, I found no agitations. All systems go. After sitting there long enough to mostly drip-dry, I put my socks back on and stepped out of the restroom with my right foot first.

The prayer hall, the muṣalla, was constructed in such a way that walking through the door meant that my body already faced the direction of Mecca. I found a spot that felt right and made the intention to myself. Raising my hands to my ears entered me into the state of worship. *Allāhu Akbar*, I mouthed in silence, my gaze lowered to the spot on the floor that my forehead would touch.

Prayer was not only the private voicing of a conviction or wish to a transcendent mystery god outside myself, but an act of my body, a thing that my arms and legs and face *did*. Like the washing, this embodied act could not be reduced to a single meaning. I did it because I did it. My body performed the standing and bending and prostrating that

Muslim bodies were supposed to do, but I prayed without a theology beyond the post-dimethyltryptamine bliss. In this condition, religion had no chance of functioning as an organized package of truth claims. There were no rational arguments or efforts at scriptural legitimation and no institutions to provide them. I possessed nothing that Muslim scholars might recognize as a systematized 'aqīda, no coherent idea of Allāh that I could articulate to a community of believers. Perhaps the movements of my external form worked toward the achievement of an inner condition—my arms and legs and spine pulling the right triggers to produce meaning in my brain—or rather expressed a condition that was already there, a devotion that could never be captured in mere text. Either way, prayer after ayahuasca could be only bodywork. What I needed most was a prayer that I could touch and feel, a prayer of my face and hands on soft carpeted floors that might restore my grounding in the world.

During the standing position, I breathed in and with my exhalation recited short excerpts from the Qur'ān, which presents itself as a collection of statements from the Lord of All the Worlds. The recitation was silent, but I moved my mouth to make the words. Years ago, I had memorized the short excerpts for this ritual use. Programming the visual, auditory, and semiotic information into my brain, processing the words in my hippocampus and then consolidating and storing them in my neocortex, I made the Qur'ān part of myself, something that I retrieve from within myself to fulfill the act of prayer, my prayer as a repetition of something. At this point, were they words? My mouth moved, but my prayer's power was almost nonlinguistic, neither a speech to myself nor to the mystery god.

Twenty feet away from my prayer, an elderly woman was teaching the same short sūras to children, and their recitations of the Qur'ān's introductory sūra made it difficult to focus on my own. I did not know if the Allāh of my post-ayahuasca prayer matched up at all to the Allāh in this old woman's heart, or the Allāh whose words these children memorized; but apart from our inner secrets, we could at least have a shared Allāh through our movements and words in this space. Their loud recitations and my silent ones blended into each other. My prayer was spacey, taking much longer than normal, and I loved the stillness between positions. In the prayer's final seated position, after extending my index finger as a physical testimony to the oneness of Allāh, followed by testimony to the messengership of Muḥammad, I lingered for a *long* time, knowing that all it took for me to leave the state of prayer was to turn my face to the right and left and say the right formula.

Who received my prayer? The act was both theological and anti-theological, affirming an Allāh that I had to know but could never know, an Allāh whose throne rested above the heavens but who became knowable in the effects of my flesh. In ayahuasca world, Allāh had expressed himself through a form. In sober world, Allāh was not represented in statues or pictures or anything accessible through my bodily senses but still promised that he was closer to me than the vein in my neck. My body, the only means through which I could begin to comprehend anything, became my sign and proof. My body gave voice to an Allāh with no body, both in my recitation of Allāh's speech and my body's existence.

Ayahuasca, like the Qur'ān, both says and unsays. I testified to a big nothing with the vague sense that this nothing was somehow benevolent, that the nothing showed me love (after torture) during my holy drug quest. I named Muḥammad as the messenger who pointed me to the nothing, and through my testimony named myself in the Muslim family. Who was Muḥammad? Our invisible father that I would chase after forever, perhaps an idea of being human that I hoped to actualize with my movements and postures. Muḥammad was an experience that I sought in my skin. Muḥammad, whoever or whatever he was, had made a brief appearance in my ayahuasca visions, during which he seemed to undergo the same kind of psychic purging and healing that ayahuasca was supposed to give me. Maybe the healing that I witnessed in Muḥammad signified only what was happening in my own self. Tradition says that if you see Muḥammad in a dream or vision, you've really seen him, because devils cannot assume his form. My relationship to Muḥammad—that is, my imagination of Muḥammad—had always been complex, but ayahuasca cleaned him out, or rather cleaned my imagination of him, allowing the two of us to start over. Yearning for Muḥammad, who was dead and buried but existed everywhere as a set of bodily disciplines, I hoped that adherence to these practices could actualize Muḥammadness in my heart—producing first a conception of Muḥammad and then a better lover of Muḥammad in me.

After my return to the East Coast, I started attending congregational Friday prayers held by the Muslim Students Association (MSA) at the University of North Carolina in Chapel Hill. Sermons by college kids, engineering professors, and community uncles were fairly hit-or-miss, but there was more to our assembly than mere discourse or even conformity of belief. I did not interrogate the brothers and sisters in those congregations for their views on scriptural controversies.

Nor am I convinced that terms like *mainstream* or *orthodoxy* could hold much power to explain every participant's private beliefs: MSA kids don't tend to be theologians. On the other side, they knew nothing of the unacceptable offenses in my head. No one asks for your beliefs at the door. Whatever they/we believed about the fundamental nature of the universe, we could become intelligible Muslims to each other through physical gestures. Moving together in accordance with a shared script, our bodies performed/created a bond between us—and also between our congregation and a larger tradition, because we did not invent those movements. We had to inherit them from somewhere. In acting out the prayer, we followed the movements of Muḥammad's body, and the bodies of those who knew him, the people who followed him and loved him and struggled and sometimes drank the water from his ablutions.

This prayer acted as a kind of medicine for me. Following my long run of doctrinal offenses, transgressive actions, questionable affiliations, and drugs, it felt as if I had exhausted the possibilities. The condition of being a Muslim might require that some things be concretized and knowable as "Muslim." For all the internal breaks and cuts and chaos in my psychedelic visions of gushing blood and theophanic genitalia, I also loved the mosque as a house of predictable behaviors. Stumbling into a mosque while in a state of shock from my interstellar voyage, I still knew what to do and how to interact with my sisters and brothers. In a head like that, perhaps a tradition of practice could anchor me down, stabilizing what had been thrown to the winds.

Embodied practices are often dismissed as irrational and superstitious, and many would see it as a hallmark of post-Enlightenment modernity that good religion does not concern itself with the minutia of ritual performance. Good religion is supposed to focus on consciousness and intentionality; bad religion means marking truth on the body itself. Belief in the importance of the flesh is seen as a primitive worldview that must surrender to the light of abstract, disembodied reason. To have an apparent fixation on "correct" practice causes some Muslims to be ridiculed by their peers, but practice might have been what I needed. After the chemically informed cracking and resealing of my selfhood at the edge of the desert, I felt thankful that being Muslim gave my body a script to follow. Sometimes I prayed because I already believed in the script, but sometimes adherence to the script transformed me into someone who *could* believe in the script. The Islam that I needed was not intellectual, but operational. After coming down from ayahuasca, you realize that what you do might actually make you what you are.

With this rethinking of my Muslim body, my practice—and the roots of my practice, the predecessors from whom I inherited this technology of Muslim selfhood—began to matter to me in new ways, and I could reconsider the discipline of my brothers at the mosque who rolled up their pant legs because they wanted to imitate the Prophet, whose garments never passed his ankles. These brothers were also the ones who taught me to sit when I pissed because it had been the Prophet's way. Maybe they weren't so bad. A lifetime ago, I had a run as one of those guys, but I ditched it all to become the kind of Muslim who consumes psychoactive teas with Amazonian shamans. Muslims often speak of the pant leg–rollers as Salafī—a weapon to use against those who go too far; but what's a Salafī? Had I been one? After the drugs and visions and Supreme Mathematics, could I be one again? If drug mysticism had opened the door for a new Salafism, could my Salafī turn also be a mystical turn?

AS LONG AS YOU FEAR SOMEONE

"Don't Fear All Islamists, Fear Salafis," declares the headline of a *New York Times* editorial dated August 20, 2012. The piece defines Salafīs as "ultraconservative Sunni Muslims vying to define the new order [in this case, postrevolution Tunisia] according to seventh-century religious traditions rather than earthly realities."[3] Salafīs are not the same as jihadi militants, says the author, Robin Wright, and many Salafīs are antiviolence and politically quietist. But nonetheless, the Salafīs' goals remain "the most anti-Western of any Islamist parties."

When an article explicitly tells you in its headline to fear people, I feel confident in calling it an example of fearmongering.

"A common denominator among disparate Salafi groups is inspiration and support from Wahhabis, a puritanical strain of Sunni Islam from Saudi Arabia," Wright explains. She is careful to say that not all Salafīs are Wahhābīs, "but Wahhabis are basically all Salafis." For Wright, the issue is that Wahhābīs are seeking influence in Tunisia by supporting the Salafīs, "as they did 30 years ago by funding the South Asian madrassas that produced Afghanistan's Taliban." But at no point does she establish what exactly separates non-Wahhābī Salafīs ("ultraconservative Sunni Muslims") from Wahhābī Salafism ("a puritanical strain of Sunni Islam"). The matter is further complicated in Wright's conclusion, in which she warns, "There is something dreadfully wrong with tying America's future position in the region to the birthplace and bastion of Salafism and its warped vision of a new order."[4] The birthplace and bastion of Salafism, according to Wright's analysis, is Saudi Arabia, which also happens to be the birthplace and bastion of what she calls Wahhābism.

So Wright's major points are that Salafism should not be conflated with the broader category of Islamism, not all Salafīs are violent, and not all Salafīs are Wahhābīs, but because all Wahhābīs are Salafīs, and Salafīs are supported and inspired by Wahhābīs, and Salafism originated in the land of Wahhābism, and well, shit, I guess Salafism *is* Wahhābism, we need to fear all Salafīs. Wright's editorial had me more confused about Salafīs than before I had read it. When it comes to the Salafiyya, this kind of thing happens a lot.

On top of these complications, we can add that self-identified Salafīs have disagreed with each other over who can rightfully claim the label, while some Muslims who might be categorized by others as "Salafīs" have argued that Muslims should not call themselves Salafī at all: They see the term as an aberration from what their "Salafism" actually represents. Similarly, the term *Wahhābism* is flawed beyond repair because it would be hard to find anyone calling himself or herself "Wahhābī"; this is a pejorative label that has been imposed on people by their opponents. Between these labels, scholar Khaled Abou El Fadl attempted to coin a third, *Salafabism*, to represent what he sees as "the Wahhabi co-optation of Salafism."[5] Because Salafism and Wahhābism are already somewhat hazy categories, I am not sure that pushing them together into a third artificial construct is all that helpful.

The New York Times has been talking about Wahhābīs since 1928, when it described them as "by nature a warlike people, who are constantly out for massacre and pillage in the name of Allah." It was "in the blood of all Bedouins, and particularly the Wahabi [*sic*]," the article explains, "not to respect any law or order, and to rob their neighbors, and even their compatriots."[6] Just four years later, however, the *Times* reported that Wahhābī rule had brought peace and stability to Arabia. The man who had been called the "Wahhabi King," Ibn Sa'ūd, is praised as "the greatest Arab of all time and certainly as one of the world's great men." The new Wahhābī state is compatible with modernity, as "the motor car has been admitted freely." Resultant social problems, such as an influx of chauffeurs from neighboring regions, "men for the most part without breeding or moral sense," are being addressed by the government.[7]

In contrast, the earliest reference to Salafīs as a distinct group in *The New York Times* appears only in 1979, after a group of armed men seized control of the Great Mosque in Mecca. The article states, "The takeover was in the name of the Salafiya [*sic*] movement," adding that Saudi royals knew of the Salafī movement's existence and that the royals belonged to a different group, the "conservative Wahabi sect in the Sunni Moslem branch." The article characterizes Salafīs by their call for a return to the ways of the Prophet and "their Moslem ancestors" and the banning of radio, television, and public employment of women. The Salafīs also called for the overthrow of the Saudi government for "what they termed its deviation from Islamic tradition" and hailed their leader as the Mahdī, based on apocalyptic traditions that are "not necessarily accepted by the majority of Sunni Moslems, including the Wahabis."[8] In its coverage of the Great Mosque standoff, the *Times* appears to identify the entirety of the Salafī movement as comprised of "nomads of the Otaiba tribe, who live in the desert northeast of Mecca."[9]

After 1979, there is not another mention of Salafīs in *The New York Times* until 2000, in an article on links between Yemeni radicals and Osama bin Laden. The article refers to "the militant form of Salafi Islam that has inspired many militant Islamic organizations."[10] The next discussion of Salafism appears in October 2001. After that, the Salafīs are referenced in at least one *Times* story every year, with the exception of 2008. The articles generally deal with Muslims murdering each other or Americans or threatening peace and freedom in various places. Business really picks up with the so-called Arab Spring, after which Salafīs are seen as preeminent forces of chaos and danger amid the newly destabilized politics of places like Tunisia and Egypt. In Libya after the fall of Gaddafi, Muslims bulldozed a Muslim shrine. The Muslims who performed the bulldozing are widely labeled as Salafī, while the Muslim body that had been entombed at the shrine is called a Ṣūfī.

On April 15, 2013, two pressure cooker bombs went off near the finish line of the Boston Marathon. The suspects were identified as two Chechen brothers. A *USA Today* column additionally marked the men as Salafīs, members of Sunnī Islam's "most radical sect." To provide some context, the writer states that "Salafi warriors swept across the Arabian Peninsula nearly a century ago, wreaking havoc in the name of the king of the new nation of Saudi Arab [*sic*]." The column's author, David A. Andelman, explains that Salafism is the "radical ideology" espoused by Al-Qaeda and "violent Chechen revolutionaries," whom he describes as "Salafis to the core."[11]

The Chechen freedom struggle is old, but this alleged Salafī core is new. Traditionally, fighters for Chechen independence were counted among the Muslims called Ṣūfīs. Sometime after the early 1990s, the resistance was taken over by Muslims who were called Salafīs and/or Wahhābīs. Then the Moscow-backed Chechen government took to promoting a revival of what it called Ṣūfism, apparently viewing Ṣūfism as the antidote to any potential for Islamically driven rebellion against the state. The government's prevailing assumptions seem to be that Salafism makes people angry and violent while Ṣūfism makes them happy and sleepy. Ṣūfism is perceived as opium for the masses in the classical Marxist sense, whereas Salafism is crystal meth.

The United States government has also constructed Salafism and Wahhābism as actual things (often interchangeable) and security threats. When "War on Terror" rhetoric needs to avoid making a blanket generalization about all Muslims, it simply generalizes against the subcategory of Salafīs/Wahhābīs.[12] In discourse pitting reformed "good" Muslims against extremist "bad" Muslims, terms like *Salafī* and *Wahhābī* serve to mark the bad ones. Salafism has been paradoxically marked as both the Islam of radical uprisings against states and the Islam of state-supported "Allāh says to obey your rulers" quietism, with its goals described as both actively waging conflict against the enemies of Islam and withdrawing from politics to purify Muslim beliefs and practices. For many Muslims and non-Muslims alike, *Salafī* or *Wahhābī* can describe any expression of Sunnism that seems archaic, legally and ritually rigid, scripturally literalist, ultraconservative on gender issues, intolerant of the diversity of beliefs and practices within Muslim communities, and the usual suspects whenever something blows up. Even for Muslims who can look past the irresponsible reportage that tags all Salafīs as would-be terrorists, the Salafiyya are often condemned as the villains in a global "war for the soul of Islam," in which the fate of not only Muslims but also the "free world," "Western civilization," etc. hangs in the balance. From this perspective, there's no reason to look closer at the Salafīs or try to examine their ideas, because clearly they're just antirational, antimodern, antihuman fundamentalists who don't deserve the time of day from us. Do they even *have* ideas to be examined?

BORDER PATROLS

Looking back on Islam as I had understood it way, *way* before my chemical turn, I remember concepts and attitudes for which I now consider my teen years to have been my "Salafī phase." This is somewhat a projection of my current awareness onto my past. In *Blue-Eyed Devil*, I discuss my youthful "Salafi fear of masturbating" and refusal to look at girls in my "Wahhab days," but there was nothing distinctly Salafī or Wahhābī about it. Thinking of my past as "Salafi," my grown-man self decides the categories into which my teen self should be placed, against which my teen self remains helpless, unable to offer a defense. My past cannot speak, so my present speaks for it. Anyway, at the time that I might have been a Salafī or Wahhābī, I did not know these terms. For me, it was just Islam.

I had become Muslim during the first half of the 1990s, a time in which the resurgent legacy of Malcolm X and the Nation of Islam—revived through Spike Lee's Malcolm biopic, Louis Farrakhan's Million Man March, and a flood of politically engaged hip-hop following the Reagan era's destruction of America's inner cities—intersected with Saudi-sponsored propagation efforts and flourishing Salafī hubs in the major urban centers of the northeast. My Islam was an effect of that collision. I converted after reading Malcolm X's *Autobiography* and literature that traveled through Saudi networks, such as Hammudah Abd al-Ati's *Islam in Focus*. It was in the Malcolm mythology that I first tasted the pursuit of religious truth as a quest for lost origins: Malcolm found himself as a Muslim in part through exposing Christian tradition as a willful distortion and manipulation of Christ's true teachings and his real identity. In the second of Malcolm's two Muslim conversions, he rediscovered his humanity by abandoning the Nation and jumping into the center of what he regarded as Islamic universalism. *Islam in Focus* gave me a concretized, bullet-pointed Islam of bodily disciplines, appeals to rationalism, and blueprints for an ideal society that resonated in complete harmony with the Islam that I had read in Malcolm. Incidentally, *Islam in Focus* was also the book that inspired the conversion of prominent American imām Zaid Shakir.[13]

The first time that I read the Qur'ān, it was a Saudi-networked reprint of Yusuf Ali's translation, in which editors had purged Ali's extensive commentary of ideas that they found unacceptable. From there I moved to the seminal Qur'ānic commentary of Sayyid Qutb, the Muslim Brotherhood ideologue who was hung by the Egyptian government one year after Malcolm's assassination. Somewhere in my readings or initial encounters with Muslims, I learned to avoid self-identification as a "convert," preferring to call myself a "revert"; I had not changed to something new, but had *reverted* to my original self. Islam had been my condition in the womb, my natural state prior to the interference of culture.

Ideas and practices can dig tunnels under the borders, and not every Sunnī who expresses a Salafī-influenced thought would necessarily identify that thought (or herself/himself) as "Salafī." I would never impose the *Salafī* label on the mosque at which I formally converted (the Islamic Center of Rochester, New York) or its leadership, but through my experience there, I encountered claims and attitudes that appear in Salafī flows of communication. The imām who witnessed my conversion and became my dearly loved mentor was criticized by some as more philosopher than imām, but he had also been a student of Ismā'īl al-Farūqī (1921–1986), a tremendously important scholar who often gets tagged as "Salafī" and/or "Wahhābī." I came to regard al-Farūqī as part of my Muslim genealogy but had no awareness of the intellectual currents that produced him. Because the books and pamphlets that fell into my hands did not clearly mark themselves as Salafī, and the well-intentioned mosque uncles who shared stories and advice with this young revert did not present their own views as Salafī, it can sometimes become hard to say where Salafism begins and ends, or whether *Salafism* is even a useful term to explain anything. This is not to play into a particular Islamophobia, specifically a Salafophobia, in which Salafī and/or Wahhābī Muslims are portrayed as a sinister fifth column that has clandestinely injected its poison into American Muslim communities. I am not interested in the conspiracy theorists who claim that 80 percent of US mosques have fallen under Wahhābī influence, nor the self-appointed voices of moderation who would marginalize Salafism by saying that it accounts for only 3 percent of Sunnīs. Salafism is not an empirically measurable quantity.

At seventeen years old, I bailed from Catholic high school to study at Faisal Mosque in Islamabad, which was named for the Saudi king who had built it as a gift for the people of Pakistan. The mosque's educational programs similarly bore the stamp of Saudi power; perhaps it was Saudi money that paid for my plane ticket. Honestly, I don't remember much of what I learned at Faisal Mosque, apart from a certain hegemonic Sunnism that wouldn't have to be "Salafī" to achieve what it did for me. While I cherished the experience of life in a Muslim-majority country, I also walked the streets of Islamabad with a guiding assumption that not everything in front of me reflected "true" Islam—that most Muslims around the world had actually diluted their religious practice with culture and innovation, and that I possessed sufficient scriptural knowledge to locate their points of departure from what God had given to the Prophet.

While at Faisal Mosque, I briefly hoped to ditch my studies and join the Chechen resistance against their Russian oppressors, but my mentors talked me out of it. I could do more good for Islam as a writer, they said, reminding me that Muḥammad had regarded the ink of scholars as holier than the blood of martyrs. Someone back then might have called me a Salafī or a Wahhābī, though this has less to do with violence (how one feels about armed struggle is not a reliable measure of Salafī- or Wahhābī-ness) than my understanding of history and the claims that I was willing to make. So I went back home, carrying an encyclopedia-size collection of ḥadīth volumes on my back, and graduated from high school. At eighteen, I was living in Pittsburgh and spending nights at a mosque that I'd later learn was the city's "hotbed of Salafism." During my alleged Salafī years, I did hear my mentors in Pittsburgh and Pakistan emphasize the primacy of the salaf as-salih, the "pious predecessors," but had no idea that this vocabulary might signify its speaker within a particular communal affiliation. The people around me who stressed that I needed to follow the Salaf believed that the most authentic expression of Islam—in fact the only vision of Islam with any legitimacy whatsoever, the only thing that could be called "Islam" at all—was that of the earliest Muslims. Being a Muslim meant that you committed yourself to following what the Prophet taught to his companions. If you couldn't make that claim for yourself and stand by it, you stood outside the dīn. I came to wager my religion on the unassailable integrity of Muḥammad's most immediate heirs: his companions and the generation directly following them and, in turn, the generation after them. These three generations, according to reported statements of the Prophet, were the greatest human beings that this planet would ever see. After their Golden Age, humanity fell into a rapid decline and never stopped.

What I call my Salafī phase ended badly, in part because of my disillusionment with the Golden Age. Every Golden Age is imagined by people who come long after that age and is made possible only by editing, erasing, rewriting, and creatively interpreting communal memory. Many Sunnī Muslims insist that belief in the Muslim community's first four rulers after Muḥammad as "rightly guided caliphs" remains an inviolable article of faith. To deny this concept would disqualify one as a Sunnī (and, for some Sunnīs, being a non-Sunnī would also mean being a non-Muslim); but "rightly guided caliphs" represents a later judgment, which the men who have been assigned this title had never claimed for themselves. The title is an act of rehabilitative nostalgia, created after the point at which right guidance seemed to go south, a longing for what appears—when viewed from a distance, with vision blurred by time—to have been an era of innocence and perfect unity.

Golden Ages are sanitized imaginaries of messy realities and generally fail to survive closer scrutiny. When I started to ask the wrong questions and Islam's sacred past became more complicated for me—that is, when I learned that my authoritative heroes fought and killed each other in civil wars—the whole edifice came crashing down. The myth of seamless unity among the earliest Muslims collapses pretty easily, and I couldn't hold up the notion of Islam's "greatest generations" when these people chopped up the body of Muḥammad's own grandson in the desert of Karbala.

For me as a teenager, everything had been based on the collective perfection of the Salaf. The tradition was what they gave us; if we could doubt them, what was left of Islam? Losing my faith in the Salaf felt like losing myself as a Muslim. To some extent, it meant losing Muḥammad, who was unknowable to me except through the mediation of those who had walked with him. Dismantling the myth of a long-lost Golden Age led me to question the image of Muḥammad that had been transmitted to us from that generation. I had previously believed in the apologetic boasts that Muḥammad's life had been more thoroughly recorded than that of any historical figure prior to modernity—we knew how he cleaned his teeth, how he stood and sat and ate, and so on—but I lost my confidence in the people who told me these things. The truth-making power of Muḥammad's life disintegrated.

In the winter of 2002, as I worked on my first novel, *The Taqwacores*, I had no confidence in my claim to be Muslim, in part because as far as I knew, there was no Muslim community that would have me. The fictional punk house in the story functioned as a kind of mosque for its residents, but a mosque with no imām, which meant that each individual had to become authoritative for his or her own self. This was the Islam of my fantasy, but I did not have faith that it could be real until distributing the book led me to encounters with real-life Muslim punk kids. The notion of a "taqwacore" community signified different things to each of us. One of taqwacore's appeals for me was its dream that we could make a Muslim community for ourselves without acting as coercive regulatory powers upon each other.

Since I had imagined myself as living in self-imposed exile from a vaguely defined blob of homogenous "orthodoxy," my comfort came through celebration of the equally slippery term, *heresy*. Rereading the sacred past as one of fracture and chaos rather than unblemished unity, I championed a positive relationship to all Muslim expressions deemed unacceptable. Instead of treating Islam as a zero-sum game, demanding that all of us are either in or out, I imagined a new binary: the Islam of the center versus an Islam of the margins. If Muḥammad's grandson was butchered by the Islam of power and authority, the only conceivable Islam for me would be an Islam that lived on the outside, far from the polished institutions and acceptable Friday-afternoon imāms. It became my quest to engage those corners of Islamic tradition that most Muslims would dismiss as absurd or dangerous. It turned out that Islam offered a rich legacy of rebel saints and charismatic weirdos, a long parade of Muslims who were called infidels by their fellow Muslims. Their presence in Islam's archive changed what the archive could tell me.

With recognition that something had gone terribly wrong in the Golden Age and the Salaf's imaginary unity, I maintained my attachment to Shī'ism, especially the story of Ḥusayn. While Salafīs have composed vicious polemical tracts against Shī'ism, charging that Shī'īs have transgressed the bounds of proper Islam, I dipped heavy not only into Shī'ism, but the expressions of Shī'ism that even the majority of Shī'īs would condemn—the radical so-called ghulat, "exaggerators," groups from long ago that had elevated members of Muḥammad's family to levels approaching prophethood or even divinity. My alternative Islam also came from people like ninth-century ecstatic Mansūr al-Ḥallāj, who allegedly called himself by God's Name and was executed for building his own Ka'ba in his yard. Retreating from the established voices of Islam's imaginary center, I found comfort in obscure characters who often amounted to only historical footnotes. One was Muḥammad al-Zawāwī (d. 1477), a North African visionary who left behind a vivid diary of his dream encounters with the Prophet, including their arguments over what ethnicity of concubine al-Zawāwī should purchase (al-Zawāwī wanted a Turkish concubine, but his imaginal Muḥammad suggested Ethiopian), and even a vision in which the Prophet personally breastfed him from his left teat, the one closest to his heart.[14] Though al-Zawāwī's motive for writing his dreambook was "first and foremost an insatiable quest for recognition," according to scholar Jonathan G. Katz, the quest failed: Al-Zawāwī became a "failed saint," more or less forgotten.[15] It was partly *because* of al-Zawāwī's failed-saint status that he appealed to me; I dreamed of an Islam written by the losers, an Islam of rejected possibilities and subaltern voices.

On the advice of Malcolm X's grandson, I picked up Ahmet Karamustafa's *God's Unruly Friends*, a discussion of tattooed and pierced dervishes from the Ottoman Empire who abandoned religious laws, smoked hashish, spread ashes across their naked bodies, begged for food, and said dangerous things about God. I also joined an Iranian Ṣūfī order, the Nimatullahis, which had been founded in the fourteenth century as a Sunnī order, reoriented itself as a Shī'ī order following Iran's Shī'ī turn in the Safavid period, and largely dropped any self-identification as "Muslim" after the 1979 revolution. "We don't advocate reading Qur'ān here," a Nimatullahi shaykh told me.

Exploring America's unique Muslim heritages, I looked beyond the standard narratives of Sunnī triumphalism that had moved me as a teenager—i.e., *Malcolm X was duped into following a charlatan cult leader until he went to Mecca and discovered genuine Islam*—to consider the teachings and mission of the Honorable Elijah Muhammad in a serious way. This led to my encountering the Five Percenter community, which had originated in 1960s Harlem with what a vast majority of Muslims would consider the most outrageous offense possible: a man naming himself Allāh. Seeing themselves as their own gods, the Five Percenters lived Islam as they personally saw fit; there were no imāms or shaykhs or 'ulama who could tell them anything. Clerics could never offer genuine transcendence: No matter how many verses they had memorized, the invisible "mystery god" for whom they claimed to speak remained invisible. Mastery of a textual tradition brought no one closer to transcendent knowledge; for Five Percenters, this made the business of religious authority a con game, because the scholars cannot claim to possess anything that you don't already have inherent within yourself. That idea nourished me for a long time, placing the Qur'ān and Muslim traditions, along with full power to determine their meanings and value, in my own hands.

Because the Five Percenter movement was young enough for me to become a student of men who had walked with that first Allāh from the '60s, I often imagined the culture with parallels to the seventh-century community of Muḥammad and his Companions. Inheriting a legacy from the first Five Percenter generation, I could be classified within the Five Percenter tradition's equivalent of what Sunnīs call the Tābi'ūn, the Followers. The righteous name that I was given reflects this inheritance: My primary teacher had been named by the first Allāh himself, and Azreal in turn named me Azreal Wisdom, which meant "Azreal No. 2" in Five Percenter vocabulary. Traveling in a young tradition, I witnessed competing memories, power struggles, and a narrowing field of possibility as debate was suppressed, and reinterpretations and innovations found themselves projected backward upon the authority of foundational figures. Similar to the constructions of orthodoxy in broader Muslim traditions, Five Percenters imagined their tradition to have emerged fully formed and coherent in an instant "Big Bang" moment, rather than having taken shape over time as a historical process. In my engagement of Five Percenter tradition, guided by the elders who taught me, I made my own choices about which texts and historical personalities I would treat as authoritative.

I also experienced community with the new phenomenon of "progressive Muslims" who sought gender-egalitarian modes of understanding the Qur'ān and reforming Muslim practice. When Amina Wadud shocked the world with her intergender Friday prayer service, I was there. One of the prayer's organizers, journalist Asra Nomani, had even named my novel *The Taqwacores*, which had depicted a woman leading men in prayer, as an inspiration for the event.[16] Within the progressive scene, which many Muslims would describe as a heretical movement in its own right, I encountered a Muslim forum in which I could speak openly and honestly about my inner conditions without fear of judgment or exile. Though the label *progressive*, like *Salafī*, covered a wide ground and signified a diverse range of priorities, I could find people in the progressive scene who did not define their community by shared faith convictions; for them, a Muslim was anyone who called herself or himself a Muslim, regardless of what the term *Muslim* meant to that individual. This allowed space not only for Sunnīs, Shī'īs, and members of other communities to come together, but also for believing Muslims to accept their brother/sisterhood with "cultural" or "secular" Muslims who did not necessarily believe in Islam's supernatural components, but still maintained an attachment to their Muslim heritage. In this hodge-podge of Muslims who felt like exiles for any number of reasons, the singular shared value was acceptance.

The terrains of my pro-heresy Islam, like those of the "orthodoxy" against which it defined itself, were always shifting. Inhabiting a borderless, deconstructed Islam that could never demand its own reconstruction, I made no claim of consistency in my sources or methods beyond a romance of the marginal. Each of these movements and figures contributed ingredients toward my own sense of what it meant to be Muslim, even when they opposed and contradicted each other. Unfortunately for my personal project, these contributors to my borderless, pro-heresy Islam were just as eager as the powers of "orthodoxy" to impose their own limits and push people out. To some Five Percenters, I remained too much of an "orthodox" Muslim to qualify for full membership; to others, my advocacy of a queer-positive Islam violated boundaries that they regarded as nonnegotiable. Meanwhile, the progressive Muslim scene as I experienced it was fairly bourgeois, frequently blind to issues of race and class, and not much interested in what groups like the Five Percenters had to say. I loved the sum of people who were tagged as heretics in part *because* they were tagged as heretics, but this did not mean that they could harmoniously merge together into a coherent countermonolith. The only thing that my teachers shared in common, at least as I engaged them, was resistance to an overwhelming matrix of "orthodox" Sunnī hegemony. By mocking and negating that power, they changed the rules of what was thinkable to me as "Islamic" and what kinds of possibilities awaited me outside the bounds of popular Muslim recognition. They provided me with new spaces to claim my own self as a righteous *Muslim* self. Perhaps all that I really wanted was a queering of Sunnism.

This borderless Islam could not have existed without borders of its own. I had defined it purely in opposition to its ultimate Other, which was represented best by what I naively tagged in terms of nation-states ("Saudi Islam") or ethnocentrism ("Arab Islam"). Progressive Muslims, Shī'īs and Ṣūfīs of various strands, Five Percenters, and taqwacore kids might have had nothing in common beyond a mutual distaste for Salafism: They could share only in an artificial unity that Salafism imposed on them from outside. But if I sought value from every corner of our vast tradition, why couldn't I approach the Salafiyya? Did they have nothing to say? Did they expose the limits of my own happy Muslim pluralism?

The consequence of my pro-heresy Islam, in which I theoretically accepted all kinds of competing interpretations and communities as equally "Islamic," was that *none* of them could have what they claimed for themselves. Each marginalized community had to share space with every other marginalized community. Because many of these discourses did in fact make exclusivist and authoritarian claims, embracing all visions of Islam ironically meant that I denied them. What if, instead of making my own mutant blend with ingredients from everyone, I just discarded all accumulated interpretation and drilled straight into the core? This is where the Salafī project, even if that project is doomed before it starts, pulls me in.

I'd love to find my own Salafism, but this isn't simply a radical turn away from the pro-heresy model, at least not in the way that you might expect. Just remember that the terms *orthodoxy* and *heresy* fail to meaningfully signify anything beyond the relations of power between competing groups, and consider the 2011 *Boston Globe* article on white convert imām Suhaib Webb. Journalist Omar Sacirbey (the same writer, by the way, who first broke "Muslim punk rock" as a national story and thus opened the floodgates for several years of awful media mythmaking) mentions the Salafiyya in passing as a tag of blame, a dangerous charge that has been hurled at Webb by his opponents. A critic accused Webb of affiliation with the "hard-line Salafī sect of Islam"; Webb, in response, "denied being a Salafī disciple and said he follows the Maliki Islamic school."[17] Without any examination of what it means to follow one or the other, the article leads us to assume that Malikis must be better than Salafīs, and then clears Webb's name of links to the undesirable latter. *The New York Times* gives a similar treatment to Yasir Qadhi, emphasizing that he sparked controversy among Salafīs for adopting a "more moderate message" while adding that he shows respect for Ṣūfīs, a "mystical branch of Islam that Salafis have traditionally denounced."[18] Perhaps the most telling moment in the article comes when the *Times* describes Qadhi's platform, the AlMaghrib Institute, as representing "an ultra-conservative movement known as Salafiya," adding that Qadhi has embarked on repackaging the institute as "orthodox with a capital O."[19] For Qadhi to find play as a fully "mainstream" Muslim leader, he had to steer his brand away from the stigma of the Salafī brand. What I've learned here: Despite our assumptions of what it means to be "orthodox" and "conservative," Salafism isn't simply "ultra-orthodox" but might ironically be the biggest heresy in town, the most problematic and marginalized affiliation available. If it has been my job description over the past decade to take seriously groups and thinkers who are almost never taken seriously, I need to look at the despised and ridiculed Salafiyya.

As Salafīs claim to represent the elite "saved sect" and argue that the majority of Muslims have gotten Islam wrong—that the legal schools and Ṣūfī orders and classical theologians and modern reformers and everyone else at best represent fallible human efforts, but also threaten to compromise, neglect, distort, or erase what the Prophet had given us—they actually push themselves beyond what most people might call Islamic "orthodoxy." At least in their impossible promise, the Salafiyya rejects everything except the Qur'ān and the prophetic Sunna as unacceptable innovation. When they take it this far, Salafīs have to be the ultimate heretics, the rebels who reject any compromise to norms that they cannot respect. Salafism is certainly a marginalized heresy for many of the Muslim circles in which I run and the most antiestablishment vision of Islam within my reach—relative, of course, to which establishment we're talking about, and also which variety of Salafism. When I wrote critically of Muslims for Progressive Values (MPV) and its leader, Ani Zonneveld, she blasted me with what must have struck her as an all-time unanswerable burn: "Michael Muhammad Knight . . . you are no better than the Salafis in the mosques." Depending on whom you want to irritate, Salafism could look like the new punk rock.

This became clear when I started writing a weekly column for *VICE* and took on popular Muslim voices with the argument that what they presented as timeless, universal Islam was just their personal construction, formulated within the limiting fishbowl of their own time and place. When a white convert Muslim chaplain at a university gave a Friday sermon about the "Islamic perspective" on sexuality, I offered the criticism that what he presented as a transhistorically Islamic position was entirely informed by contemporary and somewhat liberalized Western Protestant notions of heteronormative monogamous marriage. It worked for his audience, which consisted of university kids who were not likely to participate in plural marriage, let alone concubinage, and who believed that "Islam" fundamentally empowered everyone—men and women alike—as autonomous individual subjects. That's an appealing construction of Islam for the Muslim Students' Association of wherever this sermon was given, but it's not *the* Islam, if *the* Islam is supposed to be consistent across time and space: It's not an "Islamic sexuality" that people could have understood fourteen hundred years ago. My commentary on the sermon, after I sat back and read it a few times, seemed to operate on a kind of Salafī logic: I had basically argued that the sermon made a conflation of personal opinion with Islam and could not scripturally defend itself with our agreed-upon "authentic sources."

Conservatives can dismiss progressives as producing an Islam defined by "Western" values, but they often play by the same rules. There's a particular kind of male convert that I have in mind here, a man who fails to recognize misogyny as a deeply embedded *American* norm. Growing up in *American* patriarchy, he ingests old-fashioned *American* heterosexism and male privilege, later becomes Muslim, and then projects his culturally learned *American* antifeminism onto his newfound religious identity. Pretending that he has transcended American culture (a culture that he strangely perceives as having been overrun with radical feminists and queers who impose their hegemony on everyone), he claims to defend the Timeless Tradition of the Brown World against those who wish to dilute it with secular Western theories and methods. He picks up enough of those theories and methods and critical vocabularies to deconstruct his opponents' assumptions of universal truth and the flows of power that produce them but never turns that weapon upon his own prejudices and assumptions. As his principled heterosexism names the points at which Islam's integrity is most threatened, he rewrites American patriarchy in Timeless

Tradition's vocabulary and presents it as counterculture, a resistance against Euro-American global domination. You can either care about fighting gender inequality and homophobia, he says, *or* you can value the preservation of Islam against Western knowledge regimes. He condemns the colonization of Islam by Western neoliberals but has no fear of the same work by Western neotraditionalists, and he ironically uses anticolonial arguments to silence the voices of brown women. *It's not me*, he swears, *it's just what the Tradition says*. For his big finishing move, he justifies an arrogant and authoritarian view of the Tradition by reminding you how meek and humble its great scholars were. Watch out for these boys. They were sexists and homophobes before they ever heard of the Prophet.

Writing on popular shaykh (and another white convert) Hamza Yusuf, I discussed Yusuf's articulation of "classical Islamic tradition" as part of his carefully sculpted brand. What Yusuf offered, my piece suggested, was not reducible to "classical" or "traditional" Islam, but represented Yusuf's own scholarly imagination. I might have been issuing these critiques from my own position as pro-queer, pro-heresy, Shī'ī Nimatullahi Five Percenter consumer of hallucinogens, but my articles still challenged so-called mainstream Sunnī leaders on their own attempts to speak for the pure and real. Deconstruction had become my fundamentalism.

The move of Salafī deconstruction is unstoppable, because once you realize the critical problems of reading texts and reproducing the past and all that, then you surrender any hope for retrieving a "true" Islam that's based objectively on "what the book says." You no longer get to dismiss your rivals with the naive critique "That's not *religion*, it's *culture*," because you can't claim to have stepped out of "culture" yourself. A deconstructive read of the Salaf does not throw us into a fantasmic Golden Age of unblemished hegemony and absolute coherence but instead opens us to more fracture and disunity. Salafism is not simply antimodern as so often imagined but potentially *post*modern, shutting down empty promises of essences and universals, giving cynical smirks to the supposed light of human reason, and revealing all opponents to be squarely situated within the specific contexts and modern regimes of sense that made them possible.

The problem, then, wouldn't be that I'm too permissive with my religion, or too confident in bending and twisting the texts to make them say exactly what I want them to say. It's that *they* are—the superstar imāms and shaykhs and scholars who feed their communities an easily digestible product that they call "Islam" because neither they nor their communities want anything too complicated. Despite all their big talk about preserving or reviving "tradition," they must also take liberties with it.

Five Percenter lessons ask the question, "To make devil, what must one first do?" The lessons' answer: "To make devil, one must begin grafting from the original." For Salafism as I read it, *everything* is grafted, diluted, and corrupt. Every method is doomed. There's something potentially liberatory in the assertion that Islam as we have received it, an Islam that has taken centuries of elaboration and systematization and generations of brilliant minds to develop, represents a pollution of the pure. The great schools and methodologies offer the helpful work of humans, but if we had to, we could survive without them. A foundational intellect like al-Ghazālī was not the Prophet

Muḥammad, nor was he a companion of the Prophet or someone who had known a companion; he lived centuries too late to even know someone who had known someone who had known a companion. Al-Ghazālī represents the "essence" of Islam only if we regard Islam as something that starts *post*-Ghazālī. Ripping away the elaborations, Salafism stands to unsettle communities, which can be alternately dangerous or useful. A theoretically savvy Salafiyya—if ingesting modern critical theory didn't betray the whole point of being Salafī—could subvert the dominant narratives, tear down established norms, turn power relations upside down, and open up new possibilities. The Five Percenters had me asserting full agency over the text, creating its meaning for myself: Salafism has me doing away with interpretation, which could lead not to simple "literalism" or "fundamentalism" but to another agency altogether.

The Salafiyya look to the pristine origins as a means of anchoring and centering Islam, but what if I get the opposite result? Every interpretation, subject to the limits of interpretation, risks promoting the inauthentic. But inauthentic compared to what? When I call out others for their problematic readings, is it because I still cling to this idea that a greater authenticity awaits us out there? Where is this perfect Islam against which I measure all imperfect simulations? Without faith in the way of the Salaf as a reachable finish line, my Salafism trolls everyone, becoming the big *No* to all claims of apprehending the truth of the Qur'ān or the earliest Muslims; but this Salafī *No* comes with a price. My Salafism diagnoses the problem but gives no cure, because Salafism cannot survive its own critique. There's more than one way to bulldoze a shrine. If *everything* is bida', this includes the Salafiyya themselves, along with the premodern heroes whom they glorify as defenders of the real. Though I'd love to return to the origins of my tradition and dig up the uncorrupted Islam of the Salaf, I have to ask whether this is even possible, which means facing the consequences when such a project falls apart and I end up with nothing. Whether we denounce the tradition's diversity or speak of Islam in the plural and accept all "Islams" as equally valid, we sacrifice the potential for an absolute, pure-in-itself Islam.

"Straight to the sources," everyone says, even anti-Salafīs who produce their own ironic mirrors of Salafism. What are these sources, and how does one return "straight" to them? Can a Qur'ān website—offering multiple translations, a searchable concordance of Arabic roots, annotations of every verse with displays of the Arabic grammar, syntax, and morphology, and audio recordings of recitation—reproduce the original Islam of fifteen centuries ago? Or perhaps the original Islam awaits me in online archives of Salafī articles in PDF format? I am not sitting at the feet of a scholar to experience traditional transmission of knowledge, but some Salafīs would scroll through pristine Tradition with a cursor in the shape of a white-gloved cartoon hand.

Operating instead as a tool of alienation and negation, Salafism can perform the same destabilizing work as my pro-heresy pluralism; Salafism threatens to erase every Muslim imaginary, including mine, and then its own. If we issue Salafī critiques but confess to mediation as an inescapable fact of our lives as readers, *Salafism* then becomes as empty a signifier as *Islam* itself. In its power to deny every truth claim, Salafism ironically denies its own privilege to name the rules.

While engaging the modern phenomenon of Salafism does not instantly bring me face-to-face with the Prophet and his generation, it at least returns me to *my* origins, recovering the history that shaped me as a particular kind of Muslim. I didn't simply convert to Islam, but rather the version of Islam that could come together from the books, pamphlets, and lecture tapes that people threw at me in the 1990s. I didn't just go to Pakistan, but a particular version of Pakistan, imagined and produced by the people and institutions who brought me there and walked me through it

These white convert dudes who end up as figures in the public personality game tend to authorize themselves through overseas travel. Hamza Yusuf found his cred in the North African desert, coming home with a white-man Orientalist narrative of having learned at the feet of what he calls "living fossils" who exist "almost halfway in the dream world," custodians of a capitalized "Tradition" beyond time and space.[20] Suhaib Webb studied at Cairo's al-Azhar, the widely recognized center of globalized "traditional" Sunnī knowledge production (which, incidentally, was founded by Ismā'īlīs). Perhaps ditching high school for a brief study hermitage in South Asia (popularly viewed as lacking the authenticity cred of the Middle East), only to end up at extremes of the inauthentic—the black gods, punk rock kids, feminist imāms, and drinkers of psychoactive brews—I became an ugly failed shadow of the shining white-boy-shaykh archetype.[21]

There are tensions in my Islam that have haunted me through much of the two decades that I have been making and remaking myself as a Muslim; I want to call them Salafī tensions. As a teenager calling myself a "revert," I might have been a Salafī. But when

I called myself an ex-Muslim or pro-heresy Muslim or simply a bad Muslim, it was also as a Salafī, because my estrangement from Islam and pushback against whatever I imagined as normative was only a response to my Salafism. Reading my past work, I can find myself reacting to "orthodox Islam" and treating it as a unit of analysis as though orthodoxy is actually a thing that exists in the world. Whether I tagged myself as believer or apostate or heretic, Salafism decided the rules and named these positions. If I am not a Salafī, I was still made by Salafīs. Whether or not I should be counted among the Salafiyya, I am growing to appreciate that the Salafiyya will always be part of me, even after all my wackadoo mischief.

With bismillāh and a word of thanks to the dimethyltryptamine, here we go.

2

RETURN TO PAMPHLET ISLAM

>>> The country of the tourist pamphlet always is another country, an embarrassing abstraction of the desirable that, thank God, does not exist on this planet, where there are always ants and bad smells and empty Coca-Cola bottles to keep the grubby finger-print of reality upon the beautiful. <<< —**Nadine Gordimer**[1]

THE TRUTH STANDS clear from error, the Qur'ān tells me, and one of the dominant themes of what I called "Islam" in my teen years was Islam's awesome clarity. The message presented itself as so simple that it could fit inside a pamphlet with large font and bullet points. For me to reconsider my teen Salafism, I'd have to reconsider what Omid Safi has called "pamphlet Islam": an Islam forged in the "serious intellectual and spiritual fallacy of thinking that complex issues can be handled in four or six glossy pages."[2] These expressions of "pamphlet Islam," readily available at almost any Islamic center, bear titles such as "The Status of Women in Islam" or "The Islamic Position on Jesus"[3] and thus rely on the assumptions that (1) there is such a possibility as a definitive "Islamic position" on anything, and (2) the author has the "Islamic position" on an issue nailed down firmly under his/her control, with no room for it to move.

The term *fundamentalist* as popularly used in conversations about religion was inspired by Christian pamphlets. In the second decade of the twentieth century, the Bible Institute of Los Angeles disseminated its pamphlet series, *The Fundamentals*, with the intention to "provide intellectually sound, popularly accessible defense of the Christian faith."[4] In this context, to be a fundamentalist wasn't a bad thing: It meant that one upheld Christianity's "fundamentals" in the face of Darwinism, modern literary theories and biblical criticism, and liberalized churches that denied the Bible's literal inerrancy. *The Fundamentals* sought to prove in pamphlets' limited space that the Bible represented historically and scientifically unassailable fact, that it was only through loyalty to the Bible's literal truth that one could ground an unchanging Christianity against the unstable modern world.

Safi argues that we can and must do better than "pamphlet Islam," and I agree, but I'm also afraid that our efforts might only produce bigger pamphlets. Progressive Muslim reformism, with all its performance of theoretical sophistication, sometimes makes for its own counterpamphlet that's no less simplistic. Anyway, a certain brand of pamphlet Islam is where I come from. Once I entered into a Muslim community, pamphlets became maps to show me the straight path. I also left Islam through the pamphlets; in the period that I considered myself an ex-Muslim, it was because the pamphlets' easy answers and imaginary hegemonies couldn't hold up to the complexities of being a Muslim in my real life. The pamphlets are meant to be read once and passed along; their arguments disintegrate if you spend too much time with them.

But there had to be a time when it was really that simple, right? Wouldn't a "pamphlet Islam" be closer to the original Islam, the Islam of our Prophet? The stuff that can't fit into a pamphlet amounts to later elaboration and refinement, which, if I'm trying to recover my Salafism, is unnecessary. Safi critiques the popular catchphrase that Islam's truth lies in its simplicity, but if I imagine what Islam would look like in the presence of the Prophet, an Islam in which people did not theorize on questions of authority and interpretation, it had to be simple. Perhaps in Muḥammad's lifetime, if you upheld him as center, you could really start a sentence with, "Islam says _______________." To deny Islam its supposed simplicity is to admit the hard truth that we are functionally a prophetless community, that we have no organic center. The pamphlets aim to assure us that Muḥammad's absence changes nothing.

At a Muslim Students' Association "Islam 101" event intended to teach non-Muslim students about Islam, I sat and listened to a woman correct the audience on popular misconceptions. All her arguments were clichés that I had digested and regurgitated roughly two decades earlier: Real Islam cannot be violent, because the Arabic word *islām* shares its root letters with another word, *salām*, that means "peace"; Muslims love and honor Jesus as a virgin-born prophet of God; Islam respects women and gave them unprecedented rights; Muslims made great contributions to science while Europe was lost in the Dark Ages. Even in my post-ayahuasca love for my sisters and brothers, I felt a temptation to challenge her: When she quoted the Qur'ān as stating that Mary guarded her "chastity" and Allāh breathed into her, I wanted to point out that in Arabic, the word that she read as *chastity*—*farj*—more precisely signified *genitalia.* This matters because in 66:12, *Aḥṣanat farjahā fanafakhnā fīhī min rūḥinā* can read not only as "She guarded her chastity so we breathed into her from our spirit," but also "She guarded her vagina so we breathed into it from our spirit," and no one wants to think about Allāh or Gabriel breathing into Mary's vagina (some translations, drawing from an uneasy interpretive tradition, suggest in their parenthetical notes that Allāh breathed into the sleeve of Mary's garment).[5] I let this and some other questions go unasked. At the end of her talk, she left a stack of pamphlets on a table. I picked one up: *A Brief Illustrated Guide to Understanding Islam*, by I. A. Ibrahim. Its first edition was published in 1996, within a few years of my conversion. At a total of roughly seventy-five pages, maybe it's too big to be called a pamphlet, but it still reads like pamphlet-grade discourse. The cover shows Earth in space, with an open copy of the Qur'ān at the far end of a light beam that meets Earth in the Indian Ocean, several hundred miles from the coast of South Africa, as if to represent the Qur'ān blasting off from the Indian Ocean into space. The Earth and extraterrestrial Qur'ān appear above the Masjid Haram in Mecca, illuminated at night and crowded with white-garbed worshipers, and the surrounding cityscape. It appears as though an alternate Earth looms over Mecca in the night sky, and that this alternate Earth produces a giant Qur'ān somewhere in the southern region of its Indian Ocean, and that this Qur'ān leaves the alternate Earth to descend upon the Ka'ba of our own planet. Giving these details much more attention than could have been intended, I briefly wanted a world in which this was really how things worked.

So I considered *A Brief Illustrated Guide to Understanding Islam* as a pamphlet to start me back at the basics, a boiling down of Islam to its crucial points. This is Islam at its most simple: the sectless, undifferentiated Islam, as pure and clean as it has always been. If that is the mission, *A Brief Illustrated Guide to Understanding Islam* cannot confess to representing any particular Muslim orientation, since to do so would confess that a variety of Muslim orientations exist. There are no mentions of terms like *Sunnī* or *Shī'ī*, let alone more specific designations such as *Salafī*, and at no point does the pamphlet acknowledge that Muslims have ever disagreed with each other on anything. Pamphlet Islam can never say that it doesn't have an answer, or that we could choose from multiple answers, or that the singular correct answer might take more than a paragraph.

This is why, even if I consider the pamphlet a Salafī product, I can't call the woman who provided it a Salafī; she wouldn't have to be a self-identified Salafī to accept the pamphlet as genuinely "Islamic." The pamphlet reveals its Salafī genealogy only through its publisher (the Houston branch of Saudi-based Dar-us-Salam Publications), suggestions for further readings (including the work of Salafī scholar Bilal Philips and the Hilali-Khan translation of the Qur'ān), and directory of Muslim organizations, including groups such as the World Assembly of Muslim Youth (WAMY). An ideology is most successful when it's no longer recognizable as an ideology but accepted simply as "common sense"; religious sectarianism is best branded as the denial of sectarianism, when it no longer appears to represent one interpretation against others but simply the religion *as it is*. At that point, your rivals don't exist. What might be called "Salafī" concepts, successfully packaged as generic and universal Islam, can spread even among people who find Salafism ridiculous.

The sixty-three pages of the pamphlet's content is divided into three chapters: "Some Evidence for the Truth of Islam," "Some Benefits of Islam," and "General Information on Islam." The "Evidence" chapter takes up the first thirty-five pages, leaving just four pages for "Benefits" and twenty-four for "General Information." The "Evidence" chapter tells me that the Qur'ān expresses a harmony with modern science, which "proves without doubt" that the Qur'ān is divinely revealed. Foremost is the Qur'ān's discussion of what happens in the womb. The Qur'ān's treatment of embryonic development (which actually conforms to the stages articulated in ancient Greek medical science[6]) is presented as advanced beyond anything that human knowledge could have attained prior to modern microscopes. The Qur'ān's description of the fetus as developing from an alaqa, which can be translated as "leech" or "blood clot," is supported with diagrams comparing the human embryo at this early stage to a leech, showing the two to be similar in shape. In the next stage, the embryo is described as *mudgha*, which *A Brief Illustrated Guide* translates as "chewed substance." The mudgha-stage embryo—the somites of which "somewhat resemble teeth marks in a chewed substance"—is then compared to a photo of chewed bubble gum.[7] With a succession of charts, diagrams, and testimonials from apparently non-Muslim scientists at secular Western universities, the *Guide* proceeds to argue that the Qur'ān's discussions of mountains, clouds, and the origins of the universe all display a divine knowledge to which human knowledge has only started to catch up.

In this pamphlet's vision of Islam, the Qur'ān looks to modern science for confirmation of its claims; the Qur'ān derives its authority from non-Muslim obstetricians, biologists, geologists, and astronomers, institutions such as Georgetown University and Japan's National Astronomical Observatory, and new scriptures such as *Essentials of Anatomy and Physiology* and *Meteorology Today*. As *A Brief Illustrated Guide* frames its argument, these experts, institutions, and texts give the Qur'ān permission to say that it comes from God. For the power of such sources, the Qur'ān's heart becomes its discussion of embryos, mountains, and bodies of water. The most crucial objective in an introductory glance at the Qur'ān, *A Brief Illustrated Guide* tells me, is achieved through diagrams of the human cardiovascular system and satellite photos of cumulonimbus clouds. What's unclear in this section is how the Qur'ān could have proven itself before anyone knew that something called "modern science" would someday confirm it. There's a certain Islam that confronts me in these pages, an Islam that is presented as timeless and universal (and also a faithful and exact replication of what it had been in seventh-century Arabia) but could not have existed prior to the twentieth century.

Apart from scientific proof, the *Guide* tells me, the Qur'ān is also indisputably divine because it challenges all doubters to produce a single chapter that can match the Qur'ān in its "beauty, eloquence, splendor, wise legislation, true information, true prophecy, and other perfect attributes."[8] The *Guide* states that the challenge has not been met, though I am not sure how the contest would be measured. From there, we learn about Muḥammad's coming as foretold in the Bible, a theme that in fact goes all the way back to our earliest sources on Muḥammad. Its placement here rests on the assumption that the non-Muslim reader of *A Brief Illustrated Guide* holds a deep investment in what the Bible says.

Other proofs in the "Evidence" section include verses in which the Qur'ān accurately predicted future events, Muḥammad's performance of miracles that were witnessed by many people, and the simplicity of Muḥammad's life, which is presented as proof that he was not motivated by a desire for status, wealth, or power. The final proof of Islam's truth is its "phenomenal growth," as sources such as *The New York Times*, *USA Today*, and Hillary Clinton are quoted as affirming that Islam is the fastest-growing religion in America. "This phenomenon," says the *Guide*, "indicates that Islam is truly a religion from God."[9]

What strikes me throughout the "Evidence" pages is the treatment of humanity's purpose and ultimate destiny as a math equation. Salafīs are supposedly opposed to reason, but the pamphlet repeatedly claims that reason and empirical evidence demand our recognition of the Qur'ān as a divine revelation. Whether or not these claims to reason are satisfying isn't the question; what's interesting here is that reason itself gets treated as valuable. The "scientific rationality" pitch occupies the first chapter and over half of the pamphlet's content; by the end of it, the author has exhausted his energy and just slugs through the rest. The four-page "Benefits of Islam" chapter restates more or less the same benefit in four different ways: (1) Islam gets you into paradise; (2) Islam gets you out of hellfire; (3) Islam gets you happiness and peace; (4) Islam gets your sins forgiven. This approach once meshed with my own religiosity. If my experience of Islam is no longer compatible with something as straightforward as *A Brief Illustrated Guide to Understanding Islam*, have I moved from Islam to something else?

The "General Information" section names Islam's priorities. The pamphlet points out that "Muslims"—a categorization taken for granted as historically consistent, coherent, and full of descriptive power—produced "great advances" in a variety of sciences, because "Islam instructs man to use his powers of intelligence and observation."[10] It then tells me that in Islam, Jesus is really important, born of a virgin and performer of miracles; that Islam, "a religion of mercy," forbids terrorism; that an Islamic state protects the rights and property of all citizens, Muslims and non-Muslims alike; that Islam opposes all forms of racism; and that Islam gives women the right to own and manage their money and bestows special honor upon mothers.

The woman pushing these pamphlets promised that there was a clear difference between "religion" and "culture," but the Islam produced in *A Brief Illustrated Guide* could have been coherent only in a particular cultural moment. The cultureless, timeless, and pure Islam of this pamphlet necessarily created itself as a response to something outside it. So while the *Guide*'s claims of scientific proof for the Qur'ān might be immature, I am interested in why this section dominates the pamphlet. The need for secular and primarily Western scientists to cosign for the Qur'ān reflects the values of a *culture*; more importantly, it reflects cultural *change*, a shift from the arguments and evidence that would have been fruitful in another setting.

Muḥammad shows up briefly in the *Guide*, and he is of course a particular Muḥammad to serve the argument that the *Guide* wants to make. There are several tens of thousands of reports that depict what Muḥammad said and did, and these reports fill endless volumes. With a few pages to spare in a pamphlet, which ones get to matter? The *Guide* author chooses to highlight Muḥammad's praises of charity, mercy, community, fair wages, and kindness to animals. None of this is necessarily inaccurate or a fabrication; it all comes from canonical volumes that Sunnī Muslims tend to regard as trustworthy. The point is that from a vast corpus of material, the author had to extract what he decided were the essential themes of Muḥammad's message and reproduce these themes in a handful of short quotes. Other themes could have been chosen, some possibly in contradiction to the author's choices.

The other subjects to get attention in *A Brief Illustrated Guide* do not simply represent the "core" of Islam, but rather the questions that get thrown at Muslims in a particular time and place. The *Guide* tells us about Jesus, along with modern concepts such as "terrorism," "human rights," "racism," and of course "the status of women in Islam"; as an introduction to the eternal message of Islam, these themes would not have had the same relevance two hundred years ago. Even the specific literary genre in which this *Guide* is crafted, its style, aesthetic, and organization, and the nature of the institutions and networks that produced and disseminate it—everything between its initial conception in the author's mind to its appearing on a table at a state university's "Islam 101" event, hosted by that university's Muslim Students' Association—represent much more than "Islam." This is an Islam whose priorities are determined from outside, from what its advocates have marked as the values of non-Islam. Even when this pamphlet's vision of Islam disagrees with non-Islam, it does so within the logic of a world that it shares with non-Islam.

Where in *A Brief Illustrated Guide to Understanding Islam* can I find the Big Real? We could resort to the familiar metaphor of "old wine in a new bottle," which assumes that while a vessel might change the apparent shape and color of the liquid that it contains, what's inside remains unchanged in its eternal essence. But personally, I don't buy the wine-bottle thing. I don't know how to distinguish what's inside the bottle from its exterior appearance, and the oldest bottles that we can examine are still just the oldest bottles; we never get to see the liquid without a container. The "Basic Islamic Beliefs" section lists six doctrinal concerns that have been widely held to be crucial deal breakers. This checklist goes way back—in fact, it's represented in our textual tradition as coming out of Muḥammad's own mouth—but it also became the definitive checklist as a response to a specific historical context that emerged generations after Muḥammad's death. In the ninth century CE, these six beliefs comprised an oral pamphlet to reduce the message to clear, easily digestible bullet points that could draw a line between acceptable and unacceptable.

Dar-us-Salam offers a more explicitly Salafī pamphlet in *A Summary of the Creed of As-Salaf As-Saalih*. The pamphlet begins by explaining that our world's present religious diversity emerged as the product of distortion and corruption: The Creator sent numerous prophets to the various nations of the world, each offering the same "simple and straightforward religion," but the followers of these prophets have "changed their beliefs, thus deviating from the original religion." This even includes the case of Allāh's final prophet, Muḥammad, whose community has also suffered what *A Summary* calls the "divisions and disunity" of different groups that assert the supremacy of their own methods and interpretations. "So it is our duty now to guard against deviation from the fundamental beliefs and principles of the only one religion, Islam," *A Summary* tells me.

The difference between Muḥammad's umma and other communities, according to *A Summary*, is that amid all these departures and mutations, one group has successfully preserved the original and authentic Islam. With the double-vowel transliteration now popularly associated with Salafī literature, *A Summary* identifies this privileged group as al-Firqatun-Naajiyyah, the "Saved Sect": Ahlus-Sunnah wal-Jamaa'ah, the followers of the pious predecessors.

It is by statements of creed, says *A Summary*, that a religion or sect establishes its "fundamental beliefs and guiding principles" and thus distinguishes itself from other religions or sects.[11] *A Summary* defines the source of its creed as what "Allāh said, and the Messenger of Allāh said," as opposed to the "desires and the interference of the limited intelligence of man."[12]

The first point of *A Summary's* ten "fundamentals" includes several points of faith: belief in Allāh, his angels, his books, his messengers, the last day, and al-qadar (Allāh's decree). The Salaf, I am told, knew Allāh by his self-descriptions without further speculating or elaborating on them. The Salaf did not try to reinterpret what Allāh said about himself, nor did they compare Allāh's attributes to those of his creation: The Salaf affirmed that Allāh possesses a hand without trying to understand the nature of that hand, nor did they attempt to interpret the character of Allāh's "hearing, sight, knowledge, ability, strength, might and speech" beyond his self-descriptions. The Salaf were neither allegorizers nor anthropomorphists. The Salaf accepted that Allāh's word was not created at a particular moment of time, but exists eternally with Allāh, and they would "not allow it to be interpreted by mere opinions, as this is a form of speaking about Allāh without knowledge."[13] They also believed that everything that ever happened or would happen, good or undesirable, had been decreed by Allāh and written in the Preserved Tablet.[14]

A Summary's second fundamental declares faith to be "a statement with the tongue, action with the limbs, and belief in the heart," and that faith increases with obedience and decreases with disobedience.[15] However, the third fundamental clarifies that those on the creed of the Salaf do not declare any Muslim to be a disbeliever due to sinful actions, "unless he rejects something that is well known by necessity from the religion."[16] The fourth point tells us that the Salaf considered obedience to Muslim authorities to be a religious obligation, unless these authorities commanded disobedience to Allāh, and notes that this position constitutes "the opposite of what the misguided sects believe."[17]

A Summary's fifth fundamental says that loving Muhammad's Companions is a requirement of faith, and "hating them is disbelief and hypocrisy." It is clarified here that a Companion is anyone who knew the Prophet while a Muslim, "whether he accompanied him for a year, a month, a day or an hour."[18] This positions the true Muslim against "innovators" like the Raafidhah (Shī'as), who "curse the

Companions and deny their virtues." The Companions were capable of error as individuals but protected from error as a community. In further disputation against Shī'as, *A Summary* adds that the Saved Sect loves the family of the Prophet, and that this includes his wives, who were "pure and innocent of every evil."[19]

In its sixth fundamental, *A Summary* states that only Allāh knows the otherworldly fates of his creations, and no one can name his/herself or anyone else as destined for paradise or hellfire. The seventh point requires belief in the karaamaat ("extraordinary feats") of righteous believers, which are clearly discernible from disbelievers' acts of witchcraft, magic, deception, or that in which devils might assist them.[20]

The eighth fundamental concerns method. How do those on the path of the Salaf know what they know? "Evidences and proofs," says *A Summary*, rather than "mystical interpretations" or preference for anyone's word above that of Allāh and his messenger. They can follow qualified scholars and schools of law, but none of these are infallible, and it is acceptable that a Muslim could switch from one legal school to another based on whichever school demonstrates superior understanding and evidence for its positions.[21] Independent reasoning based on the Qur'ān and Sunna is allowed but regulated with serious disclaimers, accessible only to those who "fulfill its conditions that are well known with the scholars."[22]

The ninth fundamental is that Muslims on the path of the Salaf command the right and forbid the wrong. Finally, *A Summary*'s tenth fundamental rejects the "people of innovation who introduce new things into the religion."[23] To innovate in one's religion denies the perfection of what Allāh has provided, becoming a sort of polytheism: To deny the modes of knowledge and practice prescribed in *A Summary* essentially renders you a worshiper of idols. The followers of the pious predecessors, therefore, steer clear of innovators:

> They do not love them, they do not accompany them, they do not listen to their speech, they do not sit with them, they do not argue with them concerning the religion, nor do they exchange views with them. They prefer to protect their ears from listening to their falsehoods.[24]

Two things fascinate me about this pamphlet. First, its "fundamentals" emerged as such in response to debates and power struggles between Muslims after Muḥammad's death. What it presents as the timeless and original message can be exposed as having been formulated through a specific history. Second, though the pamphlet bears the name of a scholar who supervised its compilation, *A Summary* seems to deny its authorship. This team cannot be seen as having performed creative or productive work; their job was to deliver an item without leaving any trace of their presence. If this "creed of the Salaf" is really as clear and straightforward as the pamphlet claims, why do we need the pamphlet?

If Muslims are always arguing for Islam against others, whether their adversaries are non-Muslims or fellow Muslims that they see as illegitimate, there can never be an Islam that articulates itself with no input from outside, no culture-free Islam. There can be no pamphlet that just produces Islam as it is—apart from maybe Allāh's supreme pamphlet, the Qur'ān, which also had to speak first in response to a world of non-Muslims. But I've never known a Muslim who displayed confidence that the Qur'ān could speak for itself without help, without supplementary notes, commentaries, contextualizations, and rationalizations. No one simply hands you the Qur'ān and walks away, not even the Muslims who would proudly describe themselves as "Qur'ān-only."

Critics blame the rise of Qur'ān-only discourse on Protestantism's *sola scriptura* ("scripture alone") argument, which managed to cover the globe in part through European colonialism; but not even Martin Luther let the Bible speak for itself. Regarding the Bible as too unwieldy for common people, Luther appointed himself as a qualified mediator between the scripture and believers. He distilled what he decided were the Bible's key points into pamphlet form, writing catechisms to produce a "short summary and epitome of the entire Holy Scriptures" and prevent the kinds of misinterpretation that could spawn sectarian disputes and social chaos.

The Qur'ān may or may not be "true," but as *A Brief Illustrated Guide* reveals (perhaps unintentionally), the rules by which it must establish itself as true are always changing. The effort of this *Guide* and pamphlets like it to present Islam as a closed system only expose tradition's openness and instability. I have embarked upon a return to pamphlet Islam before knowing the frames that could determine my own pamphlet. How does the Qur'ān prove itself to me, and what does this mean for the idea of a closed system? In the mosque after my ayahuasca vision, the Qur'ān proved its value not for the truth of what it said, but for what it did: The Qur'ān had a force with which it acted upon my body, regardless of whatever claims it made about itself. I don't know how to translate that into a pamphlet. Mine wouldn't be a pamphlet that satisfies the author of *A Brief Illustrated Guide*, for whom the Qur'ān appears as a contestant on a game show, scoring points for giving right answers.

From a certain point of view, this would be the most intuitive way of engaging the Qur'ān: Either its claims are objectively true or they are not. There is certainly room to argue that the Qur'ān presents its own words this way. Some atheist thinkers operate by the same logic to treat all religion as ridiculous. The potentially heartbreaking part of this is that if I want to dive into the texts and engage the words but lack the kind of zero-sum, no-partial-credit stakes that drive *A Brief Illustrated Guide to Understanding Islam* or *A Summary of the Creed of As-Salaf As-Saalih*, I'm not always sure what I'm doing, or why. In my DMT-powered Islam and my prayer of the morning after, this was not a question: My prayer did not need a formal statement of doctrine in order to do its work. Can my Islam find its perfect expression in a pamphlet with blank pages, or perhaps a script that I find wholly unreadable, like Aurebesh? What happens when I try to confront the Qur'ān with nothing to stand between us?

3

DISCONNECTED LETTERS

>>> I used to marvel that the letters in a closed book did not get mixed up and lost in the course of night. <<< —**Jorge Luis Borges**[1]

>>> A, L, M. <<< —**The Qur'ān**, 2:1

DURING THE AYAHUASCA visions, I had asked about the Qur'ān, and I was told—either by the Qur'ān's transcendent author, or the spirit of the sacred vine, or just the dimethyltryptamine working with my brain chemicals, a message from my own self to my own self, whatever—to leave the words alone. Returning to the reality of the sober, however, the Qur'ān and its words were all that I had. In my post-ayahuasca prayer, I recited the text for a trace of what I had felt, commemorating the traumas and ecstasies of ayahuasca. The words weren't exactly words at that point.

As time pulled me further away from the chemical mountaintop, I grew more reliant on the words, but in ways that the chemicals had enabled. Feeling as though ayahuasca had washed my insides clean and opened me to the chance at a new encounter with the divine words, I decided to reconsider the Qur'ān in a serious way. The plan was to place myself in a one-on-one encounter with the Qur'ān, in which I would take the time to produce my own translation, verse by verse.

My project had one guiding assumption that would seem natural for engaging any text: that the primary way for me to approach the Qur'ān was as a source of discursive content to be investigated and understood. This was what it meant for me to have a personal experience of the Qur'ān. Assisted only by my dictionaries, lexicons, and concordances, I wanted to plunge deep into every word and retrieve everything that I could before proceeding to the next. I wasn't so naive to think that I could capture *the* meaning of the Qur'ān in some absolute, authoritative sense that transcended my own abilities and resources, nor did I share the Salafī confidence in language that could allow such a fantasy. At most, I hoped for an encounter with the Qur'ān that was my own.

This emphasis on content is not the only way to approach the Qur'ān. It's not necessarily the same experience that I would have while reciting the Qur'ān in prayer, with or without drugs; or struggling to program large portions of the Qur'ān into my memory without prioritizing comprehension; or visually experiencing the Qur'ān as calligraphy on the wall of a mosque, stylized and abstracted to the point of virtual unreadability; or writing the Qur'ān on cloth, washing the ink away, and then drinking the water as a means of physically ingesting the Qur'ān. Treating the Qur'ān as an intellectual project resonated with my youthful conception of Islam: a religion determined by divine instructions that have been made easily available to us in book form. If someone were to say the word *Qur'ān*, I would first imagine a book, and specifically a *modern* book, a mass-printed paper artifact of commerce. This itself might be a more radical departure from the origins than I can appreciate.

Before attempting to read and interpret, my first question was whether the Qur'ān encouraged or even allowed interpretation of itself. I turned to a contested verse on the matter, the seventh verse of the third sūra:

> It is he who sent down the Book to you. In it are clear verses—they are the foundation of the Book—and others unclear. As for those in whose hearts is deviation, they will follow that of which is unclear, seeking discord and seeking an interpretation. *And no one knows its interpretation except Allāh. And those firm in knowledge say, "We believe in it. All of it is from our lord."* And no one will be reminded except those of understanding.

The "you" to whom the book was sent is expressed with the singular masculine suffix *ka*, which designates its addressee as male. The Qur'ān makes frequent shifts in perspective: The man who has been addressed as "you" in this verse is referred to as "he" in others, while the divine "he" who has sent the book in 3.7 is sometimes "we" and occasionally "I."[2]

Verse 3:7 informs me that the Book's umm, its foundation or basis (or "mother"), consists of the muḥkamāt, the clear verses. *Muḥkamāt* comes from the same *ḥ-k-m* root as terms associated with wisdom and judgment. The words used in reference to "unclear" verses, *mutashābihāt* and *tashābaha*, could also be translated as "allegorical." The clear verses are the wise and authoritative, while the obscure can say one thing but mean another. According to this verse, trying to interpret the unclear verses produces discord. The word used here for "discord," *fitna*, would become the paradigmatic Muslim term for mischief and infighting; the violent power struggles that devastated early caliphates and left the Muslims forever divided are described as the Fitnas, and charges of fitna are employed to this day to shut down conversations that threaten the status quo. The word for "interpretation," *ta'wīl*, comes from the same *a-w-l* root as *awāl*, "first"; to interpret means that we seek a return to the origins.

This verse warns that obsessing over the obscure can only cause deviation and chaos, but then renders *itself* obscure, as ambiguities in the Arabic allow for two radically opposed translations for a segment of the verse:

1. No one knows its interpretation except Allāh. And those firm in knowledge say, "We believe in it. All of it is from our lord."

2. No one knows its interpretation except Allāh and those firm in knowledge. They say, "We believe in it. All of it is from our lord."

Both versions offer precise and "literal" translations, despite the dramatic difference in their consequences. The Qur'ān's orality comes into play here: Though it sometimes refers to itself (as in this verse) as *al-Kitāb*, "the Book" or more precisely "the Writing," its more recognized self-identification is of course *al-Qur'ān*, "the Reciting" (in contrast to the Bible, which is always called al-Kitāb). Because the Arabic script does not have periods or commas, sound holds as much power as sight in producing the Qur'ān's meaning: When I recite this verse in Arabic, pausing to breathe can change the message. Depending on a full stop after Allāh's name, I find different answers to the question of what a human being can know from the Qur'ān. Do those "firm in knowledge" passively accept the Qur'ān's authority without interrogation of its unclear verses, or can they understand what remains mysterious to everyone else?

For Muslim thinkers who sought an expansion of the Qur'ān's possibilities, whether theologians such as al-Ghazālī, philosophers such as Ibn Rushd (Averröes), or mystics such as al-Kashānī, reciting 3:7 without a full stop after Allāh's name suggested the existence of an elite class of knowers who could comprehend the difficult verses.[3] As we might expect, interpreters tended to identify those elite readers as the ones whose methods and arguments they shared. For philosophers, the "firm in knowledge" were philosophers, who could more fully comprehend the highest truths of the Qur'ān, which the Qur'ān cloaked in crude allegories so that it could speak to common believers and their undeveloped intellects. For mystics, 3:7 authorized mystical modes of knowledge, a privileged access to esoteric meanings through dreams, visionary experiences, and inspired intuition. For the traditionalist scholars whom modern Salafīs would count in their lineage, claims of VIP access to the Qur'ān's meanings threatened the supremacy of Allāh's words and demoted the Salaf's understanding of them as incomplete.

If there were indeed gifted knowers, who could claim to belong among their ranks? I wasn't going there. But even if I sought refuge in Allāh from the unclear verses, 3:7 still presents a problem: identifying which verses should be marked as "unclear" and thus avoided. This matter itself is left unclear, since verses do not typically make straightforward declarations that they belong to one category or the other. In perhaps the Qur'ān's supreme irony, the verse in which we learn that some verses are clear and others are unclear is itself an unclear verse. If we read an unclear verse as telling us to avoid interpretation of unclear verses, what are we supposed to do? The verse tells me, "DO NOT READ THIS VERSE," performing a double-bind, and shows that even divine revelations can play cruel literary jokes.

Numerous verses in the Qur'ān could be considered unclear because they consist only of disconnected and seemingly random Arabic letters. Some readers, however, would find the meaning of these "mystery letters" to be obvious, either through scholarly or mystical methods of analysis. If the Prophet shows up in a dream and tells you what the letters mean, what can be unclear about them? Other verses might be ambiguous because they describe Allāh's attributes, which later became a crucial point of division among Muslim thinkers; ḥadīth-based traditionalists condemned philosophers for using 3:7 to allegorize Allāh's throne and his sitting upon it.[4] Linguists argued with each other over the meaning of specific words, despite the Qur'ān's assurances that it had come down in "plain Arabic." Some questioned what it meant for the Qur'ān to label itself an Arabic text while containing words that they perceived to be foreign (for example, one of the names for the hellfire, *Jahennam*, is said to be Ethiopian). But what if we're mindful of the problems with reading, seeing the fallacies for which both premodern traditionalists and postmodern literary theorists would undermine claims upon the text's essence? Depending on how you feel about the attempt to capture meaning from texts, *every* verse is capable of ambiguity.

Because I don't think in Arabic, I must translate the Qur'ān; but every translation is an attempt to interpret the unclear, potentially violating 3:7's command. Translators perform work upon the Qur'ān to make it comprehensible for greater numbers of people and can do this only by replacing the words that the Qur'ān chose for itself. For al-Ghazālī, enhanced access to the Qur'ān was precisely the reason to *avoid* translation: Opening the Qur'ān to non-Arabic speakers only exposed it to misinterpretation by unqualified readers. Translation can have dangerous theological consequences, for which al-Ghazālī warned against translating the verses that seemed to describe God in anthropomorphic terms: Since no translation could perfectly capture all the subtleties of the original Arabic, translation only heightened the threat of misreading difficult verses.[3]

Despite the proliferation of Qur'ān translations today, many Muslims maintain that the speech of Allāh cannot be expressed in another language, and pious translators often give their work titles such as *The Meanings of the Holy Qur'ān* rather than just *The Qur'ān*. This doubt in the Qur'ān's translatability does not have to be a theologically invested claim: I want to reject the Qur'ān's translation for the same reason that scholarly study of *Beowulf* requires specialized training in Old English. The Qur'ān rewritten in new words and another author's voice cannot be the Qur'ān. "Fundamentalist" scripturalism and critical theories of translation find themselves in agreement here.

A language cannot be reduced to a glossary of words for which we should expect every other language to provide its own glossary that lines up perfectly, term for term. There's always something speculative to translation, always a gap that must be filled with educated guesses. I would have to wonder, then, about the possibilities for a Salafī theory of translation. As long as Salafī scholars are willing to subject the Qur'ān to their translation, they cannot be reduced to pure literalists. When Salafīs translate Qur'ānic verses into other languages for their polemical pamphlets, aren't they subjecting the words to their own rationalist investigation and ultimately replacing the exact words of divine speech with their personal opinions about what Allāh intends to say? For their arguments to rely on support from the Qur'ān, which a significant majority of Muslims worldwide cannot read for comprehension in its original Arabic, Salafīs must alter the words. For the Qur'ān to be shoehorned into the shape that Salafīs and other communities demand of it in an increasingly globalized world—a universal message that can be accepted and then obeyed by the entirety of the human race, all cultures and societies everywhere without distinction of time or place—the Qur'ān must necessarily adapt and become other than its own self.

Regardless of these challenges, Salafī networks have confidently flooded the world with presentations of the Qur'ān in every language. The Hilali-Khan translation, presently favored by the Saudi government's Qur'ān-printing complexes and distribution channels, has become notorious for playing the "parentheses" game, in which the translated verses are supplemented with the translator's own commentary, which appears within parentheses. The parenthesized comments, rather than clearly exposing themselves as the translator's interpretation, are disguised as part of the verse: The translator implies that what's inside the parentheses can also be found on the divinely revealed Arabic side of the page. One of the most troublesome cases could be found in the seventh verse of the Qur'ān's opening sūra, which reads in the Hilali-Khan translation as "The Way of those on whom You have bestowed Your Grace, not (those) who earned Your Anger (such as the Jews), nor or those who went astray (such as the Christians)."[6] When I read the verse in Arabic, I don't see any words that specifically signify Jews or Christians.

Even Salafīs, despite their supposed literalism, sometimes feel compelled to explain their choices. In the case of two verses that a Salafī author cites to prove that Allāh exists above the heaven (67:16–17), he clarifies that while a precise translation of the verses would place Allāh *in* the heaven (fi'l-samā'), we know that the verses really mean "above," because of course Allāh cannot be surrounded by his creation.[7]

If Salafīs wanted to interrogate the legitimacy of translation by their own methods, the answer would be to look for precedents among the earliest Muslims. It does not appear that a mass influx of non-Arabic-speaking converts who could have made the Qur'ān's translation an issue was desirable or even thinkable in the first generations: The earliest Muslims saw Islam primarily as an "Arab thing," since the Qur'ān was addressed to Arabs in their own language. Contrary to the myth of Islam spreading "by the sword," it doesn't seem that the desire to expand Muslim territory had anything to do with a desire to convert people, whether forcibly or otherwise. I am confronted by the Qur'ān's own words, which can be translated to say, "We have sent no messenger except with the tongue of his people, that he might make all clear to them" (5:44–48). Repeatedly identifying itself as an *Arabic* Qur'ān, the Qur'ān seems to relate its Arabic language to clarity and accessibility (12:2, 16:103, 26:195, 39:28, 41:3, 43:3, 46:12), which could suggest that translation only obscures the content and makes it *less* clear—and perhaps that the Qur'ān did not originally express the claim of universalism that later readers would make on its behalf.

There is nonetheless a narrative, though not found in the major ḥadīth sources, that depicts Muḥammad as authorizing the translation of the Qur'ān's opening sūra for Persian-speaking believers. This sūra happens to be crucial to the performance of required prayers, and there are reports of Muslims from the first three centuries praying in Persian prior to learning sufficient Arabic. If the account of Muḥammad allowing translation of this particular sūra into Persian is a fabrication, it might have been created to answer a controversy regarding Muslim ritual. In the second century of Islam, the seminal jurist Abū Ḥanīfa allowed recitation of the sūra in Persian, a permission that he first granted unconditionally and then narrowed to those Muslims who did not yet have knowledge of Arabic.[8]

I wanted to submerge myself within the Qur'ān and read it purely on its own terms, but the Qur'ān does not have "its own terms." As literature scholar David Bellos has remarked, "No sentence contains all the information you need to translate it."[9] When the Qur'ān mentions trees, the heavens and earth, men, women, orphans, angels, prophets, greed, mercy, and Allāh, it requires me to apply knowledge that does not exist within the Qur'ān. As the Qur'ān constructs its meaning through words whose meanings are determined outside its covers, I cannot explain any word in the Qur'ān without using other words. Perhaps this should have been self-evident when I leaned on a stack of dictionaries, lexicons, and concordances for my "Qur'ān as the best commentary on itself" project, or my own experience of life on this planet to understand what the Qur'ān means when it mentions a "garden" or "fire." I cannot speak of an unmediated encounter with the Qur'ān, because every word finds meaning through whatever stands between it and myself.

Orientalist scholars have sometimes treated the Qur'ān, particularly its larger sūras, as structurally incoherent, charging that the Qur'ān throws clusters of verses together without regard for how they relate to each other. This assumption has been challenged with closer reads of specific sūras, primarily in works by non-Muslim scholars aimed at making the Qur'ān's text more accessible for non-Muslim readers.[10] For my project, I decided to start with the fifty-third sūra, popularly titled al-Najm ("the Star"), because this sūra offers some meat on the question of gendering divinity. During my ayahuasca visions, Allāh appeared as what could be called the "divine feminine," though the Qur'ān refers to Allāh exclusively with male pronouns and can be read as condemning anyone who conceptualizes divinity as feminine. The fifty-third sūra contains some of the Qur'ān's most heated attacks on goddess worship, even dismissing the notion that angels could be female (it appears that the pre-Islamic goddesses were believed to be Allāh's daughters and/or angels). Belief in Allāh having daughters is rejected as an insult to the divine, as the fifty-third sūra notes that humans prefer sons. Amid the Qur'ān's androcentrism, what could it mean that the Qur'ān's divine "he" spoke to me as a woman? I also found the fifty-third sūra compelling because it discusses what could be a direct encounter between Muḥammad and Allāh, though most interpreters would avoid the troublesome theological implications and instead assert that Muḥammad had seen the angel Jibril (Gabriel). For its description of this meeting between the Prophet and a supernatural Somebody, the fifty-third sūra might resonate with those of us who have traveled the entheogen road.

So I began to read, starting with the sūra's introduction, "Bismillāhir Raḥmānir Raḥīm": "In the Name of God, Raḥmān, the Merciful." People usually translate *ar-Raḥmān* as something like "compassionate" or "gracious," but there's reason to suggest that it's actually a proper name that originated in southern Arabia and was associated with pre-Islamic monotheism there. In the Qur'ān's description of unbelievers in 25:60, it would seem that ar-Raḥmān was regarded as a new, alien deity, distinct from the Allāh that was already worshiped in Mecca: "And when it is said to them, 'Prostrate to ar-Raḥmān,' they say, 'And what is ar-Raḥmān? Should we prostrate to that which you order us?'" In 17:110, the Qur'ān clears up the confusion, clarifying that ar-Raḥmān and Allāh are in fact the same being: "Call upon Allāh or call upon ar-Raḥmān. Whichever you call, to him belong the best names." Early in the Qur'ān's unfolding, Allāh became the dominant name, appearing nearly three thousand times in the text, compared to fifty-seven appearances for ar-Raḥmān (not counting the *Bismillāhir Raḥmānir Raḥīm* in the superscriptions of sūras).

Following the introductory Bismillāh, the first numbered verse of the sūra is a short Wa-l-najmi idhā hawā ("By the star when it falls"). Prior to making persuasive arguments, the Qur'ān often attests to its own claims through oaths. The oath verses generally accompany issues of particular gravity, such as punishments in this world or the next. In 53:1, the oath is not by the star's usefulness for human navigation, or its beauty as an adornment of heaven, or even the star itself; we are to look not at the light, but the dark. Our attention is called not to the star's glory, but the moment at which it becomes absent. We are asked to consider the star's lack. The Qur'ān swears by the event of the star's full exposure as impermanent and thus unworthy of worship.

If the oath by a star in 53:1 is part of the sūra's polemic against astral worship, it might be notable that although the peoples of pre-Islamic Arabia had names for hundreds of stars, the Qur'ān mentions only one star specifically by its name: al-Shi'rā (Sirius, Canis Majoris), the brightest fixed star (confession: The Qur'ān itself does not explain that al-Shi'rā is a specific star, or a star at all; as with everything else, the reference can have no meaning without outside sources). The mention occurs later in this sūra (53:49), as the Qur'ān asserts that Allāh is "the lord of Sirius" (rabb al-Shi'rā). It could be reasonable to see al-Shi'rā as the star by which the Qur'ān swears in 53:1, which would also connect the start of the sūra to its later polemic against idolatry.

Using the tafsīr al-Qur'ān bi-l-Qur'ān method—meaning that I treated the Qur'ān's text as the best commentary on itself—to get a sense of what the najm might have signified in 53:1, I went heavy into mentions of stars throughout the Qur'ān. In another sūra, Abraham briefly worships a star as his god, only to realize his error when the star disappears from view. To my eyes, 53:1 read as the Qur'ān swearing by the inauthenticity of false gods and the impermanence of every object of worship other than Allāh, the darkness that comes when lesser lights flicker out.

With its mention of a star, 53:1 at least offers the illusion of a universal, because there are such things as stars within my frame of reference. I can register the verse as though it's speaking to me in my present, calling my attention to what I can directly observe. Of course, whatever meaning the word *star* conveys is a social construct and thus historically unstable. I live in an age that produces a particular knowledge about stars: When I look at a star, I cannot perceive it through the science and culture of seventh-century Mecca. Nonetheless, it's easy enough to suspend this awareness and read *star* as signifying a self-evident, natural reality, as though every person throughout history who has ever looked up at the night sky has experienced these celestial phenomena in basically the same way. I have the luxury of pretending that to read the Qur'ān's *najm* as "star," I am only rewriting an Arabic word as its best plain-sense match in English, rather than translating an experience across space and time.

With 53:2, however, the illusion collapses, and my reading hits the wall:

> Ma ḍalla ṣāḥibukum wa mā ghawā
> ("Your companion has not strayed, nor has he erred.")

Who is this person that the Qur'ān calls my ṣāḥib, my companion? I can look at the sky and think that I know what the Qur'ān means by *star*, but I cannot know this supposed ṣāḥib. To my eyes, the verse reads almost as sarcasm, because this companion cannot be *my* companion. I have never met my ṣāḥib, except in dreams and drug visions. The Qur'ān rubs this in my face.

Something gets lost in the translated *your*, because English has only one *your*, regardless of number or gender. When the Qur'ān refers to my ṣāḥib, it expresses the second-person possessive with the plural masculine suffix, *kum*. The Qur'ān here reminds me that I am not its only reader; I am one man among many men for whom he is a companion. In ṣāḥibukum, a homosocial bond is assumed: *Ṣāḥibukum* could be translated as "the male companion of you men." Because the masculine plural also serves as an inclusive, generic plural, *kum* would be used to address a mixed group of both men and women, but we don't know who is there: This *kum* is not changed by the presence or absence of women.

I do not know the name that my companion was given at birth, but the Qur'ān calls him both Muḥammad and Aḥmad. Sūra 47 is traditionally called Muḥammad, though sūra titles are not part of the Qur'ān proper. The text of the Qur'ān mentions my companion by name five times: four for Muḥammad, one for Aḥmad. The discrepancy of names has led some scholars to suggest that *Muḥammad*, signifying an object of praise, was an honorific title, not a birth name. At any rate, in these five appearances, Muḥammad's role overwhelms the details of his person. The Qur'ān tells us that Muḥammad is the messenger of Allāh (48:29); that he is the messenger of Allāh and seal of prophets, despite the fact that he is not the father of any men (33:40); that he is nothing but a messenger, and other messengers before him have died (3:144); that those who believe in what has been sent down to him will have their misdeeds erased (47:2); and that Jesus foretold to his people the coming of one who would be named Aḥmad (61:6). Other than that, we don't get much information. The Qur'ān tells me almost nothing concrete about my companion.

In contrast, Musa/Moses is mentioned by name 136 times. Ibrahim/Abraham is mentioned 69 times, as is Jesus (who is called by three names: 'Īsa, al-Masīh, and Ibn Maryam). Nuh/Noah is mentioned 43 times; Yusuf/Joseph and Lot/Lut, 27 each; Hud, 25; Sulayman/Solomon, 17. Harun/Aaron is mentioned 6 times. The Qur'ān even says Pharaoh's name more than that of Muḥammad (and all prophets except for Moses) at 76. Iblis, the Devil, is mentioned 11 times by name, more than twice the instances of Muḥammad's name; this does not even include references to Iblis as shayṭān. From a superficial first glance, it would appear as though Muḥammad is not the central character in the Qur'ān.

When the Qur'ān speaks of my companion, it is usually to argue for its own legitimacy. Such is the case with 53:2; the Qur'ān mentions only my companion, the means by which we have access to the Qur'ān, to say that he has not gone astray or spoken from his own desire. Both of the Qur'ān's other uses of ṣāḥibukum, "your companion," serve this concern, promising that there is nothing in him from a jinn (34:46) and that he is not majnūn, "jinn-possessed" (81:22). Some Muslims, arguing that Muḥammad should not be seen as representing the crucial essence of Islam, choose to emphasize the Qur'ān's paucity of direct references to him.

There's another way to look at it: The Qur'ān is *always* talking about Muḥammad and his community, because even if people hold the Qur'ān to be eternal and universal, the words must still make sense in their own world. A close read might suggest that the Qur'ān employs previous prophets as stand-ins for Muḥammad; when the Qur'ān speaks of the rejection and mockery of Noah by his people, we are supposed to learn something about Muḥammad's experience. In Muḥammad's time, the consistency of these stories—a prophet comes to warn his people, they ignore him, and Allāh subsequently removes them from the planet via natural disasters—would have served as a warning to the people of Mecca. The Qur'ān asks that its audience consider the fate of these previous peoples. If Moses dominates the Qur'ān's stories, it could lead us to consider that Moses, more than any other prophet, reflects the prophetic archetype in which the Qur'ān casts Muḥammad.

It is usually the people around Muḥammad that we call aṣḥāb; for the Qur'ān to call him ṣaḥibukum reorients our perspective. For his aṣḥāb, 53:2 referred to a man with whom they walked, spoke, and ate. My companion, as I know him, has no face; he is more or less a fictional character in my dreams. For the companions of my companion, he had a face that could be observed and remembered; after his death, they shared memories of his eyes, cheeks, hair and beard, complexion, and even the sweetness of his breath. Muḥammad was their companion in lived reality beyond the verses, so it could not have been the Qur'ān alone that made him their ṣāḥib. Instead of decentering Muḥammad, therefore, his apparent marginalization in the Qur'ān threatens to decenter *us*. We can choose to read ourselves as addressees of the *your* in *your companion*, or we can find the Qur'ān speaking to its moment with an immediacy that pushes us out. The Qur'ān first addressed people who did not need more information regarding a man who lived among them (or the man himself, who did not need to have his own biography reported to him). Grounded in its own urgent present—promising an end of the world that could come at any second and asking how believers might react *if* Muḥammad dies in the days to come, while neglecting to offer plans for such a scenario—we could question the Qur'ān's investment in its future readers. Reflecting on what the Qur'ān does *not* say, the points at which it displays no need to contextualize itself or explain its references, I confront the gulf between the Qur'ān's world and mine: The Qur'ān speaks to a here and now that I cannot touch. The Qur'ān describes Allāh's production and storage of knowledge in terms of pens and tablets; relying on the technology of its moment, the divine archive cannot shift to digital storage or even graduate from papyrus to paper.

According to traditional sources, the Qur'ān's revelation occurred in bits and pieces over the course of twenty-three years. Many of these fragments explicitly referred to incidents and controversies in Muḥammad's life, and, therefore, the lives of those around him, the people for whom the Qur'ān calls him ṣāḥibukum. The Qur'ān does not read as Allāh's monologue, but rather as one half of a dialogue. When I read about the Companions, the boundary between their lives and the Qur'ān dissolves. "They ask you" (yas'alūnaka), says the Qur'ān to Muḥammad, before giving him an answer; this occurs numerous times in the Qur'ān, including several instances within a relatively compact sequence in sūra 2 on topics such as the new moon (2:189), charity (2:215), the prohibited month (2:217), wine and gambling (2:219), orphans (2:220), and menstruation (2:222).[11] As the

German physicist Werner Heisenberg had famously remarked, "What we observe is not nature herself, but nature exposed to our method of questioning";[12] the speaker in the Qur'ān is not simply Allāh, but Allāh as produced in the Companions' questions of him. If we read the Qur'ān as a twenty-three-year series of responses to the changing lives of its audience, the Companions suddenly appear to have a degree of agency in determining the Qur'ān's content—and even its delivery, as tradition suggests that the revelations briefly ceased due to poor fingernail hygiene among the Companions. The revelations did not include women as addressees until one of Muḥammad's wives asked him why, after which the voice of the divine became more inclusive.

The Companions are said to have behaved carefully in Muḥammad's presence, fearful that they could end up as the subjects of a verse;[13] nonetheless, the Qur'ān is filled with their traces. The Qur'ān does not usually name them; those for whom the Qur'ān called Muḥammad ṣāḥibukum are rendered almost invisible as individuals. Names of figures whom later history records as important, such as Abū Bakr or 'Alī, are absent from the verses. The Qur'ān does not give us the names of Muḥammad's parents or wives or biological children. The only people from his lifetime to be mentioned by name in the Qur'ān are Zayd, identified in tradition as Muḥammad's adopted son Zayd ibn Haritha (33:37), and a figure called Abū Lahab, "Father of Flames" (111:1), presumed by interpretive tradition to have been Muḥammad's despised uncle. But the Qur'ān does make reference to people who took part in the first Muslim community, such as the mention in 80:1–2 of an unidentified blind man who went to see Muḥammad. Tradition outside the Qur'ān names him as Ibn Umm Maktum, and an incident from his life is now part of the divine revelation.

In one episode, the scribe to whom Muḥammad was reciting a verse excitedly remarked, "Blessed be Allāh, the best of creators." Muḥammad then told the scribe that "Blessed be Allāh, the best of creators" actually belonged in that verse, at the exact point at which the scribe said it. The scribe's outburst can be found at the end of 23:14.[14] Incorporating stories of the early community into my Qur'ān, I lose my sense of the Qur'ān as a singular text that preexisted the created universe, awaiting its delivery to one man in installments. Instead, the Qur'ān looks like a trace of a specific community's encounter with divine power—a power whose spontaneous bursts, localized at the site of one man's body, appeared as an ongoing exchange with that community. Maybe this view compromises the dominant Sunnī theological position regarding the Qur'ān, namely that it is uncreated and preexisted the world.

In an idealized Salafī method of reading, we would not prioritize our own eyes over those of the Qur'ān's original audience. Instead of attempting to decipher a verse for ourselves, which leaves the Qur'ān vulnerable to our prejudices, assumptions, and desires, we instead ask what the Prophet had said to his Companions about that verse, or what the Companions related to the Followers. The Companions do appear in traditional sources as Qur'ān interpreters. Ḥadīth reports portray 'Ā'isha as an authoritative teacher of the Qur'ān who intervened in debates on the text's meaning.[15] Ibn 'Abbās, the Prophet's paternal cousin (and ancestor of the 'Abbāsids), is treated as a foundational figure in the field of exegesis, and tradition represents Muḥammad as praying for Ibn 'Abbās to comprehend scripture.

According to the memory of later generations, the Companions occasionally disagreed on the meanings of verses. In conflicting opinions as to whether the fifty-third sūra discusses a personal, visionary encounter between Muḥammad and Allāh, Ibn 'Abbās believed that Muḥammad had in fact seen Allāh, while others (most vehemently 'Ā'isha) argued that no one could see Allāh in this life, neither with their physical eyes nor the mystical "eyes of the heart"; they insisted that the vision was of the angel Gabriel. Even if we suspend the question of whether these opinions really belonged to the Companions to whom they are attributed, we face the challenge of the Companions' personal subjectivities. In the case of tagging the unidentified shadīd al-qawwa of Muḥammad's vision as either Allāh or a mere angel, we should consider that this encounter took place before either 'Ā'isha or Ibn 'Abbās were born. They would have learned about Muḥammad's experience many years later, after the Muslims' migration from Mecca to Medina—a time in which Muḥammad's primary conversation partners and opponents were no longer polytheists, but Jews and Christians, who would have engaged the narrative from their own theological footings. The Qur'ān's more conservative verses regarding human access to Allāh are commonly dated from this period. Is it possible that Muḥammad's own understanding of his vision changed with time, and that 'Ā'isha's opinion represents Muḥammad's later memory? This isn't necessarily a problem, depending on how you view things like the Qur'ān's self-abrogation. On the other side, perhaps Ibn 'Abbās's understanding had come from older Companions who clung to earlier ideas about the vision; does this mean that Muḥammad had not corrected them, and that they never learned of the new interpretation? Could the report in which Ibn 'Abbās explained that Muḥammad had seen Allāh with his heart or in a dream signify a reconciliation of conflicting opinions?

The traditional accounts mention the Companions arguing not only about the Qur'ān's meaning, but also its form. In one episode, 'Umar disagreed with a junior Companion over a sūra because they had memorized it at different times. Having memorized the sūra first, 'Umar conceded that his recitation of the sūra was *less* authoritative, since the later recitation must have abrogated the sūra as he knew it.[16] In stories of the Qur'ān's compilation into what is now its recognizable form, we find Companions arguing with each other over the inclusion of verses and even suggesting that not all of the Qur'ān had been preserved.

Amid political and theological strife, the Companions, Followers, Followers of the Followers, and post-Salaf generations worked to stabilize the Qur'ān. According to popular Sunnī history, the Qur'ān was first collected during the caliphate of Abū Bakr. 'Umar had come to Abū Bakr after numerous Qur'ān reciters had been killed in battle and suggested that the Qur'ān be compiled for preservation as a textual artifact. Abū Bakr objected: "How can you do something which the Messenger of Allāh did not do?" 'Umar answered, "By Allāh, it is a good thing." Abū Bakr accepted 'Umar's position and commanded Zayd ibn Thābit, who had been Muḥammad's scribe. Zayd echoed Abū Bakr's initial concern over departing from Muḥammad's example, but Abū Bakr repeated what 'Umar had said to him: "By Allāh, it is a good thing." What I find startling here is Abū Bakr's precise order: "*Search* for the Qur'ān and *collect/assemble* it." Zayd had to *search* for something that was *out there*, beyond even the reach of Abū Bakr, to then gather what was scattered and give form to the formless. It would be unfathomable for many Muslims today to think of the Qur'ān in such terms, to imagine the Qur'ān as a chaos that must be brought to order by human effort.

In Zayd's narration of the endeavor, he relates, "So I searched for the Qur'ān, and collected it from palm leaves, stones and the breasts of men." This project resulted in a written copy of the Qur'ān, which the Companions called a *maṣḥaf* (reportedly after the Ethiopian word for *book*), produced not for public use but for archival preservation. Discussing the etymology of the Greek root for *archive*, Jacques Derrida notes that it was the holders of political power who, as makers of the law, became archons; they protected official documents in their private residences, placing the archive under a kind of "house arrest."[17] As caliph, Abū Bakr retained possession of the new Qur'ānic archive. After Abū Bakr's death, it was kept by his political successor, 'Umar; with 'Umar's death, the archive went into the hands of 'Umar's daughter, Hafsa, who was also a widow of the Prophet and regarded as an authoritative scholar of the Qur'ān.[18] During the third caliphate, the regime of 'Uthmān, a second "official" collection of the Qur'ān would be established, this time to achieve standardization of the *public* Qur'ān. 'Uthmān was driven to this project after controversies over proper readings spread among the adherents of conflicting versions (as many as fifteen different collections in the possession of individual Companions and thirteen among the Followers[19]) and also among troops during distant campaigns. For his codification enterprise, 'Uthmān is said to have borrowed the Abū Bakr archive from Hafsa. However, the ambition was not merely to reproduce Hafsa's document exactly as it appeared, as 'Uthmān assembled a team of experts to examine and confirm the text. He appointed Zayd ibn Thābit as overseer and also recruited three Meccans to assist the process—one because he was an expert in the Arabic language, the other two because they were from Muḥammad's tribe, the Quraysh—and reportedly asked that if the three ever contested Zayd's opinion regarding a verse, that they should write the verse in the "original" Qurayshī dialect.[20] In a further innovation, 'Uthmān ordered that copies of the state-supported Qur'ān be sent to major cities, and that competing local versions be destroyed. Some of these versions reportedly differed from 'Uthmān's codex in the inclusion or exclusion of particular verses or entire sūras. Similar to the way in which reports of Muḥammad's statements would be authenticated, these rival collections of the Qur'ān were associated with the prestige of specific Companions. In Kūfa, where the Companion Ibn Mas'ūd's collection had been established as the official version, there was brief resistance to 'Uthmān's state codex. What we can gather from the accounts of these variants, explains Estelle Whelan, is that early Muslims were willing to base their arguments against each other "on the premise that the Qur'ān had not been given definitive form by the Prophet to whom it had been revealed."[21] There is also a report that after Abū Bakr's collection was returned to Hafsa, the governor of Medina demanded that she hand it over to him for destruction; even if her archive had provided the foundation for 'Uthmān's project, it was not equal to the finished, official codex, and the governor feared that it would undermine the new caliphal archive. Hafsa refused; but after her death, the governor seized her collection and ordered that the pages be torn up.[22] This could illustrate a point about the ironies of preserving tradition: To safeguard the Qur'ān's integrity and unity, the oldest complete and "official" copy of the Qur'ān had to be destroyed.

What has been called the Qur'ān's "still-fluid pre-canonical text"[23] did not instantly become solid with 'Uthmān's codex, which remained capable of variation. It appears that the copies that 'Uthmān sent to cities such as Mecca, Damascus, Baṣra, and Kūfa did not match each other perfectly, perhaps including copyists' mistakes. 'Uthmān is reported to have allowed the imprecise copies, assuming that any mistakes would be corrected by knowledgeable Arabs.[24] On top of these challenges, there was the problem of instability in Arabic writing. At the time, the Arabic script was not fully developed, lacking vowel marks or dots. The government's Qur'ān, therefore, provided only a bare consonantal skeleton, which allowed for multiple vocalizations and changes in meaning. Without voweling, the word *mlk* in the first sūra could undergo a subtle shift in interpretation, recited as either *malik* ("king") or *mālik* ("owner"). Without dots to properly distinguish the letters, the word *fīl* ("elephant") could be read in numerous ways, such as *qīl* ("it is said"), *qatala* ("he killed"), or *qabala* ("he kissed"). While the variations themselves did not produce major controversies over meaning—at no point, for example, were there debates over 105:1's mention of an elephant—the mere fact of difference nonetheless enabled competing schools to discredit each other through the charge of faulty readings.[25] Roughly fifty years after the establishment of the 'Uthmānic codex, the Qur'ān's text would be further codified under the Umayyad governor of Iraq, al-Ḥajjāj ibn

Yūsuf al-Thaqafī (d. 713). Two centuries later, seven vocalizations of the Qur'ān's consonants would be established as acceptable, based on transmissions that traced back to seven well-known reciters from the cities that had received 'Uthmān's codex. The era in which the Qur'ān's vowels and dots were secured was one in which numerous fields of knowledge underwent a "shift towards the consolidation, standardisation and canonisation of concepts and doctrines."[26]

Prior to the advancements in Arabic writing, the textual copy (muṣḥaf) of the Qur'ān would not have been useful as a source of information. It functioned more as a tool for those who already knew the words to refresh their memorization or teach others, or, as in the case of a caliphal codex, to establish the proper contents and their organization. With the orthographic reforms and fixing of the Qur'ān's vocalization, however, the revelation could speak to new audiences—and these audiences could assert their right to understand the material. The revealed text, which had previously been the territory of oral reciters (qurrā') who traced their knowledge to the Prophet, became accessible to a developing field of professional grammarians (naḥwiyyūn). Efforts to understand the Qur'ān encouraged the formation of grammatical schools, which in turn transformed the study of the Qur'ān. The grammarians, boasting superior mastery of the Arabic language, competed with the reciters as privileged custodians of the revelation. Their battle for authority would be decided in part by the introduction of paper, which replaced inferior papyrus and amplified the presence of book media in Muslim debates; when the Qur'ān became a *book* to be comprehended through the knowledge of other books and fields of study, the reciters lost.[27] Though philologically centered reading had first emerged as a threat to what had been the traditional mode of authority, it became established as a "traditional" method in its own right, since the knowledge of words' precise meanings promised to push out the reader's personal subjectivity and restrain oneself within the words. For those who placed confidence in the exact wording of the Qur'ān as the means of establishing and regulating truth, the systematic study of Arabic became a prerequisite to authority.

The tradition-innovation binary loses more power here. To preserve tradition means first deciding what counts as tradition and therefore requires the work of preservation, then clarifying what had been left vague or open to dispute, sealing closed any cracks and fissures, adapting to new technologies and fields of knowledge, and redrawing boundaries. To properly shelter the tradition requires more stability than the tradition had ever secured on its own. The refined tradition ends up more guarded from misreadings, and thus narrower in its possibilities, than it could have been without these *innovative* interventions. After such a process, can it be the same tradition that it had been before getting marked as "tradition"? Even if every letter was preserved exactly as the first Companions received it from Muḥammad, the process by which Muslims protected the Qur'ān from change inevitably changed the Qur'ān. The revelation bound in book form strikes me as a memorial to the lost.

Popular Muslim history suggests that Muḥammad was illiterate, an intellectual virgin. His lack of education presents the textual Qur'ān as a miracle, like Mary becoming pregnant without a man's intervention. Muḥammad was all shaman, no scientist, no critical theorist. Revelation came to him like the ringing of a bell and made him sweat even in the cold, but he left us with these words that we pick over and throw at each other in rational debates.

Muhammad said that scholars were heirs to the prophets; at least the scholars tell us so. Funny how that works.

For scholars to actualize the role that Muḥammad had reportedly assigned them, Muḥammad must be absent; they can't inherit from a living prophet who still speaks. I don't know exactly what it meant to be a "scholar" in his time, but it's only after the death of Muḥammad, and with his death the guarantee of prophethood's closure, that the Qur'ān can become an intellectual project, the domain of scholars. If theology is what happens when the intellect negotiates with a scripture, theologians can say nothing to prophets. Theology might claim submission to text but really conquers, keeping the words intact but still assuming control over them. The Qur'ān was Allāh giving humanity his Qul, the command, "Say"—an imperative that occurs some three hundred times in the text. Every interpreter reverses the Qur'ān's flow of power, telling Allāh not what to say, but rather what to *mean* when he speaks. This cannot be helped by calling your reading "literal." Reading *is* writing, every time.

Even as the Qur'ān successfully repeats itself, speaking to times and places beyond its first audience, a text's repeatability in part depends on the potential for its old words to produce new results. A verse remains powerful not because it imposes its meaning on the future, but because it accommodates the future's needs: The verse is not bound to its author or its first audience. While the Qur'ān's references point to what's outside itself, the outside also pours in. Ideas that did not exist for the earliest Muslim community sneak into the

Qur'ān, find homes for themselves in the words, and give the appearance of having always been there. One such idea might have been the notion of human souls. Does the Qur'ān espouse belief in a soul that exists independently of our bodies? We tend to assume that it does, since the Qur'ān speaks of resurrection and we have been trained to think about resurrection in terms of souls. The text of the Qur'ān, however, consistently speaks of the afterlife in terms of Allāh's power to reassemble and revive the material body, even after the body has turned into dust; it does not explicitly argue that an immaterial aspect of every person will outlast her physical matter. The word that we now take for granted as equivalent to "soul," *nafs*, is used in numerous ways in the Qur'ān, typically in relation to selfhood—not only Allāh, but even false idols are referred to as having nafs—but never in a sense that undoubtedly produces a distinction between corporeal substance and abstract spirit. Later understandings of nafs reflect the conversation between Muslim intellectuals and Greek philosophical tradition, as found in al-Ghazālī, who, despite his defense of bodily resurrection, read the Qur'ān while upholding an Aristotelian idea of the soul that al-Rāzī rejected.[28]

In his translation of the Qur'ān, British convert scholar Muhammad Marmaduke Pickthall (1875–1936) explained the Qur'ān's first sūra in his commentary as "the Lord's Prayer of the Muslims."[29] It may be unsophisticated to think of the Qur'ān as the "Muslim Bible," but sometimes that's what it becomes: As James W. Morris explains, "virtually all the extant English Qur'ān translations are still profoundly rooted . . . in a semantic universe of allusions and parallels to the language and symbolism of Bible translations."[30] The first translation of the Qur'ān that I read had come from Yusuf Ali (1872–1953), a colonial Indian Muslim living in London. The other major English translation from colonial India was that of Ahmadiyya scholar Maulana Muhammad Ali (1874–1951). Both translators sought to present the Qur'ān within the genre of sacred literature as readers of English could recognize it: In their hands, Allāh's Arabic speech becomes King James English, peppered with *thou* and *thy* to decorate itself with an Anglo-biblical style. The divine *He* is capitalized to follow norms of Victorian-era English literature, the Qur'ān's Arabic names for Israelite prophets are Anglicized ('Īsā becomes Jesus, Mūsā becomes Moses), and the translators' extensive notes often explain the Qur'ān through references to the Bible or Christian tradition. In the mid-twentieth century, the Nation of Islam was purchasing these Qur'ān translations in bulk from a Pakistani importer in New Jersey: South Asian Muslims' experience of an English-speaking, Protestant colonial power thus produced the Qur'ān that could resonate with an African American Muslim community led by the son of a Baptist preacher. In his commentary on the Qur'ān, Elijah Muhammad also interpreted the subject headings that appeared in Maulana Muhammad Ali's translation, as though he believed that these subject headings were part of the divinely revealed Arabic text.[31] Even the "Qur'ān" as Elijah conceptualized it reflects an act of translation. Perceiving the Qur'ān through a Protestant background that taught him what scriptures were and how they worked, he expressed little interest in ḥadīth collections or Muslim interpretive traditions as conduits through which the Qur'ān must be read. A "Muslim Bible" that he could read for himself, essentially a superior version of the Bible that he already knew, was exactly what he sought and found. When presented in translation to a mostly non-Muslim society, the Qur'ān might inspire some readers to convert, but the Qur'ān undergoes a conversion of its own. Perhaps this is what it means for religious scholars in sixteenth-century South Asia to have opposed Bengali translation of the Qur'ān, on the grounds that such a project would constitute the "Hinduization of Islam."[32]

Like *soul* or *star*, words like *belief*, *prophet*, and *piety* come loaded with culturally specific baggage: They cannot help but bring new ideas or sensibilities to the original terms *imān*, *nabī*, and *taqwa*. A prime example would be *walī*, a term of special significance in Ṣūfī traditions to refer to the "friends" of God. When Orientalist scholars rewrote *walī* with the English word *saint*, and Muslim intellectuals in turn adopted this translation, a historical tension within Muslim traditions now related to a point of controversy between Protestants and Catholics. Muslim thinkers concerned with the revival of original Islam and/or proving Islam's rationality, operating within the global hegemony of Protestant empires, expressed anti-Ṣūfī prejudice with the vocabulary of Protestant anti-Catholic prejudice.

This is why I do not consistently translate the Arabic *Allāh* into the English *God*. When I converted, I changed my own name to its Arabic version (Mikā'īl) and did the same to God, attempting to reinvent both of us in a language that I did not speak. I needed a theatrically alterior word like *Allāh* to erase my previous script with God (in the constraints of my own lived experience, it was irrelevant that Arabic-speaking Christians also call upon God as Allāh). Even if *God* and *Allāh* are perfectly interchangeable, my decision to translate or not translate the name adds significations to both terms, because God's Arabic name is so widely referenced in English that it functions as an English word. English-speaking non-Muslims refer to "Allāh" in debates over Islam's perceived foreignness to America and incompatibility with Jews and Christians, alleging that Allāh cannot be the god of the Bible; these people obviously haven't read the New Testament in Arabic. While the appearance of *Allāh* in an Arabic text can refer to the god of Muslims, Christians, Jews, or any monotheist, uses of the word in English conversation exclusively point to the religion of Muslims: The word's meaning becomes "God as conceptualized by Muslims." Likewise, if I am asked to imagine Jesus or 'Īsā, two different characters appear, though these names refer to the same prophet.

Even if a word in one language can be *exactly* matched by a word in another, translation still makes an effect. Look at this extraction from 5:3, which is widely regarded as the final verse of the Qur'ān to have been revealed:

> Today I have perfected your religion for you, completed my favor upon you, and have named for you Islam as a religion.

This is a popular translation, but we could raise some questions. First, "religion" as a category isn't any more stable or consistent than things like "race," "gender," "nation," or "science"—or, for that matter, the "sun" or "moon" as produced in our culturally specific knowledges—and so we shouldn't assume that the word expresses a universal concept that exists with the same meanings throughout all of history. The modern sense of religion as a belief system or closed set of doctrines does not exist in the Qur'ān, which speaks only of communities: The Qur'ān discusses "Christians" and their beliefs but has no word for *Christianity*. In the Qur'ān's typology of communities, there are people who have scriptures from the Creator, and those who don't; there are communities that follow their prophets, and others that deviate from what they were given; but there is not a multiplicity of "religions." When translators decide that 5:3's mention of *dīn* (which translators read elsewhere in the Qur'ān as "judgment" or "duty") signifies "religion," they force their own concepts onto the seventh century.

Second, to leave *islām* untranslated only performs an alternative translation: It turns the Arabic *islām* into *Islam*, an English word found in English dictionaries. The Arabic verbal noun *islām* (signifying "submission" or "surrender") appears only eight times in the Qur'ān and never clearly as a proper name; after all, if there are no proper names for Christianity, Judaism, or Zoroastrianism in the Qur'ān, the Qur'ān doesn't have to name its own system. Within the Qur'ān and even among the works of classical theologians such as al-Ghazālī, as scholar Carl Ernst points out, *islām* is less prominent as an identity marker than *imān* ("faith" or "belief") and the holder of privileged identity is less often called a *muslim* ("submitter") than *mu'min* ("believer").[33] In the modern era of named religions, however, *islām* is not only left untranslated in English Qur'āns, but finds itself capitalized as a proper name, Islam, to work within the Protestantized category of "religion" that has just been imposed upon the verse. We make the Qur'ān report our own world back to us: The Qur'ān now tells us that we have a perfect religion and that our perfect religion has a name. We could read the proclamation another way and potentially alter the verse's consequences:

> Today I have perfected your judgment for you, completed my favor upon you, and have named for you surrender as a duty.

Besides the projection of new meanings onto the words, translation also *erases* meanings: When we decide upon a meaning, we suppress the alternatives. Qur'ānic translation threatens to conflate the translator's mind with the mind of the Qur'ān's author. We tend to make a big deal of the claim that not so much as a single letter has been added to the Qur'ān or removed from it since the time of Muḥammad, but when I think about what we actually do when we read—let alone translate—I find myself asking a "So, what?" that cannot be answered.

The original meaning isn't always the most useful. Today, the Qur'ān's 109th sūra is popularly interpreted as a statement of interfaith tolerance through its verses that have been translated thus: "Nor will I be a worshiper of what you worship, nor will you be worshipers of what I worship; for you is your religion and for me is a religion." But if your method of interpretation places a premium on historical context (and you believe that we have access to this context), reading the sūra as a message that came first to specific people at a specific moment in their lives, it becomes more difficult to project our modern values onto the words. Mecca's polytheists had reportedly offered a wager to Muḥammad: that Muḥammad worship their gods for one year, after which the polytheists would devote one year to worship of Allāh alone, and whoever ended up better off would adopt the other side's mode of worship permanently. Sūra 109 came as a rejection of this proposal, making its own wager: Muḥammad will never leave his superior, true dīn, and this particular group of unbelievers will never abandon their inferior, false dīn. Premodern commentators who situated the sūra in its historical setting did not see the verses as suggesting that all "religions" were equal roads to the same truth, contrary to the hopes of modern readers with interest in interfaith dialogue. Rather, it was a prediction that came true, as the unbelievers to whom it referred never accepted Muḥammad's prophethood. If we choose to uphold the occasion of the sūra's revelation and its original audience as the keys to its message, we lose our reading of the 109th sūra as a statement of liberal religious pluralism, and what strikes us as the clear "literal" meaning is complicated by history.[34]

Verse 20:102 describes the criminals who will be gathered on the Day as "blue-eyed." In Mediterranean antiquity's medical theories of the body, external bodily traits were regarded as clues to a person's inner character, and even the great Imām Shāfi'ī followed Hellenic physiognomy in his confidence that people with blue eyes were idiots.[35] For their racialized understandings of the Qur'ān, however, Elijah Muhammad and Louis Farrakhan are popularly imagined as heretical deviants whose theodicy of blue-eyed "white devils" distorts the Qur'ān's true message of racial egalitarianism. The irony is that in the case of 20:102, these "heretics" find themselves closer to a plain-sense reading, which pits them against "orthodox" scholars who would rather explain the verse away. When it comes to 20:102, Nation of Islam exegetes appear to be the only scriptural literalists in town.

The Qur'ān features prominently in popular "Islam was the world's first feminism" narratives: As the pamphlets tell us, people in pre-Islamic Mecca used to bury newborn girls alive, and the Qur'ān emphatically condemns this practice (16:58–59, 81:8–90). Numerous Muslim commentators have used these verses as evidence that the Qur'ān's divine author sought to advance the status of females. At no point, however, does the Qur'ān clearly link its condemnation of female infanticide to a critique of misogyny or affirmation of gender equality. While noting that parents are often disappointed at the birth of a girl and joyous for a boy, the Qur'ān does not challenge this attitude except to say that murdering your daughter is the wrong choice. Rather than express a concern with sexism, the Qur'ān associates the killing of newborn babies with idolatry and the fear of poverty. If that's feminist, then the Christian Right's antiabortion stance is feminist. Moreover, the Qur'ān additionally condemns the killing of baby *boys* (though the Arabic *awlād* could also refer to children in general) in five verses: 6:137, 6:140, 6:151, 17:31, 60:12. Interpreting the Qur'ān's prohibition of infanticide as a statement for gender egalitarianism might say less about the Qur'ān than our own needs as readers.[36]

Even when challenging these representations of the Qur'ān's message, I can't boast that what I find in the Qur'ān is its original meaning, or that an original meaning is even retrievable—or that there was even a singular "original meaning" in the first place. This is the limit that I cannot transcend, made clear to me by *ṣāḥibukum*, the word that restrains me at the sūra's second verse and keeps me from going further. A Salafī method of reading would insist that in our effort to comprehend the Qur'ān, we defer to the sayings of the Prophet and the Salaf and the scholars who mastered the knowledge that has been passed down to them; but this only adds more layers of wandering text.

I'm afraid that in the choices that we make with these words, we end up as Ariel from *The Little Mermaid*, who retrieves artifacts that descend from beyond her ocean's limits and misreads them within her own logic. For Ariel, a fork was a hairbrush and properly termed a dinglehopper. Or maybe we're Po in *Kung Fu Panda*, who attains the prophetic Dragon Scroll and learns that it's entirely blank. Po then interprets the Dragon Scroll's lack of content to be its ultimate meaning. It is not the Dragon Scroll's power that makes us believers in it, but the opposite; believers make its power. When Allāh describes himself to human audiences, or the seventh century describes itself to our present, I don't know what else we have.

The forces that brought me to the Qur'ān exist outside the book. I would never have believed in the Qur'ān's claims about itself using only the Qur'ān; before I actually read the Qur'ān, it could not have told me that it was worth reading. The Qur'ān could not even make me aware of its own existence or produce itself as a material artifact in my hands; it did not print itself or place itself in libraries or come crashing through my roof from somewhere up in the clouds. The world in which I lived informed me that there was a thing called the Qur'ān, and that this Qur'ān belonged to a literary genre that I could identify as religious scripture. My world told me that the Qur'ān made particular truth claims and that my relationship to these claims positioned me in relation to other human beings. And this is the world that put the Qur'ān in my hands in terms of its translation, material production, and distribution. There's no going "straight to the Qur'ān" if I am unable to read the Qur'ān without the assistance of a world.

The Qur'ān can provide a universal and timeless truth only when readers deny the specific histories that produce them as readers. If there can be no language without social relationships, these relationships are also what allow both the Qur'ān's language and its readers to exist. Before coming to a sense of the Qur'ān, I had acquired a sense of myself through training by a variety of structures, ranging from family and communities to government and media. Perhaps more than the Catholicism of my mother's family, the religious background through which I would read the Qur'ān was American civil religion, which consists of a vague monotheism or monism (vague enough that you can switch out *God* for *the universe*) and idea of religion as a matter of personal conscience, an inner condition of belief. Growing up with a Protestantized Catholic idea of religion as chiefly defined by an individual's relationship to scripture—rather than a bond to religious institutions or communities—I assumed that to understand Islam, it was more urgent that I read the Qur'ān with my own eyes than visit a mosque or actually meet any Muslims.

The eyes with which I encountered the Qur'ān had also been trained by the American religion of mass advertising, which upholds the individual consumer's power of choice as its most sacred value. Through Nike and Gatorade commercials in the 1990s, Michael Jordan also taught me about the limitless human potential for self-mastery and improvement, the need to achieve a legacy through consistent performance of praiseworthy acts, the importance of brand loyalty for one's personal identity, and the role of products in making us what we are. I clutched the mass-printed, bar-coded, material product of the Qur'ān in my hands as someone who had already been promised ten million times that commodities can transform me into the best *me* possible.

Attempts to live in accordance with the Qur'ān do not automatically transform this particular selfhood into a Qur'ānic self. My life outside the Qur'ān told me what to look for inside the Qur'ān; it also taught me *how* to look, how to read, interpret, and evaluate words on a page. To insist that we can objectively understand the Qur'ān using *only* the Qur'ān is more than a denial of how language and literature work; it erases the humanity of the reader.

In the creativity with which they approached their own lessons, the Five Percenters taught me to celebrate the endless possibilities of text: When you wear Allāh's name and read with knowledge that you are also the author, there are no "misreadings." As one Five Percenter elder told me, "How you see it, that's how it is." Progressive Muslim reformists have also found comfort in the instability of textual meaning and the subjectivity of the reader. When it came to difficult verses, the best (or only) Progressive Muslim move was often to argue simply that any text remains open to multiple interpretations, and that everyone reads from within his or her own context. This might be a cheap non-answer, but it's not exactly wrong.

I took that to its extreme end. A few years ago, I had retreated into the woods and attempted a William S. Burroughs–style "cut-up" experiment with the Qur'ān, rearranging words and phrases like refrigerator-magnet poetry. I'm not sure what I wanted from that, but it might have been a way of holding myself to the words—loving, revering, cherishing them, treating them as divine gifts—within the context of my dad's bunker in West Virginia. Subjected to my X-acto blades and scissors, the Qur'ān worked as both a revelation from the seventh century and also something new. I scattered and rearranged the words with realization that this is only what everyone does with the Qur'ān: We're always cutting up. Exploring an online Qur'ān concordance to see the verses in which a particular Arabic root appears, isolating a single verse as the foundation for a Friday sermon, compiling verses on a particular theme from throughout the Qur'ān in order to construct an argument, choosing which short sūra to recite in prayer, or reading verses on your phone? It's all a cut-up. Even deciding to start this project with the fifty-third sūra reflects a cutting, my tearing open a place in the Qur'ān to serve as my entry into it. The Qur'ān might look like a unified whole when we assess it from far away. When we look closer, we find many thousands of pieces that remain forever in motion, and we are the ones moving them.

Salafīs aren't going to admit that their Qur'ān citations resemble cut-ups; but paradoxically, despite their supposed adherence to pure tradition, Salafīs might act out the postmodern challenge to interpretation better than most readers. The Salafiyya are often derided and marginalized for their claims to follow the text's self-evident meaning, but their alleged opposition to reason actually strikes me as reasonable. What Salafīs seek to avoid is not reason, but the intrusion of reason—which remains inescapably limited, culturally specific, subjective, and *human*—upon the divinely revealed text's ability to speak for itself. Recognizing that the meanings of texts undergo profound transformations as their words wander between readers, Salafīs seek reliable anchors for the Qur'ān. Even with the scissors in my hand and DMT in my gut, I retain a Salafī urge, and when I read the premodern traditionalists railing against interpretation, their arguments resonate with me more than their opponents who claim to possess the powers of "objective" reason that can decipher the Qur'ān's correct meaning. My complaint about the Salafīs' method of interpretation is that they don't recognize this as in fact an *interpretation*, the product of their choices.

If faithfulness to the words cannot save us from our own misreading selves, can we avoid throwing out the Qur'ān altogether? What happens when I name the origins as the site of supreme truth, but surrender to the fact that the origins are lost? And what changes in the problems of interpretation when we're dealing not with a human Shakespeare living in his own world and language, but a transcendent author who delivered a book with full knowledge of every future context and all of its readers? What if I approach the Qur'ān as Allāh's direct statement to *me*, authored with sensitivity to *my* limitations and points of reference and all the countless and unstable contexts in which I would read it?

Scholar and activist Laury Silvers had once told me, "I know that the Qur'ān is from God, but I don't know what it is." My desire for the Qur'ān's content to make sense—and, just as importantly, my desire to experience that sense as a divine message—has taken me from a straightforward "what the Author clearly intends" approach to a reader-centered approach that privileges me as the Qur'ān's maker and owner. If I deny the efforts of others to bring my mind under their capture, but do not claim that my own interpretations offer prescriptive solutions for our problems, scriptural exegesis seems to be limited to a negotiation between myself and myself. The next step could be to back away from textual meaning, as I was advised during my ayahuasca vision.

But perhaps there's a distinction that can be drawn between meaninglessness and insignificance. If I don't know what the Qur'ān says, this could mean that the Qur'ān has become empty; or it could mean that the Qur'ān has broken open in a new way, and that I can open myself to it in new ways, including modes of encounter beyond rational interpretation. Perhaps the Qur'ān can still give me things, even without an argument.

4

DIGGING THROUGH THE CRATES

>>> The archivization produces as much as it records the event. <<<
—**Jacques Derrida**[1]

MĀ ḌALLA ṢĀḤIBUKUM wa mā ghāwa: The Qur'ān (whatever it is) tells me that my companion (whoever he is) has not strayed, nor has he erred (53:2). Elsewhere in the revealed text, I read that my companion has an exalted character (68:4), that he is a good model to follow (33:21), that to obey him is to obey Allah (4:80), and to love Allāh means following the man (3:31). The Qur'ān here turns me away from itself, toward other bodies of literature that did not exist in its own time. With caution, I go for the books.

The books themselves cannot be the origins: We do not have biographical material on my companion from within a century after his death. Nonetheless, these texts are supposed to reproduce my companion through the memories of those who had known him. The books—or at least the language *around* the books—promise that we can access the origins as reliably in their words as if the origins were happening right now, in front of us, in flesh and blood. Like the Qur'ān, these are books that do not touch the floor.

In the canonical ḥadīth corpus, each individual report of a statement or action by Muḥammad has been vetted with a rigorous evaluation of the transmitters who have passed that report through the generations. If the field of classical ḥadīth criticism did what it was supposed to do, we are to trust not only that we have a reliable record of what Muḥammad said and did, but that Muḥammad was the most intensely documented individual in the premodern world. According to these reports, we even know how he cleaned his teeth.

I don't know if such reports actually give me what they claim. The classical methods of ḥadīth evaluation developed as a response to the fact that people were already fabricating statements of Muḥammad. Most ḥadīths failed to meet the highest standards set by master critics: The reports that were sufficiently evidenced to make it into the canonical collections represent a sliver of what circulated at the time. The elite ḥadīth scholars were rigorous in their efforts, but whether they can satisfy critical historiography is another problem. For the last century, in both Muslim and non-Muslim scholarship, the study of ḥadīths has been consumed with the authenticity issue. I'm not going to unroll that entire debate, but here are the points of concern: Could the traditional science of ḥadīth evaluation reliably separate Muḥammad's authentic statements from the forged and fabricated? Was it even really a "science" in any sense that we might use the term today? If modern scholars operate on the assumption that most ḥadīths were indeed forgeries, what's the possibility of extracting an authentic core from the fictions and then reconstructing the life of Muḥammad and the history of his community?

Arguments regarding the authenticity of ḥadīths have sometimes intersected with questions of the Qur'ān's origins. Some extreme revisionist scholars have argued that the Qur'ān, rather than being revealed and compiled in seventh-century Mecca and Medina, was actually authored long after Muḥammad's death, perhaps as late as the ninth century and as far away as Syria. Fred Donner debunks this "late Qur'ān" theory with an argument that leans on the inauthenticity of ḥadīths: Studying the language and content of these literatures, he uses a "late ḥadīths" theory to argue for an early Qur'ān. Examining points of departure between the Qur'ān and ḥadīth corpus, Donner argues that the two bodies of text could not have emerged from the same historical period.

As Donner shows, the Qur'ān and ḥadīth corpus often seem to be taking part in two different conversations. The ḥadīth corpus glorifies numerous Companions, but the Qur'ān does not regard these Companions as worthy of mention. The Qur'ān remains thoroughly uninterested in tribal politics, emphasizing responsibility of the individual, mentioning only one tribe (Muḥammad's tribe, the Quraysh) and making no specific references to the political and sectarian disputes that would later ravage Muslim communities. In contrast, the ḥadīth corpus discusses numerous tribes, makes collective judgments on them, and can be shown to reflect the tribal rivalries of middle and later Umayyad rule (680–750). The Umayyad era gives us pro-Umayyad ḥadīths; the 'Abbāsid era gives us pro-'Abbāsid ḥadīths that promote Muḥammad's uncle 'Abbās, through whom the dynasty traced its lineage, while undermining Muḥammad's other uncle, Abū Ṭālib—father of 'Alī, progenitor of the Shī'ī Imamate—with narrations that

Abū Ṭālib's brain was boiling in the hellfire. And the ḥadīth corpus, unlike the Qur'ān, also takes sides in theological controversies of later generations, condemning groups that did not exist in Muḥammad's lifetime.[2]

Donner additionally points out differences between representations of Muḥammad in the Qur'ān and ḥadīths. As mentioned earlier, Muḥammad appears in the background of the Qur'ān; in the ḥadīths, he becomes the center. The Qur'ān treats Muḥammad as an ordinary mortal, while ḥadīths portray him as a "miracle-worker, able to feed multitudes, heal the sick with his spittle, procure water by pressing the ground with his heel, see behind himself, predict the future, or divine hidden knowledge such as the names of people whom he has not yet met or the origins of a piece of stolen meat served to him."[3]

Finally, Donner looks at the two textual bodies as working with different vocabularies. Between the Qur'ān and ḥadīths, words change meaning: *khalīfa*, *sunna*, and *jamā'a* signify different concepts depending on where you read them. Most importantly for my own questions, *sunna*, our term for Muḥammad's customs or habits, never appears in the Qur'ān in clear relation to him; the term signifies *any* established precedent, including the sunna of past nations that were destroyed for their wickedness. In contrast, the ḥadīth corpus explicitly refers to *the* Sunna as Muḥammad's custom, which serves as a binding precedent.[4] It's another moment at which the binary collapses: Opposition between Ahl al-Sunna (People who adhere to the Sunna) and Ahl al-Bid'a (People of Innovation, that is, everyone else) might detonate with the idea that what we call "sunna" itself is an innovation.

There remains a spectrum of attitudes about the reliability of the ḥadīth corpus. At one end, some believe that the seminal ḥadīth transmitters and critics in the early generations were completely beyond challenge: These scholars are represented as exemplars of superior piety, blessed with infallible photographic memories, and of course immune to any kind of sectarian prejudices or political dynamics that might have informed their work. Their collections can—or even *must*—be recognized as trustworthy; and even if their opinions on a specific ḥadīth can be questioned, the guiding principles of their methodologies still represent the keys to accessing Muḥammad's genuine teachings and precedents. At the opposite end, we have extreme skeptics who would throw out virtually the entire ḥadīth corpus as having been fabricated generations after Muḥammad's death. They essentially subscribe to a conspiracy theory in which a coterie of sectarian power-players forged thousands of ḥadīths out of thin air and fooled entire societies into accepting them as authentic, a project that was especially masterful because they pulled it off without leaving behind any evidence of their plot. Neither of these positions are critically satisfying. It's hard for me to imagine the scholars of the ḥadīth corpus as ideologically uninvested walking archives that transcend their own humanity, nor as megalomaniacal forgers who concocted all the ḥadīths from their imaginations. It seems reasonable to stand with scholars near the middle of that spectrum, who have carefully argued that on a case-by-case basis, we might trace *some* reports to the generation of Muḥammad's Companions.[5]

Considering the Companions' importance for my access to Muḥammad, I lose faith in the "founder" model of thinking about religion, in which a master teacher appears and singlehandedly feeds a message to masses of disciples, who passively receive and then faithfully preserve that message as an intact system. Instead, the Companions become active founders. I cannot assume the Companions to have been blank slates upon whom the perfect representation of Muḥammad was inscribed; rather, Muḥammad had no choice but to become the slate, as the Companions became active writers upon him. If we surrender to the Companions as mediators between Muḥammad and ourselves, this mediation itself is mediated in turn by their successors.

The Companions' experiences of Muḥammad mash together in the ḥadīth corpus, which looks like someone's episodic memory presented as a library—but instead of one person, it's the collective episodic memory of multiple generations, thousands of individuals collaborating to produce the appearance of one hive-mind, a community's shared mental archive and the vision of Muḥammad that rises from it. Even though the ḥadīth collections that became most authoritative for Sunnī Muslims, known simply as the "Six Books," do present the ḥadīths as narrations from chains of specific people, these identities often fade from view: Apart from the famous Companions who are centers of their own stories, many ḥadīth narrators appear in their reports as little more than names, faceless recorders, storehouses of retrievable data that together build our singular textual Muḥammad. For these Companions, we need to refer to further bodies of supplementary literature, such as the genre of biographical dictionaries, to flesh them out.

The argument upon which Sunnī ḥadīth science rests its case requires unflinching faith in the Companions as reporters; if you believe that a Companion might have distorted Muḥammad's message, the entire "science" of authenticating ḥadīths falls apart. Though they are not prophets, the Companions therefore hold a certain share of prophetic power. The Companions, though surrendering to Muḥammad's authority, become the ones who authorize him for history.

Premodern advocates for the binding power of ḥadīths argued that a well-evidenced ḥadīth equals the weight of eyewitness testimony; but is there a limit to the authority of an eyewitness? Even if we are willing to assume that a report about Muḥammad that is attributed to 'Ā'isha did, in fact, come from the historical 'Ā'isha, we have to recognize that an eyewitness reporter is still an editor, author, and *creator*: With her words, she produces the only Muḥammad that we can know. As reporter of his life, she possesses a degree of personal power over what she reports, or what she considers to be worth reporting. It is for this reason that scholar Sebastian Günther, advocating the use of modern literary theories in our study of the ḥadīth corpus, has suggested that we consider ḥadīths with an eye for fictionalization. By "fictionalization," Günther is not making a judgment on the historical authenticity of the accounts; even if all the data in a ḥadīth is reported truthfully, fictionalization still occurs when the narrator enacts his or her authorial sovereignty over the narrative.[6] In other words, telling a story—even a *true* story—requires there to be a storyteller. Our storyteller must decide which details are essential to the plot, which ones can be erased, and where the story begins and ends. In the ḥadīth corpus, we can find narrations in which a long stretch of time is covered with just one or two sentences, or the narrator reports events that s/he did not witness firsthand. Sometimes, perspective shifts between a firsthand "insider" perspective and that of an "outsider" who reports from a detached but omniscient vantage point, i.e., "The Prophet left me and went into the city, ________________ happened to him, and then he came back to me and said ________________." Organizing the facts into a coherent narrative, the Companion must decide *how* to tell the story. Before considering narrative strategies, however, the Companion must first decide that a sequence of events can even become a story worth telling: The Companion needs to endow the events with meaning and significance and then shape the events into a narrative that conveys the intended meaning and significance. The Companions cannot be imagined as mere transmitters of empirically observed facts regarding the Prophet, even if this was how they saw themselves. With every word, the Companions became interpreters.

It has been called a foundational claim of Sunnī Islam that the Muslims who took part in the first three degrees of ḥadīth transmission—Muḥammad's Companions, the Followers (Companions of the Companions), and the Followers of the Followers (Companions of the Companions of the Companions)—faithfully preserved what they had received and taught it to the ones who came after them. These are the salaf as-sālih, the pious predecessors. Before recognizing the Salaf and accepting their ḥadīth narrations as authoritative, however, we have to define the Salaf as a class; and to define them is to risk doing violence to them. As we exalt the Salaf above us, we also hang something over their heads: the power of naming.

Salafism's conception of the Salaf draws from ḥadīth reports, attributed to Companions such as 'Ā'isha, Ibn Mas'ūd, and Imran ibn Ḥusayn, with minor variations, in which Muḥammad names the best people as those in his qarn, followed by the next qarn, and then one qarn after that. These ḥadīths are employed to justify the Salafiyya's belief in a three-qarn Golden Age but then force the question: What's a qarn? Is it a class of people or a unit of time? Scholar Abed al-Rahman Tayyara has recently argued that meanings for *qarn* evolved gradually and in response to a developing historical consciousness among the early Muslims.[7] In the Qur'ān, *qarn* appears to generally signify "generation," "people," or "nation" (synonymous with *umma*) Tayyara shows the term to make slight shifts in meaning between two ḥadīths that are both attributed to Abū Hurayra. In the first, Muḥammad says that he came from the best of the qarns after Adam, and that "qarn after qarn until the qarn in which I was born came about." This ḥadīth could support a definition of *qarn* as "generation" or perhaps "nation." In the second ḥadīth, *qarn* more explicitly points to "nation," as Muḥammad links the Hour of Resurrection with a coming age in which his umma imitates the ways of the qarns that preceded it; when asked for further clarification, Muḥammad affirms that he was referring to the Persians and Byzantines. Though the Persians and Byzantines had preceded Muḥammad's community, they could not be considered as separate "generations," since these nations had existed for many generations and survived into Muḥammad's own era; *qarn* thus appears not to mark a measurement of time, but instead corresponds to *umma*.[8]

For those who conceptualized *qarn* as a category defined by time, identifying the three best qarns in history meant answering a question that had not been clearly addressed in the Qur'ān or ḥadīths: How many years makes a qarn? Different spans of time were theorized, reflecting "Muslims' concern to portray significant events in their early history in chronological order."[9] Some posited ten years as a qarn, based on the period in which Muḥammad lived in Medina; others suggested twenty years, roughly corresponding to the length of Muḥammad's prophetic mission; still others defined a qarn as forty years because it was at forty years of age that Muḥammad became a prophet, or sixty years because it approximated Muḥammad's lifespan. As an effort to "highlight certain stages in Islamic history representing the genuine spirit of Islam," thirty- and fifty-year qarns were suggested: thirty years because this measurement represented the four regimes that would be later designated as the Rāshidūn ("rightly guided") caliphates; fifty years included both the Rāshidūn period and Muḥammad's prophetic career within the Golden Age. All these numbers were supported by prophetic statements and associated with specific Companions.[10] Parallel to the emerging genre of biographical dictionaries organized by generation (ṭabaqa), some defined *qarn* as a period of seventy or eighty years, corresponding to the lifespan of a ṭabaqa. Other interpretations stretched the number to one hundred twenty years, marking the first qarn as starting with Muḥammad's birth and concluding with the caliphate of Yazīd ibn Mu'āwiyya. The conception of *qarn* that would become dominant corresponded to one hundred years, supported by traditions associated with the Companion 'Abd Allāh ibn Busr al-Māzinī, who was said to have reached the age of one hundred. When al-Māzinī was a small child, Muḥammad reportedly touched the mole on al-Māzinī's face and predicted that the boy would "live one qarn."[11]

Companion, like *qarn*, was a social construction and potentially unstable. Early traditionalists sought to nail down the concept as they increasingly attached power to the Companions as undoubtable reporters of Muḥammad's statements and actions. It could be for this reason that we don't seem to have a reference to the "Companions" as a clearly defined class prior to the accelerating development of ḥadīth evaluation in the ninth century CE.[12] The evolving field of ḥadīth science not only sought to preserve the legacy of the Companions, but it also, as support for its methodology, at least partly *created* the Companions as a category.

To properly follow the Companions meant knowing whom to include among their ranks. Anas ibn Malik, when asked whether he was the last surviving Companion, answered that there were indeed some people alive who had "seen" the Prophet, but they had not "accompanied him" (ṣaḥibahu). In the view of Anas, merely seeing Muḥammad did not make someone a Companion. The last surviving person to have laid eyes upon Muḥammad, Abū al-Ṭufayl, died in 718 CE, roughly a decade after Anas, and reportedly self-identified as someone who had *seen* rather than *accompanied*. Even if he had not claimed Companion status, traditionists of later centuries would designate Abū al-Ṭufayl as the last surviving Companion. His death, dated roughly a lunar century from the start of the Islamic calendar, might have also supported the view of *qarn* as equal to one hundred years, the age of the Companions as corresponding to the first Islamic century, and thus the age of the Salaf as the first three centuries. The possible irony here is that when it came to defining *Companion*, those scholars who regarded the Companions as custodians of pure Islam overruled the Companions themselves.[13]

The second generation of Muslims, the Followers (Tābi'ūn), also appear to have defined *Companion* in ways that would become too restrictive for later scholars, including the notion that to qualify as a Companion, one had to accompany Muḥammad for a full year and take part in at least one of his battles.[14] As the Companions became increasingly crucial to ḥadīth projects, the category of "Companion" adjusted. Fu'ad Jabali argues that it was in the third century of Islam (roughly the ninth century CE), as ḥadīth scholars asserted that their body of knowledge was sufficient for silencing all controversies, that the definition of *Companion* expanded to become as inclusive as possible. The more people who could be counted as Companions, the more ḥadīths that could be endorsed as authentic, thus the deeper the archive from which ḥadīth scholars could draw evidence for their arguments.[15] Anyone who had met the Prophet and died as a Muslim counted; *met* became the preferred verb over *seen* to avoid excluding Companions who were blind. Requiring that one remained Muslim until his/her death denied Companion status to apostates; but even people whom Muḥammad had personally disliked, such as al-Ḥakam ibn Abī al-'Ās al-Qurashī al-Umawī, still qualified as Companions if they had remained Muslims. The possibility of nonhuman Companions was discussed, with scholars deciding that while jinns could qualify for inclusion (as some jinns did apparently meet Muḥammad and accepted him as their prophet), angels could not (because it was not part of Muḥammad's prophetic mandate to teach them). The pre-Islamic prophets who had met Muḥammad during his visit to paradise, such as Adam, Noah, and Moses, could not be counted as Companions, because they had actually died centuries prior to meeting him; the exception was Jesus, who, having escaped crucifixion and ascended to the heavens without dying, was still alive when he met Muḥammad. A difficult point of contention was the matter of child Companions; some scholars charged that to be a Companion, one had to have met and followed Muḥammad while an adult. This position failed to take hold, since it would have meant downgrading the rank of numerous child Companions, most notably Muḥammad's grandsons, Ḥasan and Ḥusayn.[16]

Ḥadīth reports tell us that because the devil could not assume Muḥammad's form, anyone who saw Muḥammad in a dream *really* saw him, but claims of encounters in dreams or the realm of the unseen were not granted the power to qualify someone as Companion, lest the whole regulating function of "Companion" status fall apart.[17] Nonetheless, Muḥammad's relationship with Uways Qaranī, whose tomb was detonated by ISIS in May 2014, might complicate the Companions as a category. An ascetic contemporary of Muḥammad, Uways had nothing to wear but what he received in charity; he scavenged from dunghills; he either shaved his head bald or had a mass of disheveled hair; and he traveled through society inviting mockery and revulsion. Unable to leave his mother's house because she depended on his care, Uways never had a face-to-face encounter with Muḥammad; but the two apparently engaged in telepathic communication, granting Uways a privileged status that was recognized by the likes of 'Umar and 'Alī. Uways wasn't *exactly* a Companion, but the prestige of his unique relationship with Muḥammad contributed to a tradition of what would be called Uwaysī Ṣūfīsm, in which initiatory knowledge could be passed from teachers to students outside the normal routes of personal contact.[18]

So how many Companions were there? Muḥammad began his career as a fringe street preacher with a handful of followers but died as the head of a metatribal federation. Some put the number of Muslims in his lifetime at more than one hundred thousand, but not all these individuals had necessarily met him in person, and not all Companions became equal contributors to the communal memory. Just a little more than 1,000 Companions, approaching just 1 percent of the higher estimates, are named in the Sunnī ḥadīth corpus as reporters of Muḥammad's statements and actions. Of this 1,000-plus, only 208 and 213 are respectively included in the two compilations regarded as most authoritative by Sunnī Muslims, and just 149 find their way into both. Nearly half of these Companions are credited with offering only a single ḥadīth each; 55 have given 100 reports or more; 11 have given more than 500 reports. Within the top 10 most prolific transmitters, the numbers make big jumps: The single greatest transmitter, Abū Hurayra, reported 5,374 ḥadīths, more than twice as much as the second most prolific transmitter ('Abd Allāh ibn 'Umar, 2,630) and nearly 5,000 more than the tenth-ranked transmitter, the caliph 'Umar (537).[19] Each of the top 7 transmitters, distinguished as the Mukaththirūn, provided 1,000 reports or more.

Looking at the most productive narrators among the Companions, we find an important trend: long lives after the death of Muḥammad. In a culture of oral tradition that preserves its archive in flesh-and-blood bodies rather than written documents, longevity can become truth-making power; of the Companions who were properly positioned, those who lived longest naturally became the owners of history. Muḥammad died in the year 632 CE; of the top ten transmitters of ḥadīths, only two died within twenty years of him, and the rest all survived him by at least forty-four years. Abū Hurayra almost reached the age of eighty; Abd Allāh ibn ‘Umar approached ninety, and Jabir ibn Abd Allāh saw ninety-four. Anas, who might have been the last surviving Companion depending on your criteria, lived to be over one hundred, passing away roughly eighty years after Muḥammad. ‘Ā’isha, who was married to Muḥammad while still a child, became the fourth most prolific narrator of ḥadīths. She served as a crucial resource for information on Muḥammad due not only to her intimate access to his daily life, but also to the fact that she lived well into her sixties, which enabled her to teach generations of students for whom Muḥammad was only a phantom of the distant and unknowable past.

Compare ‘Ā’isha’s prominence in the Sunnī ḥadīth corpus to the virtual invisibility of Muḥammad’s daughter Fāṭima, who was roughly the same age as ‘Ā’isha but died less than a year after Muḥammad. ‘Ā’isha and Fāṭima were connected to the two men whose short power struggle would define Muslim futures: ‘Ā’isha was the daughter of Abū Bakr, recognized by Sunnī Muslims as the first successor to Muḥammad’s political authority; Fāṭima was married to ‘Alī, regarded in Shī’ī traditions as the rightful successor whose position had been usurped. ‘Ā’isha and Fāṭima also apparently despised each other, but the caliph’s daughter triumphed over the Prophet’s daughter, in part because ‘Ā’isha had a greater opportunity to push her memories into the future. In canonical ḥadīth scholar Nisā’ī’s *Sunan al-Kubra*, for example, ‘Ā’īsha is named as the source for 1,285 ḥadīths, while only two ḥadīths are attributed to Fāṭima. Fifteenth-century scholar Ibn Ḥajar al-‘Asqalānī even stated that one-fourth of Islamic legal tradition was based on teachings from ‘Ā’īsha.[20] What if they traded lifespans and political fortunes, and ‘Ā’isha’s voice was silenced while Fāṭima survived to transmit her legal opinions, scriptural interpretations, and recollections of her father? What might have changed in our views of Muḥammad's life and personality, or Islam as we know it? This could have massively impacted the tradition, since not only would we trade 'Ā'isha's perspectives for Fāṭima's, but these perspectives would have been transmitted to different heirs and thus transformed scholarly networks in the following generations. Among 'Ā'isha's students was her nephew, 'Urwa ibn al-Zubayr, who became known as one of the foundational jurists of Medina and a teacher of Ibn Shihāb al-Zuhrī, who in turn became an Umayyad court scholar, teacher of caliphs, pioneer in the use of transmission lineage (isnād) for ḥadīth studies, and a prolific contributor of material to the next generation of ḥadīth masters. Without 'Ā'isha's transmissions or the brand prestige that her name lent to students, we would not be working with the same tradition.

As the generations rolled on, 'Ā'isha and Fāṭima would both become appropriated as emblematic Muslim women for rival traditions and visions of history—'Ā'isha for Sunnism, Fāṭima for Shī'ism—based on not only their respective relationships to Abū Bakr and 'Alī, but also their special closeness to the Prophet. This would have impacted the words that are put in their mouths and the details of their lives that would be recorded or forgotten. Whether historical or not, reports that Muḥammad praised 'Ā'isha's superiority over other women served a political purpose, defending 'Ā'isha's legacy against her opposition. Likewise, for transmitters to report that Muḥammad said, "Fāṭima is a piece of me, and whoever hurts her has hurt me," also becomes more than an ideologically innocent portrayal of a father's love. Muḥammad's words against those who would offend

Fāṭima serve a sectarian polemic and ironically a pro-*Sunnī* one: Muḥammad issues his warning in response to ʿAlī's attempt to take a second wife, implicating ʿAlī as the offender.

Multiple ḥadīths highlight ʿĀ'isha's young age and her playing with dolls, while sometimes representing her interactions with Muḥammad with a vibe more daughter-father than wife-husband; in the same Sunnī corpus, Fāṭima's childhood receives no comparable attention. Even if Fāṭima herself did not live long enough to present her memories to the next generation, one might expect to see more of her in the recollections of others. It has been suggested that as the Sunnī ḥadīth corpus developed in part as one community's assertion of its superior roots against the claims of other Muslim communities, these presences and absences were politically purposeful. Through its portrayal of Muḥammad acting in a fatherly role toward ʿĀ'isha, the literature siphons away some of Fāṭima's importance as Muḥammad's favorite daughter, reassigning that role to his favorite wife.[21]

Memory is not politically neutral. Things are remembered because people deem them worthy of remembering: first the original rememberer, followed by those with whom s/he shares the memory, and in turn those to whom they transmit the memory. What happens if we operate on the assumption that traditional methods of ḥadīth evaluation can reliably trace reports back to specific Companions of Muḥammad, but cannot surrender our heads to the Companions as mini-prophets beyond question or criticism? One tradition has Muḥammad telling us that his Companions are like stars in the sky: We can follow one and be guided. Unfortunately, the stars accuse each other of having faulty memories or even lying. In the same canonical ḥadīth collections that have Abū Hurayra attributing misogynistic statements to Muḥammad, we also read 'Ā'isha denouncing these narrations as false. If we are to regard the Companions as possessing universal probity in regard to their ḥadīth reports, it doesn't seem that the Companions themselves engaged all "Companions," whatever that term might have meant to them, with such confidence. Political struggles split the Companions into rival camps, and 'Ā'isha even raised an army against 'Alī. What if I maintain a Salafī logic in which truth rests with the original community, while preserving a Shī'ī recognition that the original community was broken? The generations immediately following the Companions remained bitterly divided over which Companions ought to be privileged over others. The gradually developing idea that all Companions were noble and trustworthy, enforced by ḥadīth reports against insulting them and scholars asserting that to disrespect a Companion amounted to heresy or disbelief, might have developed as a healing mechanism for a community that had been traumatized by power struggles and civil wars—or, more cynically, as a means of consolidating voices from the past to better authorize the present.

After the Companions, another round of creation takes place with the Followers, a category that requires—as in the case of the Companions—acts of definition. Many ḥadīths appear as taking place in question/answer sessions between Companions and Followers: A Companion is asked about the practice of the Prophet and relates what s/he had witnessed. Even when a ḥadīth is not explicitly presented as such, it can often be imagined as emerging in this kind of setting. In treating the Companions as authoritative holders of the Prophet's legacy, asking questions on matters that were important to them, and constructing memories of the Companions just as the Companions had done to the Prophet, the Followers become creators and foundational figures in their own right.

In the class after the Followers (the Followers of the Followers), we begin to see the emergence of ḥadīth science as a professional field and also the start of a communal identity forming around networks of ḥadīth scholars. Developing methods to assess the authenticity of prophetic reports (an enterprise that demanded the systematic evaluation and ranking of transmitters and creation of new categories), organizing the collected ḥadīths in various formats, and perceiving their methods both as the basis for authority and as an identity defined against the advocates of other methods, these ḥadīth scholars kept the past alive in ways that could not help but change its form, making the past into something new.

The humanity of the transmitters is perhaps easier or harder to notice depending on the ways that ḥadīth collections are structured. The collections of the generation that preceded the Six Books' master compilers were often presented in musnad format, which meant that ḥadīths were arranged not by topic, but rather the Companions who reported them. While musnad works are insanely difficult to use while researching specific questions, they also emphasize the fact of these reports coming from individuals, allowing us to recognize our Muḥammad as the composite that he is, an assemblage of stories from those who remembered him. Though the variations, disagreements, and personal conflicts between Companions can still shine through in the collections organized by topic, the topic-based collections might speak more to an era after the collective reliability of Companions had already been established, when there was no longer a reason to refer to one Companion's reports before another's. The topic-based collections would thus represent an intensified territorialization of the corpus, dissolving much of the Companions' presence as individual subjectivities. Through a different choice of structure, multiplicity becomes unity, communal chaos moves toward a coherent system, and Muḥammad becomes more efficient as supreme lawgiver.

In a circle of self-authorization, our scholars act as trustees of the Companions, who are made to speak for the Prophet, who tells us to follow the Companions, who in turn affirm that we must follow our scholars. Without upholding the necessary assumptions to keep this wheel turning, the whole edifice falls apart. Even if I were to accept every canonical ḥadīth as really coming from the Companion to whom it was attributed (a leap that I don't personally make), I would still have to face the ḥadīth corpus as a battlefield of memories, a site of winners and losers, and consider the voices that *aren't* there, the memories that failed to become canon, the voices that were edited, adjusted, forgotten, or erased.[22]

Whether or not the Prophet's given name was actually Muḥammad, he became *muḥammad*, "site of praise," through those for whom he was the object. He cannot be *my* Muḥammad without their collective reconstruction of him, their shared authoring of him, a process in which his agency was limited or nonexistent. Even in his own lifetime, Muḥammad could not have claimed full authorial power over his body. Depending on whether you read Bakhtin or Sartre, the Salaf's authoring of Muḥammad can be seen as either an act of love and generosity or one of theft and enslavement. At any rate, the Muḥammad whom

I claim to love is an image that I have received from others, rather than Muḥammad's image of himself. Muḥammad cannot be reduced to an individual self who appeared at a specific moment in history. Instead, he is that self as produced by the gaze of his Companions, and his Companions' gaze as transmitted to the Followers, and then the Followers' reception of the gaze as processed by the Followers of the Followers, and this collaboration as reprocessed by all of us since. Muḥammad's body, which places me in relation to many, many people other than him, and contexts other than his own, remains an inescapably communal body.

Imagining Muḥammad's body as a communal one is not a problem if I believe in the first three qarns as fundamentally united in their vision of his life and their own history. Something changes when I look closer at the chaos within the so-called Golden Age and the potential for celebrating multiplicities within it. Examination of the ḥadīth corpus gives me a fluid, malleable Muḥammad who shapeshifts over the generations, as narratives mutate in adaptation to the changing political contexts and needs of Muslim communities.[23]

The Muḥammad that we have received from this process, of course, would speak to the needs of some more than others, depending on who could take part in his construction. Examining the chains of ḥadīth transmitters, we can track changes. In the earliest generations, as one could assume, most ḥadīth transmitters were Arab. However, the demographics of ḥadīth scholarship shifted over time; later in the chains, the majority of transmitters are non-Arab, primarily from the lands east of Iraq.[24] It has been suggested that Persians and Central Asians took over ḥadīth scholarship as a means of compensating for their position on the "fringe" of Islam and insecurities over proper Muslim practice; ḥadīth mastery enabled this mimesis by non-Arabs to become the new measure of authenticity.[25] We also need to look at gender. Though 'Ā'isha and other women in the early community were recognized as ḥadīth transmitters, careful investigation of the chains of transmission reveals that women were progressively excluded from reporting ḥadīths, due to factors such as the evolving professionalization of ḥadīth study and the male-privileged rihla culture of traveling to learn ḥadīths in distant cities. By the time that women found their way back into ḥadīth scholarship, the field had already crystallized, having produced its canonical texts.[26] These various marginalizations mean that when a report presents itself as the firsthand account of an Ethiopian woman who personally knew the Prophet, her textual representation comes to us through scholars who were overwhelmingly neither Ethiopian nor women. Perhaps we should remember this when reading about Umm Ayman, the Ethiopian woman praised in ḥadīths and sīra for her exceptional piety while also portrayed as a bumbling comic figure who cannot properly say *as-salāmu alaikum* and who unknowingly drinks an entire bowl of Muḥammad's urine.

Muḥammad's shapeshifting occurred alongside, among other things, the development of formalized methods for evaluating ḥadīths. The science by which premodern scholars sought to authenticate ḥadīths was not simply a legal science or act of apolitical devotion, but as much a polemical, sectarian enterprise, a performance of inclusions and exclusions, projection of contemporary prejudices and assumptions onto earlier generations, and the formation of an orthodoxy.

Ḥadīth transmitters were not necessarily disqualified as reliable sources for holding unacceptable theological opinions or affiliating with reviled groups, but again, a close look at chains of transmission reveals that the ḥadīth networks did tend to marginalize sectarian reporters.[27]

The proto-Sunnī ḥadīth scholars' particular methodology of stabilizing history and speaking for the Prophet, resting upon absolute trust in the Companions as reporters—in opposition to a competing methodology that prioritized Muḥammad's biological descendants and the specific Companions and Followers who supported them—is how ḥadīth science gave us the thing that we call "Sunnism," which did not exist at the time that the project started. Assumptions that (1) Muḥammad's Sunna is the necessary supplement to the Qur'ān, and (2) this Sunna is knowable to us through the canonical ḥadīth corpus and the methods upon which it rests, represent ideologies that branded themselves so powerfully that people could conflate them with Islam at large. For many, the urgency of an accessible ḥadīth-based Sunna has graduated from sectarian ideology into common sense.

Some argue that the ḥadīth corpus contains its own undoing. A report attributed to Abū Sa'id al-Khudrī states that Muḥammad had prohibited the writing of any words from him beyond the Qur'ān; in an Abū Hurayra report, Muḥammad finds a group of Companions writing down what they had heard from him and expresses his disapproval.[28] Ibn Mas'ūd is said to have washed the ink away from pages of written ḥadīths.[29] Among the Companions, 'Umar appears to be the foremost opponent of writing ḥadīths: It is reported that 'Umar had once considered writing the sayings of the Prophet into a collection, and had consulted with other Companions on the project, but then decided that it was a bad idea after remembering a past nation that had grown devoted to books other than the book of God. In another report, ‘Umar commands that written statements of Muḥammad be destroyed, comparing them to the Jewish Mishnah. The most provocative report depicts Muḥammad in his final illness, requesting that writing materials be brought to him so that he can leave his people with something that will keep them from going astray. In one version of the story, the people around Muḥammad start to quarrel over whether to obey him, some suggesting that he is delirious, and Muḥammad never gets his chance to provide a final written statement. In another version, ‘Umar personally shoots down the request, insisting that the revealed word of God is sufficient. There are also reports in which Companions such as ‘Umar and ‘Ā’isha express skepticism or outright disbelief at what they hear presented as prophetic statements, and ‘Umar is said to have warned against growing distracted with ḥadīths in a general sense, advising his companions to instead "bare the Qur’ān."[30]

The evidence, however, does not compel us to assume that transmitters of these "anti-ḥadīth" reports actually interpreted them as discouraging interest in ḥadīths altogether. Reports of the Prophet or a Companion that appear to reject the transmission of ḥadīths tend to focus on the act of *writing* ḥadīths. Writing, particularly in the still-developing Arabic script, was a relatively new and controversial technology. It seems that for the ḥadīths' early transmitters, the concern was not over the authority of ḥadīth itself, but rather the question of writing versus memorization, a debate with important social consequences.

In his examination of the antiwriting ḥadīths, Gregor Schoeler finds them to trace back to four transmitters. Two of these transmitters were from Medina, one was from Baṣra, and one was from Kūfa but later moved to Mecca. The Kūfan, Sufyān ibn 'Uyaynah (d. 811), also appears as a transmitter in one version of the report of Muḥammad wanting to write while on his deathbed. While other reports of this incident include Ibn 'Abbās expressing regret that because of their quarreling, the Muslims had missed their last chance at Muḥammad's guidance, this detail is absent from Ibn 'Uyaynah's version. What's interesting is that despite their status as transmitters of ḥadīths against the writing of ḥadīths, Ibn 'Uyaynah and other figures are themselves reported to have transmitted ḥadīths in writing.[31] Despite 'Umar's apparent resistance to ḥadīths in general, his son 'Abdullah also transmitted ḥadīths, even in writing.[32]

According to Schoeler, debate over the proper method of preserving ḥadīths was politically loaded, intertwined with ḥadīth scholars' feelings toward the empire. The first collection of written ḥadīths was reportedly produced under orders of the Umayyad ruler Umar II (r. 717–20), "for fear the tradition might vanish and its supporters might die out."[33] Observing the prominence of opposition to writing ḥadīths in Baṣra (Ibn Ḥanbal, who did not oppose writing, even described memorization as the Baṣrans' method), Kūfa, and Medina, Schoeler connects the rejection of writing ḥadīths to anti-Umayyad sentiment in these cities: "Outside Syria people were not prepared simply to accept ḥadīths that had been codified and circulated under the aegis of the Umayyad government."[34] In cities such as Mecca and Sana', which were farther removed from the Umayyad power base of Damascus, opposition to writing ḥadīths did not find the same intensity, and it appears that there were written collections independent of the government.

Challenging the popular narrative that early Muslims were resistant to writing ḥadīths, Schoeler suggests that writing had been important among the earliest Muslims, including "books" that existed primarily in the form of scholars' lecture notes. Additionally, he argues that opposition to writing ḥadīths in Medina and the scholarly centers of Iraq related not to the questionable status of ḥadīths or the absolute centrality of the Qur'ān, but to a broader fear of writing's destructive power in government hands. The Umayyad regime's ambition to concretize and standardize in books what had been a fluid, malleable, and charismatic "oral doctrine" constituted an attempt at religious hegemony, a power grab. For this reason, Schoeler argues, Iraqi ḥadīth scholars resisted the state-sponsored codification of ḥadīths just as they had earlier resisted the state-sponsored codification of the Qur'ān.[35]

Questions surrounding the rise of ḥadīth books also highlighted an epistemological problem familiar to Greek philosophy: the tension between speech and writing. What did it mean to access knowledge through a book without the physical presence of its author? Could the knowledge retrieved from a book be considered as reliable as that obtained in face-to-face instruction from a human being? The shift of ḥadīth transmission from a flexible oral tradition to an inflexible text-based one threatened to destroy the established structures of learning and teaching ḥadīths and also cancel the social relevance of ḥadīth transmitters as a professional class—a danger that would be partly realized in the generations after the great ḥadīth scholars compiled their canonical collections. It has been suggested that ḥadīths in which Muḥammad forbids the writing of ḥadīths originated as expressions of traditionists' political and professional anxieties, while pro-writing ḥadīths emerged later as responses to them.[36]

What we now take for granted was once contested. When the great al-Shāfi'ī (767–820) argued for the supremacy of ḥadīths, he had to do so because not all Muslims shared his views. Al-Shāfi'ī's treatments of the Sunna and ḥadīths did not reflect what everyone would recognize as the obviously "traditional" point of view but needed to triumph over opposing arguments to *become* traditional. Al-Shāfi'ī's view of ḥadīth was not the only choice available at the time. The jurist Mālik ibn Anas (711–795), while a ḥadīth scholar himself, resisted the privileging of ḥadīths as most representative of the prophetic Sunna. Rather than a ḥadīth-based concept of the Sunna, Mālik argued that the Sunna was best found through amāl, the collective precedent of the Medina community, in which Muḥammad had established his preferences as the public norms for an entire city. Advocacy for Medina's amāl was not necessarily in opposition to transmitted ḥadīths; the two resources could, and often did, serve to confirm each other. When they disagreed, however, Mālik privileged amāl, being the reflection of knowledge in Medina's public habitus, over ḥadīth reports, which consisted of individuals reporting what they had heard from other individuals.[37] Prioritizing the city of the Prophet over the ḥadīth-transmitter networks centered in Iraq, Mālik remarked, "The Qur'ān was not revealed on the Euphrates."[38]

The cluster of ninth-century ḥadīth scholars who relied on ḥadīths' primacy for their own claims became the nucleus of what we now call "Sunnism."[39] The various local schools, which came to be branded under the names of seminal scholars associated with them (i.e., the Mālikī school named for Mālik), were consolidated into a developing communal consciousness that amounted to more than being simply non-Shī'ī. In the generations following the ninth-century traditionalists, a growing culture of canon around seminal ḥadīth collections provided a common textual ground on which these schools could argue with each other, enabling them to come together as "Sunnī" Muslims.[40] Rather than simply the system of Muḥammad and the early community, then, Sunnī tradition is in fact a *tradition*, a process, a construction that accumulated over the course of centuries.

In what I now call my Salafī years, it never occurred to me that the development of our ḥadīth corpus took place in competition against rival traditionalisms. To me, the great ḥadīth scholars were simply the natural heirs to the original Muslims, cataloguing straightforward knowledge of Muḥammad's life in a political vacuum. I remember myself in 1995, carrying all nine heavy volumes of the most authorized Sunnī ḥadīth collection, Ṣaḥīḥ al-Bukhārī, on my back through the Islamabad airport and some twenty-plus hours later, the Rochester airport, feeling as if this had been a devotional act that amounted to carrying the Prophet himself. The textual tradition has since lost that kind of power over me; it cannot be what had once made me so urgently lug it across the world. The books do not add up to make

Muḥammad, but present only a particular Muḥammad who has been assembled by conflict and factionalism at every step. My Salafī desire is not satisfied with what Salafism can offer in response to the problems of memory, history, and interpretation. These days, my hands are empty. My burden has been lightened, you could say.

But I don't throw out the ḥadīths. I recognize both my dependence on the Salaf and the limits of what they can give. I attempt to sit at their feet and hear these stories, knowing that they're stories. Human lives, perhaps even the lives of prophets, are too complex and contradictory to shoehorn into singular themes or messages. There are almost ninety thousand seconds in a day, and Muḥammad lived more than sixty years. Any attempt to make his roughly two billion seconds on this earth—the overwhelming majority of which went unreported and are lost to us forever—into a coherent story with a clear point at the end is always going to be mythmaking. When you think about it that way, biography is forever doomed to be fiction. What the ḥadīth corpus offers is vast enough that it tends to give people the Muḥammad that they want to find. I search for the communal Muḥammad, the hologram of Muḥammad that we create together in our conversations, and also for traces of *my* Muḥammad, the Muḥammad who appeared in my ayahuasca trip, after the dimethyltryptamine bound itself to my brain's nerve receptors and my brain experienced increases of alpha activity in its occipital lobes and increases of theta amplitudes in both the occipital and frontal areas. Some ḥadīths will touch me in the right ways and cause my brain to release oxytocin and dopamine, chemicals associated with human bonding, trust, love, and pleasure. The right texts can work in my blood like drugs.

Here's an example of that kind of ḥadīth:

> When the Prophet (ṣ) emigrated to Medina, aṭ-Ṭufayl bin 'Amr emigrated to join him, and another man from his people emigrated with him, but the climate of Medina did not suit them and he fell sick. He was unhappy, so he took an iron arrowhead and cut his finger joints, and his hands bled until he died. Aṭ-Ṭufayl bin 'Amr saw him in his dream, looking good but with his hands bandaged. He said to him: "What did your Lord do with you?" He said: "He forgave me because I had emigrated to join his Prophet (ṣ)." He said: "Why do I see your hands bandaged?" He said: "It was said to me: 'We will not set right anything of yours that you damaged yourself.'" Aṭ-Ṭufayl told his dream to the Messenger of Allāh (ṣ) and the Messenger of Allāh (ṣ) said: "O Allāh, forgive his hands too."[41]

Relating this ḥadīth to others, I'd get a quiver in my voice. Reading it privately, I have felt the water in my eyes and electric charges in my chest. I imagine the Companion first heartbroken at his friend's suicide, then confused and troubled by the appearance of his friend in a dream—in a setting in which dreams were treated with the utmost seriousness—and presenting his confusion to the Prophet. Then I picture Muḥammad, his tender heart devastated by the suicide, reflecting on what the hardships of refugee life in an unfamiliar city had done to this man, and then overwhelmed with Allāh's compassion and love for a broken creation. He also witnesses the suffering of the survivor, the grieving friend who stands before him, hoping for him to make sense of it all. Muḥammad pleads with Allāh for the man who had injured himself to be healed and made whole again; his prayer might also be an act of mercy for the friend who was left behind. This story does something to me every time, even while I know that other ḥadīths might undo it. I don't assume that every episode that I find in the ḥadīth collections will resonate with me in this way, nor am I even committed to the logic of salvation that underpins this whole story; but I am not always convinced that I need to care. In my attempt at surrender to the origins, which aren't even the origins beyond doubt, I still have to decide things for myself, namely, which pieces are useful.

It sounds like a slacker move, but this is how I navigate the immense textual sea of ḥadīth. Like the original eyewitnesses who shared their experiences of Muḥammad, we're all editors: We select what deserves to be remembered and how we should remember it. Consider modern discussions of Muḥammad's marriage practices. Among the early generations, Muḥammad's vigorous sexuality wasn't a problem; there were even ḥadīths asserting that Muḥammad had the sexual power of forty men, and that he had received the blessing of supernatural virility after drinking a potion given to him by the angel Gabriel. In postcolonial modernity, however, after Victorian England ruled over half of the world's Muslim population and a celibate Christ became the globalized image of a perfected religious body, Muḥammad's polygamy couldn't be denied but had to rewrite itself. Today, the possibility of Muḥammad having even a normal human sex drive, let alone an exceptional or superhuman one, makes some people uncomfortable; in modern pamphlets, Muḥammad's multiple marriages are explained away as tribal network-building projects, acts of charity for widows who were considered unmarriageable, or lessons in antiracism and religious pluralism. In another time, these defenses would not have been necessary. The Salaf do not appear to have been troubled by the idea of a prophet who loved sex,[42] nor did they take issue with details of Muḥammad's sex life, which includes not only plural marriage but also child marriage and concubinage, that are controversial today. The data might remain mostly intact, but points of emphasis undergo significant shifts. There's no room in the pamphlet for every ḥadīth, so pamphlet writers must locate the essence for themselves and work from there.

I've been reading articles at Suhaib Webb's online home, SuhaibWebb.com, considering how Muḥammad's biography and the ḥadīth corpus are used to construct a certain kind of American Muslim masculinity. Many of the contributors to the site, while disavowing terms like *feminist*, nonetheless employ Muḥammad's own conduct as a means of correcting gendered injustices and inequalities in their communities. They show examples of Muḥammad empowering women in leadership roles and use Muḥammad's own behavior as a counter against contemporary stereotypes of masculinity.[43] It allows for significant blind spots, of course, and amounts to a slightly progressive and uncritical pamphlet. It's not "science," and it can't be; there's no method that could make any of this objective.

On the other side, I was recently added to a Facebook group called "Radical Muslims." As a mission statement, the group offered the following:

> We believe the Prophet Muhammad [saw] was a radical-feminist-environmental anti-racist community organizer,

> activist and freedom fighter that believed in freeing people from the status quo and freeing them from oppression through Islam and Allah [swt]. And we believe in following that tradition.[44]

These people are not "Salafī" in the popular sense, but they're doing what Salafīs do. Like Salafīs, they represent their own values as true to the origins. Like anyone who wants a conversation with a man who died nearly fifteen centuries ago, they have to do most of his talking for him. Was the Prophet a feminist? How would one find out? Did he identify himself with this term? Were there Arabic words for *feminism* or *sexism* in the seventh century? The claim that Muḥammad was "antiracist" also becomes complicated when confronted with a closer reading. It's not a question of whether Muḥammad endorsed or opposed racism; because "race" itself is a modern fiction, there could not have been "races" in seventh-century Arabia, and thus no possibility for anyone to express racism or antiracism. Asking what Muhammad said about racism is like asking what he said about the Internet. Yes, there was skin color prejudice and ancestral/tribal prejudice, and we can talk about what Muḥammad said on these issues, but to make an argument regarding Muḥammad's views on "race" would require at least some educated guessing. One report of the Prophet that is used to support his image as antiracist has him saying that people must obey their ruler, even if the ruler is an Ethiopian slave. In addition to being Ethiopian, the hypothetical leader in this tradition is marked by bodily peculiarities such as amputated arms, a mutilated face, or, in the most popular version, a head like a raisin. Perhaps this ḥadīth was intended to condemn what we would call racial prejudice; or maybe the point was to stress the importance of obeying one's ruler by using as an example a man who, by a particular setting's preferences for ancestry, social status, and physical appearance, would have been the least likely to rule. Is this ḥadīth about promoting equality among all human families or simply upholding political order at all costs? One reading is not more straightforward or "literal" than the other: To understand requires that we make a choice. There are also Qur'ānic verses and prophetic statements that interpreters have applied to modern concerns about nationalism. Among the earliest Muslims, however, the notion of Islam as being uncompromisingly egalitarian was not yet fully developed; non-Arab Muslims such as Bilāl had to align with Arab tribes as honorary members or "clients," which often amounted to a second-class status. Al-Shāfi'ī, writing at a time in which newly Arabized non-Arabs (al-'ajam) threatened the stability of Qur'ānic interpretation, argued that non-Arabs should defer to the authority of Arabs due to Arabs' superior grasp of the Qur'ān's language and what he saw as their innate connection to its logic.[45] The Shu'ubiyya movement of the ninth century, which challenged Arab claims of religious privilege over non-Arabs, was regarded by such a seminal figure as Aḥmad ibn Ḥanbal as subversive and touching on heresy.[46]

As for the "Radical Muslims" group's presentations of Muḥammad as an environmentalist, community organizer, freedom fighter, and so on: Rather than say that they are right or wrong, we can recognize such claims as acts of translation, which means that they must be acts of interpretation and innovation. These issues aside, the Radical Muslims' idea of Muḥammad personally resonates with me. This feminist, antiracist Muḥammad isn't the least charming Muḥammad that you could invent. More power to them, even if they wouldn't survive a Salafī critique.

Modern Salafīs, invested in the binding power of authentic ḥadīths, have evaluated the veracity of ḥadīth transmissions with new rigor and iconoclastic rebellion, even challenging the most canonical collections.[47] Salafī scholars such as Nasir al-Din al-Albani, the most prominent Salafī ḥadīth critic of the twentieth century, subject ḥadīths to heightened scrutiny because they retain faith in traditional methods of ḥadīth evaluation: They insist that the science of transmitter criticism does what it is supposed to do. They believe that through the methods that made these texts possible, they can retrieve the historical Muḥammad and achieve certainty. This is not where my own Salafī project could go, because I'm not subscribing to the same assumptions. If a Salafī wants to question more than the results of the great ḥadīth scholars' methods—questioning the methods themselves, looking closer at the string that holds this tradition together—the whole thing might fall apart.

The ḥadīth corpus, like the Qur'ān, comes to us as literature. Historically reliable or not, it comes with all the problems of reading literature. When our hologram of 'Ā'isha says that Muḥammad's character was the Qur'ān itself, she tells us that the key to one indecipherable text is another indecipherable text, another locked door that needs its own keys. But if I'm looking for experiences of the Qur'ān beyond its argument—namely, a way to renew the Qur'ān through my own presence in the world—the ḥadīth corpus at least gives me some means of embodying whatever I experience through the Qur'ān. To imitate Muḥammad in even minor acts can contribute to what Michel Foucault called a "technology of self," through which individuals perform "operations on their own bodies and souls, thoughts, conduct, and way of being, so as to transform themselves in order to attain a certain state of happiness, purity, wisdom, perfection, or immortality."[48] Because the ḥadīth corpus gets much more detailed than the Qur'ān regarding bodily practices, "Qur'ān-only" Muslims often dismiss ḥadīth-oriented Muslims as overly concerned with trivial matters such as bathroom habits. Really, I can open up ḥadīth collections and read about how the Prophet squatted, where he went, what direction he faced, how he cleaned himself, and which of his Companions held the water for him. I can read Companions debating over whether he ever stood to urinate. Muslims in the early days were mocked for this attention to detail, as a polytheist heckled the Companion Salmān al-Farsī: "Your prophet has taught you everything, even how to shit!"[49] Maybe this is what I actually want, and I want it more than I want to decipher lectures from mystery gods. I am looking for myself as a human being, and I want a way to shit that calls me to my fullest humanity. Shitting in a particular way can actually do this, if it points to the man who touches my heart, or an idea of that man, a fiction of him that negotiates with other fictions. My Sunna-compliant anus becomes a site of truth, a new text to read. If I am always trying to act out an image of Muḥammad-ness, even my bathroom habits can become triggers to activate a better self. Just as pretending to be sick might produce real symptoms, perhaps my pretending to live in Muḥammad's way can give me the symptoms of a real Muslim.

While the Qur'ān becomes an event in my body through scripts from the ḥadīth traditions, I also have a life outside myself, the world that I share with my brothers and sisters. For whatever the Qur'ān is/says, I hope at least to make my body a Muslim one, and then place my Muslim body in a room with other Muslim bodies. In corporeal experience, the ḥadīth corpus finds special power as the source of a lived Islam that writes itself on our flesh. The ḥadīth corpus gives us details that become our shared behavioral script, through which I could function in the mosque even after ayahuasca had cleared my head out. Honestly, it's more important to me that I know how to act in a prayer line than that we're all praying to the same thing.

It seems hard to fathom, considering the trillions of plant combinations possible in the Amazon, how people could have discovered the recipe for ayahuasca. Because I am ignorant to the traditional botanies of indigenous peoples in the Amazon, it strikes me as a beautiful accident: In the infinite randomness of the rain forest, someone stumbled upon a miracle, real baraka in drinkable form. This also frames my imagination of our sacred archive. I approach the volumes of prophetic reports less as a coercive law or sectarian polemic than something like a two-million-square-mile rain forest in which we can wander and explore, pulling leaves from trees and mixing them into experimental brews. Some would find the comparison distasteful, but when it comes to manipulating reality, texts and drugs might not be so far removed from each other.

When I play in the archive, critical rigor does not give me the Muḥammad who opens himself to encounter. The Amazon model doesn't give me a new theory or method for dealing with ḥadīths, nothing that will reinvent Islamic legal and ritual tradition if you care about such things. I only find justifications for no longer taking much interest in theories and methods. My best hope with these textual sources is to fall into glimpses of a Muḥammad whom I love irrationally, and who binds me to the communities that love him.

5

IBN ḤANBAL ACTION FIGURE!

>>> . . . it is only through the knife of the anatomist that we have the science of anatomy, and that the knife of the anatomist is also an instrument which explores only by doing violence. <<< —**Norbert Wiener**[1]

"WITH WHOM FROM the past will the coming generations of thinkers commune?" asks Ebrahim Moosa in *Ghazālī and the Poetics of Imagination*.[2] Building on Derrida, Moosa discusses the ways in which engaging thinkers of the past anticipates the intellectuals of the future, speaking to future philosophers who already exist; they exist because we visualize them; we make them possible and speak to them. Introducing his work on al-Ghazālī (1058–1111), Moosa considers al-Ghazālī's "ambivalent relationship" with Manṣūr al-Ḥallaj, who had been tortured to death a century earlier, and in turn the engagement of al-Ghazālī by 'Ayn al-Quḍāt al-Hamadhānī (d.1131), who was executed roughly twenty years after al-Ghazālī's death. Each of these figures, Moosa explains, "signaled a mutation" and "refused to yield to the hegemonic discourses of his day," for which they were "exposed to varying degrees of suffering and dangers within the confessional community" (Moosa notes that while al-Ghazālī himself was not executed, his books suffered the violence of burning during his own lifetime).[3] Even if their relationships to Islamic tradition were challenged, these figures nonetheless became contributors to that tradition and, to different degrees, would be seen as representatives of the tradition itself. In this sense, al-Ghazālī is treated not as an innovator who *added* to Islam, but rather as someone who articulated the highest truths of an essence that was *already there*. But that depends on whom you ask.

I am interested in the process by which radical becomes classical, which means that I am interested in mutation. "There is a compelling reason why we declare our friendship with some figures more than others," writes Moosa. For him, it is because these thinkers point to what Dipesh Chakrabarty calls "the plurality of the 'now,'"[4] the "lack of totality, the constant fragmentariness, that constitutes one's present."[5] Sa'diyya Shaikh draws on Moosa's treatment of future friendships in *Sufi Narratives of Intimacy*, her effort to rethink Islamic conceptions of gender and sexuality through the work of thirteenth-century mystical theologian Ibn al-'Arabī. For Shaikh, Ibn al-'Arabī appears as one of those "frontier thinkers" who, despite the marginalization that they experience in their lifetimes, "wrote courageously and daringly right into the future."[6] Observing that these thinkers "would not have been in a position to determine the future impact of their work or the ways in which their ideas might wedge open the future horizons of human imagination," Shaikh engages Ibn al-'Arabī's work to approach questions about gender that could not have been asked in Ibn al-'Arabī's world.[7]

Just as our tastes in things like music and fashion remain bound in social relations and can become strategic power plays, our choices for premodern conversation partners situate us in the Muslim intellectual fields of today. Al-Ghazālī, for many Muslims and non-Muslims alike, represents the apex of "classical" Islamic thought. Ibn al-'Arabī is recognized as a foundational thinker for systematized Ṣūfīsm and the paragon for various mystical, intellectual, and artistic traditions that are positioned today as foils to modern "Wahhābism." The works of both al-Ghazālī and Ibn al-'Arabī have inspired entire bookshelves of academic investigation while also remaining iconic figures in popular Muslim discussion. Of course, you have to be careful about the past heroes to whom you become the future friend: Ibn al-'Arabī's name could be gold in some places, dirt in others. Even dropping al-Ghazālī's name fails to authorize you in some contexts; Salafīs would approach his work with extreme caution or reject him altogether. These names are like game pieces on a board, their movements and powers limited by the rules of the game that you choose to play. So when Shaikh writes her discussion of gender in Ibn al-'Arabī's thought, whether or not the book achieves its desired impact depends partly on whom she's talking to. If the intention is to authorize Progressive Muslim commitments to gender justice with the credibility of "orthodoxy" or "tradition," seeking endorsement from a figure as suspect as Ibn al-'Arabī can get us only so far. For certain audiences, any positive reference to Ibn al-'Arabī immediately disqualifies the project.

In terms of our tradition's past elders whom I have engaged as conversation partners, you could question my choices. I have tended to opt for countertradition, the rebels and antiheroes who become meaningful to me specifically because in many Sunnī circles they can have no authorizing power, no orthodox cred, no legitimacy to lend. They are either holders of ambiguous status, like al-Ḥallāj, whose passion was deemed threatening enough to warrant his execution but who found his way into mystical and poetic traditions of later centuries, or they are attached to communities that have been reviled and stigmatized, like First Born Prince Allah of the Five Percenters. There aren't many places in which you can use these names to make an argument; there's *no* setting in which all my cited elders could legitimize my case. Collectively, they serve only to authorize my loneliness: They tell me that it's okay to stand outside whatever people have designated as the mainstream; it's okay to be weird.

The premodern figures to whom modern Salafism performs as a future friend are also the types to be privileged as canonical in some places, demonized in others. In Progressive Muslim contexts, their names should come with trigger warnings. Some Ṣūfīs would treat them as representing everything that went wrong in the tradition. In journalistic attempts to explain the Salafī/Wahhābī menace in eight hundred words or less, these names enable a quick narrative that claims to locate the roots of modern "terror," "fundamentalism," and so on. Maybe this qualifies them as rebels and misfits for my heretics' parade, at least for certain audiences. That doesn't mean that I'd expect them to join the parade willingly. I am not the kind of Muslim that they could have regarded with any seriousness, but this is probably true for most of the figures to whom I thought myself a "future friend." Maybe "future friend" is the wrong way to put it.

For the people who are called Salafīs and/or Wahhābīs, these names can be similarly appropriated to give the presentation of a lineage, a straight feed that connects them to the greatest generations. The assurance of lineage is that the origins have been made available to us by a reliable delivery system. Amid the declining generations of departure and deviation from pure and original Islam, *someone* had to be getting it right. Salafism is not the clean, unmediated "back to the sources" project that the Salafīyya advertise, but rather turns to the sources as *re*mediated through a particular tradition of scholars. The obvious paradox is that when we're supposed to shed accumulated tradition to find the original Islam, another accumulated tradition becomes our tool for doing so.

Theoretically, when it comes to Islamic law—using *law* in the broadest sense, including not only things like criminal justice, marriage contracts, and such, but also how to pray, wash before prayer, and so on—Salafīs don't need to subscribe to a particular school, since their method is just to follow the precedent of the Prophet and the Salaf as set forth in what they regard as authentic sources. In practice, they typically follow the Ḥanbalī school, named for the great scholar Aḥmad ibn Ḥanbal (780–855). Some would say that Ibn Ḥanbal wasn't really a legal scholar; Jarīr aṭ-Ṭabarī (839–923), famed historian, Qur'ān commentator, and eponym for his own failed "Jarīrī" madhab, in fact said this, for which the Ḥanābila threw rocks at his house. Today, the Ḥanbalī school stands as the government-supported madhab of modern Saudi Arabia, and it's often unclear how journalists differentiate between traditional Ḥanbalism and extreme Wahhābism, or whether they've even asked this question of themselves. My sense is that they just define a "Wahhābī" as a Ḥanbalī who's really, really enthusiastic.

Here are some things that I want to say about Ibn Ḥanbal: He was described as tall, with dyed hair and very dark skin.[8] He sat with his head bowed, smiled at people, and gave them his full attention.[9] He refrained from discussing popular topics but spoke when conversation turned to matters of ḥadīth.[10] He loved transmitted knowledge but disdained books of personal opinion.[11] He avoided spending much time with people because he hated good-byes.[12] He ate crusts of bread with salt, sometimes dipping them in vinegar.[13] He slept on a dirty mattress with a single quilt.[14] He said that his happiest days were when he woke up and nothing was in his house.[15] He wore clothes with patches of different colors.[16] Whenever he saw a Christian, he closed his eyes, explaining, "I can't look at anyone who lies about God."[17] He bought a concubine and named her Rayḥāna, after the Prophet's concubine.[18] He has been called the last man who could be counted among the generation of the Followers,[19] and it has even been said that he did more for Islam than Abū Bakr, since Abū Bakr had friends and allies and he had none.[20] Men who wandered the deserts or became lost at sea reported encounters with the mystical being Khiḍr, the immortal prophet Elijah, and the angel who watches over islands, asking the men to extend their greetings to Ibn Ḥanbal upon return to Baghdad.[21] Ibn Ḥanbal said that the inkpots of ḥadīth scholars were the lamps of Islam[22] and personally put one million ḥadīths to writing, by his own estimation.[23] After the government issued an order for him to be whipped, he forgave the one who carried it out.[24]

The whippings and other torments fell upon him in the Miḥna, which is often (and problematically) described in comparison to the Spanish Inquisition. The short and simplified version of the story: The caliphate had endorsed the methods and arguments of the Mu'tāzila school and persecuted scholars who held opposing views. Having emerged amid the 'Abbāsids' major translation project and the absorption of Greek, Indian, and Persian philosophical traditions into Muslim thought, the Mu'tāzila sought to reconcile the Qur'ān to new challenges these traditions posed through rationalist interpretation and resort to allegorical readings. References in the Qur'ān to Allāh having body parts, for example, couldn't literally mean that Allāh had a body, since this defied their idea of what was reasonable. One of the Mu'tāzilī positions held that the Qur'ān was a created thing, to which the ḥadīth-based traditionalists objected that the Qur'ān, as the speech of Allāh, was necessarily eternal and uncreated. While the government forced scholars to profess the new caliphal creed under threat of imprisonment and torture, Ibn Ḥanbal famously refused to surrender his positions, becoming the people's champion in the process. As tales of his courage and fortitude spread, they reached the level of miracle tales that believers told about prophets. When Ibn Ḥanbal was being whipped, one story claimed, his garment fell and nearly exposed his nakedness, but a hand descended from the heavens above to pull his garment back up and protect his modesty.

The Miḥna has been popularly treated as a defining watershed in Muslim history, the moment at which the scholars ('ulama) defeated the caliphate in a confrontation over the power to make orthodoxy, and tradition-based knowledge defeated personal reason as the dominant mode of interpretation. Recent scholarship suggests that the Miḥna's importance has been overestimated.[25] Whatever the Miḥna was or wasn't in terms of caliphate-'ulama relations or the fate of Muslim rationalism, the conflict between the Mu'tāzila and the traditionalists made a lasting impact on Sunnī creeds that would continue to include affirmations of the Qur'ān's uncreated status, even up to the Pamphlet Islam of our own time.

AGAINST HISTORY

Ibn Ḥanbal is revered not only for his stand against the government, but perhaps even more for his immense scholarship: His musnad contains something in the neighborhood of thirty thousand ḥadīths that he had assessed and graded worthy of inclusion. Considering the unwieldy awesomeness of Ibn Ḥanbal's collection and the inherent challenges of the musnad format, I wondered how it might have looked if Ibn Ḥanbal had chosen to present his vast archive in a different literary genre—perhaps refined into a sīra, a narrative biography of the Prophet. This might be an illustration of Marshall McLuhan's dictum, "The medium is the message": The manner in which Ibn Ḥanbal presents his information says something about how he perceived it.

The writer of the most significant early sīra, Ibn Isḥāq, was not an exceptional ḥadīth scholar and lacked street cred among the hardcore traditionist crowds of his day. A work of sīra by the great Ibn Ḥanbal would surely have supplanted Ibn Isḥāq's work as the seminal treatment of Muḥammad's life from the first three centuries of Islam and would have made later scholar Ibn Kathīr's voluminous sīra—the preferred prophetic biography for modern Salafīs—unnecessary. To write a sīra, however, would have gone against Ibn Ḥanbal's whole understanding of how sacred history should be handled. For this, even if nothing else about Islam as I process it would make sense to Ibn Ḥanbal, I want to hope for one point of agreement between us.

Here's where I meet Ibn Ḥanbal's rejection of sīra: Following the modern linguistic turn and challenges of poststructuralism, historians have grown increasingly mindful of the limits of what they can say about the past, or what sources from the past can say to them; the claim to do history as a purely empirical report of "what really happened" has been all but surrendered. There is no longer much confidence in a retrievable "actual past." Instead of direct access to "the past" as the thing itself, historians deal in the limits of traces and representations. Unable to step out of their present, historians must perceive the past within the bounds of what their present allows. Moreover, the difference between raw data and "history" is the presence of storytelling, interpretation, and editorial manipulation of the data into a coherent narrative with possibilities for meaning. Without acts of fictionalization, there can be no history; this is more or less the postmodernist charge that Ibn Ḥanbal made against historians roughly twelve centuries ago.

Ibn Ḥanbal scorned historians such as Ibn Isḥāq and Wāqidī (745–822), famed chronicler of the Prophet's life in the maghāzī literary genre, due to their distortions of ḥadīths for the sake of narrative coherence. Both Ibn Isḥāq and Wāqidī were known to blend differing accounts of Muḥammad's actions or sayings into what has been termed *combined reports*. The practice of using multiple narrations to assemble a single story was said to have originated with the great ḥadīth scholar Ibn Shihāb al-Zuhrī, for which al-Zuhrī has been credited with making an "important step towards continuous historical writing."[26] While combining reports might have made for smoother storytelling, however, it wasn't necessarily superior historiography: Where there had once been a diversity of accounts and meaningful disagreements between transmitters, we would now have a single, streamlined version of the event in which variances and uncertainties were erased. For Ibn Ḥanbal, such editorial hegemony and suppression of differences to produce an "orderly narrative" amounted to vandalism on the tradition.[27] He charged that to pull elements from varying reports together to produce a story, the writer had to make choices, thus corrupting the transmitted knowledge with personal subjectivity. According to Ibn Ḥanbal and the ḥadīthī crew, writes Robert G. Hoyland, it was better that "one should efface one's own self and not let one's own ideas and thoughts intrude, but simply be a medium for a report to pass from one person to another. Only in this way could the continuity of the teachings and practices of the Prophet Muḥammad among the Muslim community be preserved."[28] In contrast to the creators of mash-up ḥadīths, Ibn Ḥanbal was known for his rigorous attention to accuracy, even when a difference of wording or vowelization between two reports made no impact on the content.[29] Ibn Ḥanbal's discipline was imitated by his students such as Bukhārī, who articulated the ḥadīth scholar's duty as the passing down of ḥadīths exactly as they were received, with no alterations to the content or chain of transmission.[30] Hoyland calls Ibn Ḥanbal's position "basically anti-intellectualist," but Ibn Ḥanbal's wariness of editorial subjectivity could place him in greater harmony with (post)modern ideas about history. Ibn Ḥanbal recognized that whenever an editor makes a choice, the Prophet who survives only on our pages becomes a little less of himself.

It was also Ibn Ḥanbal's fear of clouding sacred sources with the pollution of human opinion that informed his method of reading the Qur'ān. Ibn Ḥanbal was famous for his refusal to interpret verses beyond their most straightforward meaning; for this he has been called a literalist and anthropomorphist. For his supposed textual literalism, however, I find him useful in ways that he would probably find horrifying.

IGNORE THE THRONE

In the early period of Islamic theological battles, the charge of anthropomorphism was thrown at just about everyone. Rationalists pegged it on traditionalists for refusing to read the Qur'ān's descriptions of Allāh's body parts as allegorical. Traditionalists threw the accusation back at them, countering that if rationalists demanded that Allāh's "face" be read allegorically, it was because of their insistence that the meaning of *face* could correspond only to *human* faces. The traditionalists charged that readers who required allegorical meanings were ironically the true anthropomorphists. The approach offered by Ibn Ḥanbal and what became his school was to accept challenging verses bi-la kayf, "without asking how." Allah is as Allah describes himself in his own statements, and we can say no more about such statements than whatever explanations might have been offered by the Prophet to his Companions. This deferral to tradition is a response to the same problems as the Isma'īlī method of ta'wīl through an infallible imām: the unreliability of individual reason, the differences that may arise from personal speculations, and the necessity of knowledge that transcends logical proofs.

Bi-lā kayf has led many to dismiss the premodern Ḥadīth Folk and modern Salafiyya as having no critical reading skills. It's easy to see Salafīs as intellectually stunted and uncreative, but my dissatisfaction with progressive Muslim reworkings of the Qur'ān led me to see something beautiful in the refusal to interpret. Here's what I read in the Qur'ān: Allāh possesses something called a yad. The word seemingly corresponds to a body part of human beings, but because the Qur'ān also says that Allāh is like nothing in the created universe, identifying the yad on a human body does not allow us to use it as a basis for knowing Allāh's yad. We cannot even speculate as to why Allāh's yad should be called a yad. Unable to read Allāh's yad as a yad in the most straightforwardly anthropomorphic sense, and barred from making up our own allegorical meanings for the yad, our consequence is that the Qur'ān's mention of a yad in reference to Allāh has no useful meaning at all. For readers who do not understand Arabic, reading a verse bi-lā kayf means that the Qur'ān's descriptions of Allāh might as well be left untranslated; to look up the Arabic *yad* in Hans Wehr's dictionary and learn that it corresponds to the English *hand* does nothing to make Allāh's yad more comprehensible.

Sherman Jackson explains that for the traditionalists, Allāh's incomparability indeed meant that his attributes were rendered "*sui generis*, i.e., abstract and essentially devoid of concrete meaning," though the bombastic Ḥanbalī jurist and hero of modern Salafism, Ibn Taymiyya (1263–1328) later sought to concretize the divine attributes in his own articulation.[31] Ibn Taymiyya accepted the truth of Allāh's attributes while affirming that any likeness between Creator and creation existed entirely within the mind of the creation, rather than in shared reality.[32] For all his supposed antirationalism, Ibn Taymiyya was nonetheless a theologian and needed a workable system; he could not resist asking how.

Despite its apparent defense of embodied anthropomorphism, bi-lā kayf's affirmation of the words can ironically deny them and become apophatic or "negative" theology, an unsaying of whatever Allāh says about himself. Bi-lā kayf recognizes the inability of language, even Allāh's language, to convey Allāh's reality; bi-lā kayf could reduce the text's infinite possibilities not to one absolute meaning, but to zero. If the Qur'ān's word for *hand* no longer signifies a hand or anything concretely handlike when used in reference to Allāh, which words *can* safely describe Allāh, and how can Allāh describe himself? What could it mean to say that this "Allāh" authored a text, or that this Allāh can be called merciful, powerful, forgiving, just, wise, lord, or creator? The only working construction of Allāh would be to write the word *Allāh* and then cross it out, because Allāh is not Allāh.

The Qur'ān loses some of its power to produce an imagination of Allāh, and human theologians lose their power to come between the Qur'ān and the reader. The consequence of bi-lā kayf's atheology/antitheology could be that while outward expressions of what it means to be a Muslim are stabilized, allowing for a mosque to be filled with humans who share in a collective statement about God, our interior possibilities remain limitless. Without a rationalizing system to demystify the words, we might experience God's self-descriptions through our own secrets.

> We are in no need of knowing the meaning of what God intended by his attributes. For they require no action and there is no duty connected with them other than belief in them. And belief is possible without knowing the meaning intended by them.
>
> —IBN QUDĀMA AL-MAQDISĪ (D. 1223)[33]

This is where I find Salafism rubbing against postmodern challenges to language and text: Ibn Ḥanbal loved Allāh without knowing the secret of Allāh's self-descriptions in the words, in fact denying that he could *ever* know the secret of the words or even that the words contained a secret at all. Bi-lā kayf sounds like Deleuze: "There is nothing to explain, nothing to understand, nothing to interpret."[34] There is no unitary core to Allāh's self-description for a skilled hermeneuticist to decipher, no hidden jewel to excavate. You want to dive into the sea and reach the depths, but what appears to be the water's surface is actually a solid mirror: There are no depths, and there is no diving in. Bi-lā kayf refuses to let us think beyond or inside the Qur'ān, since the bare surface of its language is all that we have. Anything more is what you conjured up yourself.

Bi-lā kayf was formulated to restrain the Qur'ān's meaning and guard what were seen as the essentials of Muslim faith against dangerous speculation, but what does it change for *me* when I stop asking how? To read bi-lā kayf, meaning that I accept the Qur'ān's statements about Allāh without asking how these statements are true, could also mean that I don't really have to accept them, since my acceptance of these statements does not require my comprehension. Deciding on the truth of the Qur'ān's claims about itself, I am like a small child signing legal contracts. My relationship to the Qur'ān and its author cannot be reduced to matters of belief or disbelief, because bi-lā kayf leaves me unable to interrogate the terms. Strictly in its (anti-)theological dimension, reading bi-lā kayf struck me as a means for suspending some big questions.

The more that I considered bi-lā kayf as a means of dealing with the Qur'ān's representation of God, the more that it resonated with what I had learned as Five Percenter thought—the Salafī affirmation of a mystery god with real but unknowable hands—and the Five Percenter rejection of that god's very existence landed me at the same place. Five Percenters with interest in the revealed text would argue, as hip-hop legend Rakim boldly asserts, that "It even tells us we are gods in the Holy Qur'ān."[35] The Qur'ān, after all, states that Allāh is closer to human beings than the veins in their necks. The Five Percenters' lessons also mention the Qur'ān as authored by the Asiatic Black Man, enabling a Five Percenter claim upon the revelation. Apart from the Qur'ān, Five Percenters have frequently found their views to be most resonant with Ṣūfī traditions, both in terms of apparent Ṣūfī self-identification with God (as in the ecstatic utterances of mystics such as al-Ḥallāj and Bistāmī) and seemingly disdainful attitudes toward ritualism, dogmatism, and religious law (as in Bullhe Shah). Meanwhile, a vaguely defined "orthodox" Islam, often conflated with the equally vague notion of "Arab Islam," is placed at the far end of the Muslim spectrum as the antithesis of both the Five Percenters and Ṣūfism. Even if the Salafiyya could be imagined as upholding divine anthropomorphism, which would appeal to some Five Percenters (taking the anthropomorphic Allāh as evidence for a theomorphic Black Man), the Salafī god remains wholly other, a "mystery god" on his throne above the heavens. Whether or not Ibn Ḥanbal believed in prophetic reports of Allāh appearing as a beardless youth who placed his cold hand between Muḥammad's shoulder blades,[36] or Muḥammad forbidding men from striking each other in the face because Allāh had created Adam in Allāh's own form,[37] I am not sure how far a theological dialogue between Salafīs and Five Percenters could go. The Salafī god, hands or no hands, throne or no throne, does not grant human beings a share in his divinity; meanwhile, Five Percenters denounce this mystery god's very existence as a falsehood. End of conversation?

Perhaps not. I return to my lessons.

> Who is that mystery god?
>
> There is no mystery god. The sons of man have searched for that mystery god for trillions of years and were unable to find this so-called mystery god. So they have agreed that the only god is the son of man, so they lose no time searching for that which does not exist.
>
> —KNOWLEDGE CIPHER DEGREE, 1–40

This is where bi-lā kayf becomes Five Percenter manhaj. In the Five Percenter lessons, I read an emphatic denial of hope that human beings might achieve that VIP access. With this denial comes an important social consequence: No human beings can claim secret knowledge by which they would be privileged over others. Five Percenters often quote Ibn al-'Arabī when he says something that they like, but if he were alive, they would not follow him as their guide to the unseen. Though I know Five Percenters who have dabbled in Ṣūfī orders popular in North America, such as the Nimatullahi order, Five Percenters are generally uninterested in submitting to Ṣūfī masters claiming mystical privilege. The Five Percenter response to tariqa-based Ṣūfism might be analogous to the former Clarence 13X's response to the Nation of Islam, which itself was a kind of initiatory lodge led by a master teacher (Elijah Muhammad) who boasted of having received special instruction from a transcendent supreme knower (Master Fard Muhammad). The former Clarence 13X, having dropped his *X* and renamed himself Allah, recalled his estranged wife trying to put his mind "under the capture" of Elijah Muhammad. The former Clarence 13X wanted none of it. In his breakdown of *Islam* as I.S.L.A.M., "I Self Lord And Master," he shot down the possibility of anyone telling him how to live out Islam as he understood it. Ironically, his act of individual resistance gave rise to a new community: A brotherhood of gods.

The Five Percenters are often seen as esotericists due to their interest in assigning symbolic meanings to letters and numbers and using their own unique systems, the Supreme Mathematics and Supreme Alphabets, as tools for engaging texts, particularly their own lessons. While some Five Percenters certainly jump into the deep end of the pool when it comes to their creative engagement of texts, I remain wary of thinking about Five Percenter tradition as esoteric. For many Five Percenters, there's nothing esoteric about their knowledge. The truth that they see is as plain as day; it's not hidden (bāṭin) but in fact the complete opposite, clearly manifest (zāhir).

More than once during my time with the Five Percenters, the gods warned me to avoid "Willy Wonka Math." I understood the *math* part as a reference to Supreme Mathematics. When I asked for an explanation of the Willy Wonka reference, my teachers told me that Willy Wonka Math represents the kind of esotericism that transports someone into a "world of pure imagination." It was not a positive valuation; these Five Percenters looked at such activity as frivolous. Reading interpretations of the Qur'ān based on progressive Muslim hermeneutics or complex systematized Ṣūfism, I couldn't help but feel that I had fallen into Willy Wonka Math. Similarly, the controversies of classical Islamic theology—free will and predestination, the createdness or eternality of the Qur'ān, the nature of Allāh's attributes, or Allāh's material resurrection of human bodies—meant nothing for me in my engagement of Islam: They did not change my prayers, fasts, or marriage. None of it moved money into or out of my pocket. At least for the world in which I lived, these questions amounted to Willy Wonka Math, and I couldn't bring myself to care.

Ibn Ḥanbal, of course, believed in the mystery god, and he also believed that we could have some limited knowledge of the mystery god through information that this god himself provided: the text of his divinely revealed, uncreated Qur'ān and his guidance to the Prophet Muḥammad. For Ibn Ḥanbal, Muḥammad was exactly the kind of privileged mystical knower that Five Percenters would reject, as were Muḥammad's Companions, who became authoritative in Muslim communal memory through their closeness to him. By Ibn Ḥanbal's time, however, the Prophet and his Companions were long dead, having become what Five Percenters might call "Mystery Salaf" and unattainable.

The Ḥadīth Folk presented themselves as the most authentic heirs to Muḥammad's authority without claiming to be prophets themselves: Their authority rested on custodianship of transmitted knowledge. I am not naive enough to imagine the Ḥadīth Folk's mode of knowing as purely egalitarian, since for numerous social and economic reasons—lack of specialized training in ḥadīth sciences, lack of access to material resources, wrong gender[38] sectarian backgrounds,[39] bad politics, injured reputations, and so on—not everyone could join the elite cliques of master scholars. But their epistemology still makes a claim against mysticism and high-end philosophy: No one gets a private window into the unseen. We must engage each other using materials to which we at least theoretically have equal access. While mystics and philosophers have depicted the Qur'ān's truth as unevenly parsed out between the ignorant masses and more privileged elites who could really "get it," Ibn Ḥanbal won't allow us to claim that we have retrieved hidden treasures that had somehow been hidden from the rest of the Qur'ān's readers. In my encounters with both the Ḥadīth Folk and the Five Percenters, I found a refusal to speak on what one cannot know, and guards set up against individuals who might claim transcendent control over the tradition.

Just as no position can ever be truly neutral, my refusal to interpret can inflict its own harm on the text. The phrase *bi-lā kayf* does not appear in the Qur'ān. It is not necessarily how the Qur'ān tells us to approach its words, nor was it even a "traditionalist" method prior to being privileged as such. Having developed as a response to an expanding range of choices, attempting to govern the chaos of interpretation, place limits on theology, and defeat competing schools, bi-lā kayf emerged—like everything else—as an innovation in its own right. It is not a given that this strategy of fidelity to the Companions is what the Companions themselves would have advocated had they lived in Ibn Ḥanbal's time: Bi-lā kayf's advocates, arguing for this approach, must become mediators between the original community and ourselves. Everything that we write to conceptualize, explain, and regulate bi-lā kayf as a method cannot help but become its own mode of asking how, a way of elaborating on the text as we argue against elaboration. Bi-lā kayf, while seeking to protect the original content from history, inflicts history's effects upon the content anyway. The verses are still covered in our fingerprints.

Despite the inconsistencies and impossible ideals, bi-lā kayf's attempted choice of no choice strikes me as my truest possible surrender (islām) to Allāh's transcendence. Bi-lā kayf means that no reader can expose the Qur'ān's secret insides: not the elite philosophers, nor the visionary mystics, initiated masters, classically trained 'ulama, state-supported clerics, or institutionally pampered academics.

Ḥadīth reports tell us that Muḥammad had predicted a future in which people asked unnecessary questions to such a degree that eventually they would ask, "Who created Allāh?" It does not seem impossible that Muḥammad could have really made this prediction; or the quote might have come from the early centuries following his death, when an expanding corpus of ḥadīth literature developed partly in antagonism against speculative theologians. "Who created Allāh?" reads like the logical conclusion to hair-splitting debate over doctrines of divine attributes, the nature of divine authorship, secondary causation, and the tension between affirming Allāh's absolute power over all things and the moral responsibility of every individual for his/her actions. But what do you do after the question has already been asked?

Embracing bi-lā kayf doesn't erase these acts of "asking how" from my memory or reinvent me as someone who had never asked. Bi-lā kayf does not serve me as a technology of faith, but it might work as a technology of love—a way to keep me in the mosque with my Muslim family after the doubts, confusions, and even disbeliefs have inflicted their cuts. I can affirm, like the slave girl in a famous ḥadīth, that Allāh lives above the clouds, and I can join others in surrender to this Allāh without having to decide what any of it means. Maybe this is a cop-out, since it excuses me from having to bother with the text and its difficult questions. But bi-lā kayf has also given me comfort in strange times, like joining in chants of *lā ilāha illa Allāh* ("There is no god but God") or *Allāhu Akbar* ("God is the greatest") during a funeral procession. There's no surrender like the surrender to divine empty nonsense. When we put our faces to the ground and mourn the senselessly dead, mouthing words that cannot explain anything, bi-lā kayf can hold us together without the fraud of theological rationales. Bi-lā kayf allows a space for grief without pretending to have answers.

Bi-lā kayf's applications are limited. It never allows me to fully drop my guard, and it's not redemptive for questions of ethics or law or social justice; but if I'm willing to pray without a systematized theology that can tell me who exactly I'm praying to, bi-lā kayf at least builds a bridge for me to other communities of human beings. When there is nothing beneath the Qur'ān's surface, no depth that we can access without first fabricating it, we must share the surface together. Bi-lā kayf becomes a way to love the Qur'ān even when it loses the power to tell me things. Instead of reinventing meaning, I will kiss the Qur'ān, place it on my top shelf, and leave it safe from my polluting touch. Or I will walk with recitations of the Qur'ān in my earphones as a comfort and shelter against the outside world. I hope for my love of the Qur'ān to match that of my Muslim aunties and uncles who do not understand Arabic but nonetheless read through the entire Arabic Qur'ān multiple times in a year, running their fingers along verses that can say almost nothing to them beyond the occasional appearance of Allāh's Name. When my acts of reading are no longer pursuits of meaning, they can survive as acts of love.

IN THE NAME OF ALLĀH, WHO CAME IN THE PERSON OF IMĀM AḤMAD

In Ṣūfī traditions, we can find numerous figures who were either persecuted in their lifetimes or reviled by later generations for the accusation that they claimed to be Allāh. Ṣūfism also became my strategy for negotiating with the boundary dividing Five Percenters from "classical Islamic tradition"; in *Why I Am a Five Percenter*, I devote an entire chapter to placing Five Percenter thought in conversation with Ibn al-'Arabī, whose teachings of wahdat al-wujūd ("unity of being") and provocative visionary experiences led to the charge that he placed humanity on some level of association with divinity. Premodern scholars whose names later became important in modern Salafī thought accused Ibn al-'Arabī of atheism and even working as a vanguard for the coming Dajjāl, the "antichrist" figure of Islamic eschatology.[40] As I saw it, the ambiguities in Ibn al-'Arabī's systematized mysticism as well as the ecstatic utterances attributed to figures such as Abū Yāzīd al-Bisṭāmī and al-Ḥallāj enabled me to walk some theological tightropes.

We frequently play into the assumption that Ṣūfism is above all else a quest of the individual, a search for intimately personal knowledge of the divine that occurs beyond the social and institutional trappings of "organized religion." This assumption is at least partly derived from the contexts in which many people encounter Ṣūfism: lines of Rūmī's poetry posted on a Facebook page, qawwālī music that people listen to in their cars, or premodern works of mystical and allegorical literature that are now printed in mass quantities, stamped with bar codes, and made easily available for purchase by anyone, anytime. In these contexts, Ṣūfism can be entirely personal, sure; but this isn't simply the "traditional" Ṣūfī way, because it neglects the heritage of Ṣūfi orders as rigidly hierarchical institutions, in which human mediators, the order's master and shaykhs, name the terms and facilitate access to the divine. To imagine Sūfism as free of elements that folks commonly find undesirable in religion today—rules and regulations, codes of behavior, centralized human authority—isn't universally *wrong* for all times and places, but it's not exactly historical; it leaves a lot out.

In the contours of our present world, there is no self-styled "Islamic republic" that has appropriated Ṣūfism as its official version of the "Islamic." This grants us the luxury of pretending that a withdrawal from political or legal interests expresses some inherent, timeless quality of Ṣūfism—relegating Ṣūfism's concern to the inner conditions of the heart, an ideal religiosity for secularist states—while avoiding reflection upon the possibilities of Ṣūfism as an instrument for claiming or wielding power. In previous eras, however, Ṣūfī institutions were deeply embedded in the affairs of government: Mystical masters and the heads of orders often used their spiritual power as a bargaining chip in negotiation with monarchs.[41] Visiting the mosque at the tomb of Ibn al-ʿArabī in Damascus, I prayed in a structure that an Ottoman sultan had constructed upon his conquest of the city, a monument to both his Muslim piety and imperial power. In the later nineteenth and early twentieth centuries, Salafī anti-Ṣūfism related significantly to resistance in Egypt and Syria against a Ṣūfism-infused Ottoman regime.

In the narrative of Ṣūfism as private, interior, and removed from politics, Salafism makes for an easy villain, the extreme darkness opposing Ṣūfism's light—selectively ignoring the Salafīs who avoid political activism, disdain the Muslim Brotherhood, and prefer to focus on the purification of one's inner belief and ritual practice. Salafism and Wahhābism, after all, remain our labels for the official ideology of Saudi Arabia, as well as for Muslims who go around bombing Ṣūfī shrines and other holy sites in the name of purifying Islam. The attacks of 9/11, it has been charged, could never have happened if only Ṣūfism, with all its love and beauty and poetry and spiritual pluralism, had triumphed over Salafism/Wahhābism in its battle for Islam's heart and soul.

A closer look at Ibn Ḥanbal's life and post-life might undermine our modern Ṣūfī/Salafī opposition. Ṣūfism and the Ḥadīth Folk—the formative nucleus of later Sunnism—emerged from the same milieu of ninth- and tenth-century Iraq.[42] Ibn Ḥanbal lived in a time in which categories like "Ṣūfī," "Salafī," or even "Sunnī" did not yet exist in the ways that we use them now.

Though modern Salafīs are popularly reduced to shrine-razers who oppose the reverence of relics, Ibn Ḥanbal attached great significance to artifacts associated with Muḥammad. He reportedly carried hairs of the Prophet with him at all times, sometimes washing them and then drinking the water as a medical treatment, kept them sewn into his shirt as he endured his flogging, and left instructions that they should be buried with him: two on his eyelids, a third on his tongue.

Because modern Sunnī go-back-to-the-origins revivalism frequently intersects with a desire to prove Islam's science-friendly modern rationality, we don't treat dreams and visions as proofs as we used to: Going back to the origins is supposed to be limited to the trustworthy data that texts have preserved for us. After his death, however, Ibn Ḥanbal made numerous appearances in believers' dreams.[43] One dreamer saw Ibn Ḥanbal in paradise, walking with an unusual swagger, and asked him about it. Ibn Ḥanbal answered, "This is how the servants walk in paradise," and explained that for his testimony to the Qur'ān's uncreatedness, Allāh bestowed upon him a crown and sandals of gold. Muslims also learned through dreams that Allāh had appointed Ibn Ḥanbal as a guard over the gates of paradise (the only human alongside angelic guards Jibrīl, Mīkā'īl, and Isrāfīl), and that the bridge to paradise could be crossed only by those wearing Ibn Ḥanbal's signet ring.[44]

When Ibn Ḥanbal objected to proto-Ṣūfīs, it was more on the grounds of their relationship to systematized theology (kalām) than the mysticism or renunciation for which later critics would take them on. Similarly, the "proto-Ṣūfī" ascetics often behaved more in line with the stereotype of modern Salafīs than the romantic image of Ṣūfīs as drunken, lawless poets. These figures exemplified "Salafī" values of correct ritual practice, bodily discipline, and "ordering the good." When proto-Ṣūfīs found themselves in trouble with the government, it was not simply because they were seen as subversive for having transcended the constraints of ritual and law, but more often the exact opposite: They denounced rulers who failed to meet their standards of piety and would even destroy shipments of wine that had been headed for the caliphal palace.[45]

Praised in hagiographic literatures for his asceticism, self-negation, and connections to miracles, even Ibn Ḥanbal might read as the kind of character that we would call "Ṣūfī." In fact, he was seen as such by later Ṣūfīs. The important mystic al-Hujwirī (990–1077) includes Ibn Ḥanbal in his roster of Ṣūfīs, noting his piety, humility, miracles, and martyrdom (alleging that he had died from his tortures in the Miḥna). According to al-Hujwirī, Ibn Ḥanbal refused to answer the question "What is love?" instead deferring to the authority of his proto-Ṣūfī contemporary, Bishr ibn al-Ḥārith al-Ḥāfī (d. 841): "I will not answer it while he is alive."[46] This account serves a particular political function, in that it portrays the ḥadīth scholar as confessing to the greater authority of a mystic. For such an endorsement to mean anything, it must grant legitimacy to the ḥadīthī side as well.

For my own needs, a particularly compelling intersection of Ibn Ḥanbal and the proto-Ṣūfīs remains the relationship between the early Ḥanābila and Ṣūfism's paragon of ecstatic martyrdom, al-Ḥallāj. Here was a supreme knower who allegedly said crazy things (like calling himself by al-Ḥaqq, one of the Names of Allāh), did crazy things (like building his own Ka'ba in his yard), found himself at odds with the religious establishment, received a death sentence that was signed by his own Ṣūfī teacher, and danced on the way to his execution. For many of us, al-Ḥallāj expands our field of thinkable Islam. It should also be noted that my initial access to al-Ḥallāj came through the mediation of Western scholars, who sometimes rewrote him as a spokesman for their own prejudices about Islam and religion at large. As Edward Said points out in *Orientalism*, the Western scholarship on al-Ḥallāj has popularly rendered him an Islamic Christ figure, using al-Ḥallāj to locate self-annihilating mystical love as the innate "core" of Islam while denying love within the rest of Muslim tradition and undermining any concerns for ritual or law that Muslims might find valuable.[47] In short, al-Ḥallāj became a case study for how nineteenth-/twentieth-century liberal Protestant values (heart/"spirituality" = good, ritualism/legalism = bad, institution/hierarchy = bad, Jews and Catholics = clueless) and the construction of "mysticism" as a category of academic analysis mapped the Western study of Ṣūfism and Islam. Just as I've been swimming in those prejudices (even while growing up Catholic), they also drove my image of al-Ḥallāj. Ibn Ḥanbal is supposed to signify cool Ṣūfism's ugly and uncool antithesis, and this is how many liberal and Ṣūfī-oriented Muslims like to position him today. But what if the supposed grandfather of mean Wahhabism was my favorite Ṣūfī's favorite Ṣūfī? Al-Ḥallāj used to spend nights in prayer at Ibn Ḥanbal's tomb, engaging in the devotional behaviors for which modern Sunnī revivalists sometimes destroy tombs. Al-Ḥallāj was revered and memorialized by the same Baghdad populace that had honored Ibn Ḥanbal; after al-Ḥallāj's execution, the followers of Ibn Ḥanbal even broke out in riot.[48] Looking closer at the Ṣūfīs and Ḥanābila, or rather the proto-Ṣūfīs and proto-Ḥanābila, our categories lose at least some of their clarity. Al-Ḥallāj can no longer be essentialized as the antidote to Ibn Ḥanbal, and whatever Ibn Ḥanbal represents might be less in need of an antidote. Even in the notoriously anti-Ṣūfī modes of contemporary Salafism, the boundary between Salafīs and Ṣūfīs isn't always so clear. Ethnographic work in Cairo has shown Salafī scholars to incorporate Ṣūfī concepts into their own interpretations, even if they do so cautiously and avoid explicitly branding these concepts as "Ṣūfī."[49]

I had once wanted to write a "Heretics' History of Islam" project, in which I would catalog all the important figures who, for lack of a better term, bore the stigma of "heretic" throughout Islamic tradition and present them as a countertradition against the Salafī-ish "orthodoxy" from which I had exiled myself. The issue (besides the fact that using vocabulary like *heresy* and *orthodoxy* threatens to cast the conversation within a Christian framework) would be that constructs like "margins" and "mainstream" are not historically secure. If we wanted to glorify Muslim history's rebels and misfits as our answer to all of Salafism's problems, our countertradition would have to include the same people who give modern Salafism its foundation. In certain times and places, figures such as Ibn Ḥanbal, Bukhārī, and Ibn Taymiyya were all seen as heretics and subjected to persecution. On the other side, Ṣūfism—which we like to romanticize for what we perceive as its valorization of individual spirituality and resistance to the legalistic Islam of modern state power—has often enjoyed greater social and economic privilege with imperial regimes than the traditions of the Ḥadīth Folk.

Reading the Ṣūfī/Salafī binary through the paradigm of my Five Percenter lessons, I can see movement across categories of "bloodsucker" and "poor righteous teacher." Though Five Percenters might engage Ṣūfīs as more compatible conversation partners in terms of theology, Salafīs can also do the work of poor righteous teachers. Sure, Ibn Taymiyya comes off as an elitist prick in his disdain of folk religion; but when he condemns medieval Ṣūfī groups that attempt to operate as bloodsuckers (Ten Percenters), using false miracles and claims of magical powers to deceive the uneducated masses (Eighty-Five Percenters), he almost reads as liberatory Five Percent.

My imaginary of Ibn Ḥanbal might amount to nothing but appropriation and theft, but Ibn Ḥanbal had once come to me in an initiatic dream. He appeared in the form of an Ibn Ḥanbal action figure, mint in an unopened package of hard bubble plastic and cardboard backing. The dream ended without my retrieving the figure from the package, but I wondered what it would have meant to do that. It was in this question that I found Ibn Ḥanbal's lessons for me. An Ibn Ḥanbal action figure, of course, is not Ibn Ḥanbal himself, but a plastic body that cannot move or pose its own limbs without my manipulation. Should we simply admire through the clear plastic, protecting Ibn Ḥanbal's action figure from the oil of our fingertips and the weather of our world? Or should we play?

6
SALAFĪ PLANET

>>> The starting point in critical elaboration is the consciousness of what one really is, and is "knowing thyself" as a product of the historical process to date, which has deposited in you an infinity of traces, without leaving an inventory. <<<
—**Antonio Gramsci**[1]

FOR PEOPLE WHO mess with "religion and modernity" questions, Islam often gets treated as the prime reason that these questions are asked: The problem of religion's place in our modern world becomes principally a concern over whether Muslims can make Islam work within modernity's rules. Some folks, imagining a universal timeline of progress, present modernity as a uniquely Muslim crisis because Islam happens to be six hundred years younger than Christianity and therefore needs time to "catch up" (but they don't follow this logic to assume that Christianity needs to catch up to Judaism, nor do they take Zoroastrianism to be more advanced than all these "Abrahamic" traditions). For whatever reason, Islam is often represented as the religion that might someday agree to "become" modern, but has not yet, at least not fully. In the extremes of this idea, the world is imagined as accelerating toward an epic battle in which *either* Islam or modernity will survive, but not *both*, at least not without one being humiliated, subjugated, and transformed by the other.

We find it on both sides of the equation: those who believe that religion is inherently antirational, antimodern, and the enemy of all progress, as well as those who believe that a return to Tradition can save us from the poisons of our spiritless modernity. Experts who try to articulate what they call Islamic fundamentalism often give the impression of a straight line proceeding from the Salaf to Ibn Ḥanbal to Ibn Taymiyya to contemporary Salafism, which both affirms the Salafī claims of representing "real" Islam and treats this "real" Islam as incompatible with whatever they define as *modernity*. Even if we followed the straight-line model, there's still the question of how an uncorrupted, unchanging, "real" Islam manages to find a home in this modern world that allegedly opposes it at every step. As always, a closer look makes our simplistic categories dissolve. If modern seekers are capable of recognizing truth in the premodern, then scientific rationality and secularism have not fully killed the spirit, and the border that shows us where "Tradition" dies and "soulless modernity" is born gets a little more blurry. On the other hand, if premodern wisdom can make itself intelligible to modern readers, maybe it's not "premodern" at all, but only an alternative modernity disguised in the garb of the ancients. Contemporary Muslim intellectuals who present themselves as voices of capitalized Tradition against what they see as diseased modern life, such as Seyyed Hossein Nasr and Hamza Yusuf, are not time travelers. They have never seen the premodern world that they promote to their constituencies (despite Yusuf's narrative of the

Mauritanian desert as a place that time forgot), but can only promote a simplified, exoticized, and ultimately self-referential image of classical Islam, just as Euro-American New Agers might fetishize and commodify India or Tibet as lands of "spirituality."

A premodern intellectual luminary such as al-Ghazālī becomes a whole Tibet in his own right, a blank screen on which various imaginaries can be projected. As many of us read him, al-Ghazālī becomes sufficiently isolated from history to appear as the source of a "timeless wisdom," representative of "classical Islam" and the superior scholarly life from a lost golden age. Assessing al-Ghazālī's timelessness by our own measures, we can extract profound statements from his body of work and quote them without much sense of the world that produced his thought. The same al-Ghazālī who was wary of translation for fear of unqualified readers now has a Twitter account and tweets in English to thousands of followers with decontextualized wise aphorisms about knowledge, piety, and the struggle against the ego. Running on the assumption that al-Ghazālī's universal truths can be easily distinguished from the culturally specific aspects of his thought, or that his thought can be isolated from the broader field of knowledge in his time, al-Ghazālī's Twitter account doesn't quote him on the structure of the solar system or the benefits of female genital mutilation for a young woman's complexion. The Tradition to which al-Ghazālī calls us via Twitter represents an editorial process through which al-Ghazālī—and the Tradition itself—cannot possibly speak for the purpose of *correcting* modernity, because the editors themselves are modern and decide what our timeless shaykh should be telling us.

If it is the modern that creates the "premodern" as a concept and decides its value, the fact that Nasr and Yusuf idealize premodern/traditional cultures as providing the tools to fix "modern" ones only traps them forever on the side of the modern: They search for a cure to the modern, but can only look with modern eyes and through modern histories. In their diagnosis of the "modern West" as diseased and prescription of a return to classical Islamic Tradition, they participate in a narrative informed by antimodern Christian thinkers, as well as Orientalist scholars writing in the age of colonialism.

Resonant with this "modern premodernity," Elijah Muhammad presented Islam as the Original Asiatic Black Man's pure and timeless way of life, "older than the sun, moon, and stars," to which those lost in the depraved wilderness of North America must revert. As Elijah Muhammad articulated the pure and timeless Islam, its valorization of hard work, bodily discipline, respectability, economic self-reliance, rationality, nation-building, "traditional" family values, heterosexual monogamy, and (especially female) modesty actually reads a lot like Victorian-era Protestantism.[2] Five Percenters likewise present their big arguments—that there is no invisible creator deity, and that black men must be their own gods and free the masses from religion—as rooted in a global and transhistorical blackness even more universal than Islam or pan-Africanism. While justifying their particular universalism through eclectic sources such as the Qur'ān, Ṣūfism, Egyptian hieroglyphs, Sumerian tablets, Vedic texts, and East Asian philosophies, however, Five Percenters nonetheless process these sources through the lens of the American wilderness that they claim to transcend, informed by neoliberal constructions of individual autonomy and contemporary Western ideas about what constitutes "race" and "religion."

Within Sunnī traditions, the Salafī call to purification and return to origins wasn't new. In the late eighteenth and early nineteenth centuries, several revivalist projects emerged in association with leaders in a variety of Sunnī contexts: Muḥammad 'Alī al-Sanūsī (1703–1787) in North Africa; 'Uthmān ibn Fudī (1754–1817) in West Africa; Shah Wali Allāh (1703–1762) in India; and most famously Muḥammad ibn 'Abd al-Wahhāb (1703–1787) in what is now called Saudi Arabia. In his comparative investigations of these thinkers, scholar Ahmad Dallal demonstrates that they advocated markedly different ideas regarding matters such as politics and social reform, the permissibility of taqlīd (unquestioning adherence to a particular legal school), the legitimacy of Ṣūfī theology and practices such as the veneration of pious people's tombs, and the conditions by which someone can issue takfīr, declaring fellow Muslims to have apostatized from Islam. Dallal thus argues that the assumptions of a homogenous, monolithic "modern fundamentalism" are unfounded. These leaders and their movements cannot be easily assigned to shared "intellectual family trees," nor can their emergence be reduced to a singular cause, such as the crisis of European colonialism or challenge of modern Enlightenment rationality, let alone something inherent and inescapable within Islam itself.[3] Similarly, an effort to look at the emergence of modern Salafism in the late nineteenth century should consider this phenomenon within its own world rather than simply as a resurgence of generic "Islam."

Whether or not the division of premodern versus modern really means anything, the notion of Islam as premodern or even antimodern still provokes some questions. I want to ask what we're comparing it to: When Muslims were supposedly freaking out over the crisis of modernity, what was everyone else doing? In the era that produced Salafism as an ironically *modern* antimodernism, what did other religions look like?

Salafism showed up in the same nineteenth century in which European Christianity was confronted by challenges both structural and intellectual: the intensifying separation of church from state and an emergence of scientific rationality as a rival to divinely revealed knowledge. The pressures to divorce religion from political power moved theologians toward a depoliticization of Jesus and the location of religion's essence within the individual's conscience. While the threat of positivism moved some Christians to assert the privilege of scripture over science, others sought to bring them into harmony with each other. It was also late in the nineteenth century that the Catholic Church formally declared papal infallibility as a point of dogma.

The dramatic transformation of religion in Christian Europe produced "religion" as a category that was imagined to be universal, appearing in some form or another in every human culture throughout time. The developing conceptualization and study of "religion" tended to evaluate this phenomenon through prevailing opinions about civilizational progress, meaning that religions, like societies, could be deemed "advanced" or "primitive." This model assumed that all religions would necessarily pass through the same phases on their way to religion's most advanced stage: full harmony with science and reason, freedom from superstitious rituals and abusive priesthoods, and complete absence of interest in the affairs of the state. The universal phenomenon of "religion" in its most advanced state, according to elite scholars of nineteenth-century western Europe, looked remarkably like an idealized image of nineteenth-century western European Protestantism. The life and teachings of Jesus Christ also underwent revision to fit this model, as numerous intellectuals sought to deprive Jesus of miracles and supernaturalism, constructing him instead as a genius philosopher who was concerned less with scriptures and dogmas than with guiding the intellectual and moral progress of the human race.[4]

As the advent of "modernity" has been marked by Europe's dominance over the rest of the planet, the emerging category of religion cannot be separated from European colonialism. Western powers, primarily Protestant nations, conquered the world and brought their categories with them. When Western scholars posited a thing called "religion" as universal, various modes of European and American power—military, political, and economic dominance; scientific and technological supremacy; and Christian missionary enterprises—actually made it so, as everyone everywhere now had to confront the category and its relationship to other categories, like science.

Let's start in Japan. Originating in the late eighteenth century, the Kokugaku ("National Science") movement sought to recover Japan's pure and original national essence through a philologically driven study of ancient Japanese texts. The movement eventually shifted toward an interest in demonstrating that classical Shintō cosmology anticipated the findings of modern Western astronomy. The claim for Japanese gods as the teachers of the West was then extended to other branches of knowledge and advances in technology, including medicine. Hirata Atsutane (1776–1843) made the claim that modern medicine, "though introduced to Japan from abroad, appears originally to have been taught to foreign countries by our own great gods." As the nineteenth century progressed, National Science scholars asserted that Shintō narratives of creation were more directly compatible with modern science than the Bible, that study of Shintō teachings could further the progress of astronomy, and that knowledge of modern science would in turn help readers to more profoundly understand Shintō texts.[5] Japan's gods were both the teachers of the world and the makers of natural laws that were only beginning to be comprehended by non-Japanese scientists. For the National Science movement, all human knowledge was perceived as indigenous to Japan; this meant that for Japan to adopt European science was not to fall under foreign influence, but to reclaim what had always been its rightful property.

The desire to obtain European science without also falling to Christian influence led Japanese censors to purge all Christian references from translations of European books. Jason Ānanda Josephson suggests that the editorial prohibition also extended to Islam, references to which seem to have been interpreted as references to Christianity.[6] In seeking to completely de-Christianize the scientific literature coming from Europe, editing out even the most vague nod to monotheism, Japanese intellectuals thus achieved an explicit binary between "religious" and "scientific" discourses that Europe itself had not yet fully constructed.[7] "It would be only a slight exaggeration," Josephson suggests, "to say that Japan is where European knowledge first came to be secularized."[8]

In the course of the Meiji Restoration, "religion" as a means of grouping ideologies and communities would become intertwined with the project of nation-building. "Rhetorically," writes Josephson, "the Restoration embraced simultaneously a technological futurity and a return to the divine age," when "the workings of the state harmonized with rituals devoted to the imperial ancestors and the great gods of Japan."[9] The state offered a construction of its prehistory that suited the needs of its scientific, rationalist future, while seeking to erase what it perceived as alien transgressions against eternal, essential Japan-ness. This meant that recently adopted European science, presented as indigenously Japanese and having originated with Shintō gods, was privileged as more authentically "Japanese" than Buddhist and Confucian traditions, which had been in Japan for centuries.

Prior to 1853, when the United States forced Japan to treaty conditions that included freedom of religion, there was no word for *religion* in Japanese. It proved challenging for Japanese translators, who read *religion* to signify numerous things, including culture, a type of education, and basically a synonym for Christianity.[10] After trying several terms with a considerable range of meanings, Japanese intellectuals and diplomats in the 1870s came to popularize *shūkyō*—a compound of words for *sect/lineage/principle* and *teachings*, adding up to mean "the teachings of a sect" or "principles of the teachings"—as the proper Japanese analog to a Euro-American concept.[11]

Following the creation of a new category came the question of which items belonged within it. For the Meiji-era Japanese state, the pivotal distinction was not exactly between "religious" and "secular" realms of knowledge and practice, but rather between "religion" and "superstition." Indulgence in superstition was seen as impeding the advancement of the nation.[12] The emergence of "religion" as a category also allowed new possibilities for plural "religions" and divisions between them. The nineteenth-century construction of Shintō as a unique body of concepts and practices required its clear separation from other traditions. The state took this division as its responsibility, issuing national proclamations against the mixing of Buddhism and Shintō. Anti-Buddhist prejudice had flared in the years prior to the Meiji Restoration, as nativists categorized Buddhism as one of the foreign influences that corrupted an otherwise pure and united national spirit. Under the Tokugawa regime, Buddhism was additionally condemned as a parasite upon the people. Buddhist temples were accused of wasting material and human resources: Anti-Buddhists argued that the metals that went into temple bells and Buddha images should have been melted down to make cannons, and they viewed Buddhist priests as beneficial to society only if they learned useful trades.[13]

Faced with increasing hostility in their own country, Japanese Buddhists looked beyond Japan to coreligionists in Korea, China, India, Sri Lanka, and elsewhere, taking refuge in a sense of global Buddhist community. As growth in commercial shipping led to new opportunities for private travel throughout Asia, and European colonialism became a shared crisis virtually everywhere, the development of transnational Buddhist networks contributed to rhetoric of pan-Asianism as a collective resistance against the encroaching power of the West. The chief obstacle to worldwide Buddhist unity, as some Japanese clerics saw it, was the immeasurable diversity of Buddhist ideas and practices. Japanese Buddhist reformers such as

Shaku Kōzen (1849–1924) argued that for Buddhism to survive in modernity, Buddhists must purge their tradition of whatever doctrines, practices, and cultural differences threatened to divide them. In this vision, global Buddhist solidarity could only be achieved on the basis of what all Buddhists shared as common ground: the historical person of the Buddha. For Kōzen and other reformers, Buddhists needed to do away with inauthentic innovations and return to the Buddha's original teachings and the precedents that he had established.[14] As a modern reified Buddhism, presented as the faithful restoration of original Buddhism, became seen as the key to overcoming European power, an element of Japanese exceptionalism entered into pan-Asianism, with Japan embarking on a "civilizing mission" to act as intellectual and political savior to colonized Buddhist nations.[15] Though Buddhists had been demonized and persecuted for much of the Meiji Restoration, Buddhism would later become vital to Japanese imperial ideology.

Emphasis on reviving the pure message of the Buddha also developed as Buddhists throughout Asia engaged a growing body of Western scholarship on their tradition. Informed by growing academic investigation of the historical Jesus, and the nascent field of comparative religion—which, having emerged through a Christian context, privileged the "founder" model, in which great religions were treated as the singlehanded works of great men—European scholars of the nineteenth century became increasingly interested in the historical Buddha. Even the term *Buddhism* (like *Mohammadanism*) emerged as a result of European scholars viewing the tradition through their own Christocentric framework.[16]

Buddhist revivalism developed in conversation with Western scholarship, particularly as Buddhist intellectuals struggled with the intersecting concerns of European colonialism, Christian missionary activity, and the new truth-making power of empirical science. The Buddhist thinker Anagarika Dharmapala arrived at 1893's Parliament of World Religions in Chicago to offer an image of Buddhism that not only countered racist imaginaries of the "Asiatic mind" as inferior, but also addressed the spiritual crisis of Victorian-era disillusionment with Christianity, while playing upon anti-Catholic prejudices. "The message of the Buddha that I bring to you," he told an audience in New York that same year, "is free from theology, priestcraft, rituals, ceremonies, dogmas, heavens, hells and other theological shibboleths . . . a scientific religion containing the highest individualistic altruistic ethics . . . a cosmology which is in harmony with geology, astronomy, radioactivity and reality."[17] Though Dharmapala's claims did not exactly match Buddhism as a lived reality in Ceylon, these arguments became popular for Buddhist apologists.[18] In an act of "reverse orientalism" or "strategic occidentalism," Dharmapala flipped the dominant narrative upside down, arguing that when Christian Europe was lost in the dark ages, Buddhists in Asia enjoyed advanced scientific knowledge and a rational way of life.[19] The notion of Buddhism as offering spiritual fulfillment in full compatibility with modern science attracted converts such as Henry Steel Olcott, who became a significant contributor to reformist Buddhist thought.[20] Olcott stressed the need to distinguish between the Buddha's original message and its corruptions that one would find among the ignorant masses: Eternal Buddhism could not be conflated with the cultures of people who happened to call themselves Buddhists. Olcott argued that Buddhism needed increased systematization and purging of ignorant folk practices, which he sought to achieve in part through promoting his own "Buddhist Catechism." To restore original Buddhism as taught by the Buddha, Buddhism had to adopt new tools and become something that it had never been.

As a Theosophist who believed in the esoteric unity of religions, Olcott extended his reformist insights to other traditions, offering a prescription for Zoroastrian revival. Zoroastrianism, he lamented, had originated as a "highly spiritual faith" but had decayed over the centuries into a "purely exoteric creed fully of ritualistic practices not understood" and "the shriveled shell that once held a radiant soul."[21] The cause for Zoroastrianism's decline, according to Olcott, was ignorance on the part of both its priesthood and laypeople. He suggested that the restoration of Zoroastrianism to its original integrity could be achieved through education on both fronts: The priests should engage in study of world languages and literatures, while the lived religion of the masses must be cleansed of its ritualism and superstition. This would be achieved in part, as Stephen Prothero explains, by "translating prayer books into English and vernacular languages, by explaining those texts in simple language in footnotes, and by publishing commentaries that reconcile hoary Zoroastrian truths with the laws of modern science."[22] Additionally, Zoroastrians must engage in archaeological research to confirm the truth of their scriptures, similar to the mission of the Christians' Palestine Exploration Society.[23]

In colonial India, as Christian missionaries condemned indigenous communities for their superstitions, exploitive clerics, child marriages, degradation of widows, blind ritualism, and denial of moral agency, these critiques directed the new shapes that indigenous traditions would take. In other words, Hinduism became Hinduism significantly in response to what European Christians—who had brought the term *Hinduism* to India with them—said about it. The global Protestantization of religion meant that there was now a thing called Hinduism, existing as its own set of clear-cut norms, and that this Hinduism must defend itself by the colonists' terms. The Brahmo Samaj, founded in 1828, promoted Hinduism as universal, monotheistic, rational, and grounded in the authority of scriptures rather than popular practices. The Arya Samaj, founded in 1875 in Bombay, argued for free will and moral responsibility, insisted that all science had originated with Hinduism, and marked a clear difference between the "pure religion" and later distortions. These efforts would inform later Hindu nationalism and mythic reconstructions of Indian history: The Westernized construction of Hinduism that emerged through British colonialism became a language of anticolonial resistance.

Other communities engaged in similar projects. The Singh Sabha, established in Amritsar in 1873, sought to restore Sikh tradition to its original purity, which meant rejecting elements of Punjabi popular culture, escaping the influence of both Hinduism and Ṣūfism, and answering the question, "Are Sikhs Hindus?" with a resounding negative.[24] Each religion's integrity depended on its isolation from other religions; what the British would have regarded as "syncretism," or the mixing of materials from traditions assumed to be naturally distinct from one another, could not justify itself in the new "world religions" model. In the eyes of the colonial power—enforced through mechanisms such as the census, which enforced constructions such as "Muslim" and "Hindu" as lived realities—syncretism signified illiteracy and irrationality, and to mix religions meant that one was unsophisticated and "confused."[25] It was in this milieu that Muslims, like Hindus and Sikhs, increasingly defined themselves through forced isolation from other communities, which required a return to original Islam. Parallel to the Hindu and Sikh purification projects, Muslims developed revivalist and reformist movements of their own, such as the Deoband madrasa network, the Ahl-e Hadith, and the Tablighi Jama'at, led by Muḥammad Ilyas (1885–1944), which sought to cleanse Islam of folk practices and outside contamination.[26]

The Ahmadiyya, whom many people seem incapable of discussing as anything but a "heretical" or "quasi-Islamic" group, also emerged in this setting to defend Muslims against the polemics of Christian missionaries—and additionally against the Hindu and Sikh reformists and revivalists in a heated pamphlet war. The Ahmadiyya movement, formed in Qadian in 1880, showed up with its own answers to the problems of Islam's supposed decline, the failures of religious scholars, and the need for a worldwide renewal of what Muḥammad had brought in the seventh century.

Comparative history has its problems; it would be naive to simply point out similar trends taking place in different regions and assume that whatever conclusions we can draw from one context must also apply to the others. If little else, we can at least say that everyone faced the effects of intensified print culture, greater opportunities for transnational networking and global media, the new authority of empirical science, and the crisis of European hegemony, and that we can observe some shared responses to these new contexts. At any rate, this all makes Salafism look a little less of an aberration.

Before recovering the golden age, Muslims had to decide what that golden age signified, and what exactly made it golden. They rummaged through the past for what it could say to their present, which is where the project necessarily became creative and presentist. The constructed Muslim past ends up looking not all that different from the Hindu, Buddhist, and Shintō pasts that were constructed in the same period. While Shintō thinkers asserted that European science originated with Japanese gods, Muslim thinkers—including proto-Salafī figures—placed a premium on past centuries in which Arabic reigned as the dominant language of science and scholarship for the Mediterranean world. As Buddhist intellectuals reconstructed Siddhartha as a freethinker who extolled science and condemned all superstition, Muslim intellectuals promoted Muḥammad's statements about the virtues of seeking knowledge and the holiness of scholars' ink, while marginalizing reports of Muḥammad's supernatural powers and miracles. Muḥammad and Buddha become repackaged as rationalist philosophers at roughly the same historical moment. Contrary to both the "Islam is incompatible with modernity" argument and the Salafiyya's own self-imagination, Salafī discourse moved in the same inescapably modern global currents as a litany of thinkers and movements, both Muslim and non-Muslim. In seeking to create their futures by looking backward to a golden past, the Salafiyya seem to have been doing *what everyone else in their present was doing.*

RISE OF THE SALAFIYYA

People sometimes represent the mysterious globetrotting activist, Jamāl ad-Dīn al-Afghānī (1838–1897) as a foundational figure for modern Salafism, though this gets tricky. Salafīs, for reasons that should be obvious, don't want anyone to be seen as Salafism's founder. Regardless, Salafīs wouldn't typically accept al-Afghānī as one of their own, since this founder-figure doesn't meet the standards of authenticity for the movement that he had supposedly founded.

Some details on al-Afghānī: He was born and raised in Iran during a time of sectarian uprisings, particularly involving the Babi movement, whose leader had declared himself the Bāb (gate) to the hidden Twelfth Imām and which would become the forerunner to later Bahā'ism. Coming from a family of sayyids, he received a Shī'ī education in the holy shrine cities of Iran and Iraq. His particular engagements of Avicennan philosophy, mystical knowledge, and alpha-numeric esotericism apparently alienated the religious scholars in Najaf.[27] In 1857, while still a teenager, he journeyed to India, where he had his initial encounters with European sciences as well as colonial oppression. Biographer Nikki Keddie describes his developing religiosity as the blend of a "Sufi mystical streak with extraordinary political activism."[28] He would continue to wander, leading café discussions over tea and cigarettes, collecting disciples, hustling for financial and political support among social elites, starting or joining secret societies, preaching of glorious ancient heritages—Egyptian, Indian, Persian, always customized for local audiences—as alternatives to Western models of knowledge,[29] and eventually finding trouble with governments or clerical authorities, often leading to his exile or retreat. He concealed his Iranian origin with aliases like *Istanbūlī* and later *al-Afghānī*, perhaps to avoid the challenges of a Shī'ī background as he preached in Sunnī-majority countries. Seeing himself as the "Islamic Luther," he advocated a Muslim adaptation of European religious reform models[30] and sought the rationalization of belief and practice as the key to Muslims' material and political progress.[31] Islam, he insisted, was in fact "the only religion that censures belief without proof and the following of conjectures; reproves blind submission; seeks to show proof of things to its followers; everywhere addresses itself to reason; considers all happiness the result of wisdom and clear-sightedness."[32] However, in his famous exchange with Ernest Renan, who had asserted not only that Islam was fundamentally hostile to science and philosophy but that these disciplines were incompatible with the "Semitic mind," al-Afghānī accepted part of Renan's claim. Al-Afghānī allowed that Islam was hostile to science, but he employed the now-familiar evolutionary argument that Islam, being centuries younger than Christianity, needed some time to catch up, and he admitted that all religions were fundamentally antagonistic toward science and free thought.[33] Al-Afghānī was a hard one to pin down.

In Cairo, where al-Afghānī landed a stipend through political friendships and taught classes at the global gravity center of Sunnī knowledge production, al-Azhar University, the university shaykhs accused him of conspiring to start his own atheist sect.[34] During his troubled stint at al-Azhar, however, his private discussion circles attracted a young man named Muḥammad 'Abduh (1849–1905), for whom meeting al-Afghānī would amount to a conversion experience. "In Egypt," writes Keddie, al-Afghānī "apparently took his disciples at whatever point he found them and was able in many cases to lead them to his own combination of Islamic philosophy, concern with self-strengthening via religious and other reforms, and hostility to Western encroachments."[35] Twenty-three-year old 'Abduh was a student at al-Azhar and exposed through family contacts to the Madaniyya, a reformist/revivalist Ṣūfī order that emphasized strict rigor of practice in opposition to the popular folk Ṣūfism of local shrines and saints' holidays. Al-Afghānī welcomed 'Abduh into his group, inviting him to study thinkers such as Avicenna, al-Farābī, and Ibn Khaldūn, who were commonly read in Iran but had fallen out of favor in Sunnī intellectual circles.[36] Al-Afghānī initially appealed to 'Abduh's mystical inclinations but gradually steered him toward more rationalist modes of interpretation.[37] 'Abduh also joined the Kawkab al-Sharq masonic lodge, of which al-Afghānī was a member and later the president; through the lodge, 'Abduh entered the world of al-Afghānī's elite political contacts.[38]

After the failed 'Urabī revolt, 'Abduh fled British-occupied Egypt for Syria in 1883. He reunited in Paris with al-Afghānī, who had been exiled from Egypt in 1879, and the two collaborated on publications of religious and anti-British interest. 'Abduh returned to Egypt in 1888 and rose to the rank of national mufti in 1899. Though 'Abduh experienced a dramatic split with al-Afghānī, apparently due to 'Abduh's softening views on Europe, he maintained his mentor's position that true Islam was rational, advocating allegorical, nonmiraculous, and "scientific" interpretations of stories in the Qur'ān.[39] He condemned what he regarded as superstition and argued that while the original Ṣūfīs were superior Muslims, later Ṣūfīs misunderstood their teachings and resorted to tomb worship and other unacceptable innovations. Though a classically trained jurist and the most powerful judge in Egypt, ʿAbduh opposed blind adherence to legal schools, a value that would survive through his own disciples into later Salafism. So I pause here. Maybe ʿAbduh wasn't the founder of Salafism either, but he did become the hub around which a network developed, and that network would become the hub for networks, and then we ended up with something called Salafism. I am left considering what it means for Salafism to have entered the world through all these decidedly non-Salafī pathways: an esotericist Shīʿī freethinker, Ṣūfism, Avicenna, and freemasonry.

When ʿAbduh passed away in 1905, we didn't have Salafism yet, but the pieces were coming together. In 1897, ʿAbduh launched a transnational newspaper, *al-Manār*, with his Syria-born disciple, Rashīd Riḍā, who would outlive ʿAbduh by thirty years and work on *al-Manār* the full length of that time. Riḍā's thought shifted and evolved alongside a sequence of developments that ʿAbduh could not have anticipated: World War I, the collapse of the Ottoman Empire and dissolution of the caliphate, conflation of reformist circles in Syria and Egypt with the menace of "Wahhābism" (which ʿAbduh had criticized for its ideological excesses), and so-called Wahhābism achieving its own kingdom, Saudi Arabia. If someone had to be modern Salafism's founder, maybe it's Riḍā.

Or maybe we should think of networks rather than singular founders. Network analysis of the Damascus-Cairo relationships (which become triangulated with the Hijāz) that gave rise to the Salafiyya movement problematizes assumptions that Sunnī revivalism proliferated as a response to Western colonialism and hegemony (or even to the problem of "modernity" when modernity is viewed as the crisis of European dominance). While the Cairo reformers functioned within a context in which Europe was indeed the problem, the Damascene reformist scene developed in resistance to the Ottoman Empire.

Tāhir al-Jazā'irī (1851–1920), described by one disciple as "the Muḥammad 'Abduh of Syria," was born in Damascus, the son of the city's Mālikī mufti, who had emigrated from Algeria in 1846.[40] Al-Jazā'irī was educated first by his father, who died when al-Jazā'irī was seventeen years old; he then studied with numerous other teachers, attended the new Jaqmaqiyya college (the first official school in Damascus), and at the age of twenty-two began teaching at a madrassa. Amid major educational reforms during the governorship of Midhat Pasha, al-Jazā'irī was appointed inspector of education. He not only evaluated the qualifications of teachers but also wrote textbooks on a variety of subjects, including a textbook on religion that was translated into Dutch for use in Indonesian Muslim schools.[41]

With the abandonment of many of Midhat Pasha's reforms following his death in 1883, as well as opposition to al-Jazā'irī from religious conservatives, al-Jazā'irī's post was closed in 1885 or 1886.[42] In 1898, al-Jazā'irī became inspector of libraries. To more effectively preserve and centralize the manuscript collections of the city's mosques, he founded the Ẓāhiriyya Library and required that the mosques surrender their archives.[43] In the process of collecting and cataloging rare manuscripts, which he had started years prior to his official post, al-Jazā'irī renewed what had apparently been a lifelong admiration for the works of Ibn Taymiyya, which he attempted to distribute "clandestinely and cheaply."[44]

In al-Jazā'irī's view, Ottoman rule had been disastrous for Arab civilization. He asserted that Arabs could reclaim their rightful place in the world only through rediscovery of their ancestors' literary, linguistic, and historical glory, a process that necessitated a return to Islam.[45] Regarding the Arab Muslim past as the solution for problems of the present, al-Jazā'irī emphasized the Islamic philosophical tradition as evidence of Islam's compatibility with scientific rationality. Central to his argument was the Mu'tāzila of the ninth century, not for their specific positions but as reflective of a past age in which elite Muslim intellectuals could direct the flow of culture and civilization and enjoy freedom of expression. To this end, he argued against the charge that Mu'tāzila thought had been solely the product of Greek influence, and therefore owing more to Western intellectual tradition than Islam itself.[46] Asserting that the Mu'tāzila had emerged before the mass translation of Greek texts into Arabic, he repositioned the movement as an organic and internal Muslim phenomenon.[47]

From the 1890s onward, al-Jazā'irī cultivated a following among students from the government schools, including the top secondary school in the city, Maktab 'Anbar.[48] Students at Maktab 'Anbar received an education in Arabic, Ottoman Turkish, Persian, and French and studied modern sciences as well as religion. In salon-styled meetings, al-Jazā'irī engaged the students in discussions of science, religious reform, Arab history, and European advancements.[49] These discussions are said to have contributed to al-Jazā'irī's dismissal as inspector of libraries by the Ottoman authorities in 1902.[50]

Al-Jazā'irī's Damascus salons came to be known as two groups, the original "senior circle" (al-ḥalqa al-kabīra) and a later "junior circle" (al-ḥalqa al-ṣaghīra) that emerged in 1903 with members roughly ten years younger who would also attend the senior circle's meetings. Among the members of al-Jazā'irī's junior circle was Muḥibb al-Dīn al-Khaṭīb (b. 1886), the son of a prominent local 'alim who had died when al-Khaṭīb was thirteen. While enrolled at Maktab 'Anbar, he had studied religion directly under al-Jazā'irī, who supported al-Khaṭīb's simultaneous engagement of multiple bodies of knowledge; in al-Jazā'irī's view, all aspiring scholars of Islam should also develop other vocational or commercial skills to reduce their financial dependence on the rulers or pious endowments (awqāf).[51] Al-Jazā'irī additionally hired al-Khaṭīb to transcribe manuscripts in the archives of Ẓāhiriyya Library, leading al-Khaṭīb to have his own encounter with the thought of Ibn Taymiyya and related figures.[52]

Al-Jazā'irī discovered a new enthusiasm for Ibn Taymiyya at roughly the same time as 'Abd al-Razzāq al-Bīṭār (1834 or 1837–1916), who would later be described by Rashīd Riḍā as the "renewer of the Salaf's way in Syria" (mujaddid madhab al-salaf fī al-Shām).[53] Al-Bīṭār was the student of Muḥammad al-Shaṭṭī, a member of the leading Ḥanbalī family in Damascus. In the early 1880s, Al-Shaṭṭī had authored an essay that contributed to the Damascene renewal of interest in Ibn Taymiyya.[54] While al-Shaṭṭī's essay supported unquestioning adherence to legal schools (taqlīd), al-Bīṭār claimed that he had been inspired by God to reject legal rulings without proof and advocate direct interpretation of the only authoritative proofs, the Qur'ān and Sunna.[55]

In 1896, a weekly study group to which al-Bīṭār belonged became embroiled in controversy due to rumors that it was a "mujtaḥids' club" that practiced individual reasoning (ijtiḥād). The group was called the "Jamālī school" after its member Jamāl al-Dīn al-Qāsimī. Al-Qāsimī had grown up in an 'ulama family, though his education included both traditional study and enrollment at the government school. He briefly accepted initiation with the Naqshbandī Ṣūfīs but did not last long in the order. He would later attack Ṣūfīs as mostly charlatans and frauds who performed fake miracles and made Islam look bad in front of foreigners.[56] Al-Qāsimī argued for a Ḥanbalī position on God's attributes, rejecting attempts to decode God's self-descriptions and denying the possibility of attaining knowledge of God beyond what is said of him in the Qur'ān.[57] Following the "Mujtaḥids Incident," al-Qāsimī wrote a poem in which he affirmed that his "school" consisted only of the Qur'ān and sound ḥadīths, and that he found taqlīd to be ignorance and blindness. In this poem, he also declared, "The truth is that I am of the Salafī creed."[58]

The reformist scene experienced more tension with the Ottoman authorities in 1901, when Abd al-Ḥāmid al-Zahrawī (1871–1916) published a sixty-page tract, *Jurisprudence and Sufism*, in which he viciously attacked the maḍhab establishment and Ṣūfism. Prior to the tract's publication, al-Zahrawī had already had a troubled relationship with the Ottoman government: His newspaper, *al-Munīr*, had been shut down for its commentary on despotism; after writing more articles calling for reform, the government exiled him from Istanbul to Damascus; while under house arrest in Damascus, he continued to write articles for Egyptian publications in which he charged that Abdul-Ḥamīd did not fulfill any prerequisite qualifications for the caliphate.[59]

Arguing in *Jurisprudence and Sufism* that analogy (qiyas) and scholarly consensus (ijma') had no basis as legal proofs, criticizing the position of near-infallibility accorded to the classical scholars, and presenting ijtiḥād as the way of the Prophet's Companions, al-Zahrawī rejected all claims to legitimate authority with the conservative 'ulama. In his discussion of Ṣūfism, al-Zahrawī decried Ṣūfī tradition as a syncretic blend of Greek thought and other sources, charged Ṣūfīs with greedily exploiting the masses for their own interests, and argued that Ṣūfism was largely destructive to society for its alleged lack of interest in worldly affairs.[60] The tract sparked major controversy with the conservative 'ulama. In the hysteria that followed, the police confiscated copies (including the one in al-Qāsimī's house), Zahrawī was deported, and the situation of the proto-Salafīs became more delicate in the face of 'ulama intimidation.[61]

In the face of rising government hostility toward the religious reformists, Aleppo-born 'Abd al-Raḥmān al-Kawākibī (1854–1902) fled Syria for Egypt, anticipating more persecution with the release of his book, *Umm al-Qurā*. In this work, al-Kawākibī imagines a secret society of Muslim scholars who hold an assembly in Mecca to discuss a revival of the Muslim world. The scholars discuss "causes of stagnation," which are divided into three categories: religious, political, and moral factors, in addition to Ottoman policies. The fictitious conference produces a condemnation of Ṣūfism, listing asceticism, superstitions (introduced by "deceivers and worshipers of the dead and their shrines"), astrology, magic, the "liars and flatterers" who believe in esoteric knowledge, and popularity of "manifest or hidden polytheism" among the religious causes of Muslim stagnation.[62]

Additionally, al-Kawākibī blames the religious scholarly establishment, citing belief in predestination, "deceitful 'ulama," the assumption that religion is incompatible with science and philosophy, "surrender to taqlīd and the abandonment of reflection and the quest for guidance," and "undue allegiance to madhabs, and the opinions of recent writers, forsaking scriptures and the path of the pious early Muslims."[63] Finally, the "religious causes" category concludes with the "requiring of what would not be required if one sought guidance from the Book and the Sunna."[64] Al-Kawākibī's concern for religious revival was inseparable from his interest in pan-Arabism, as the thesis of *Umm al-Qurā* asserts that the resurgence of the Muslim umma can become possible only with the end of Turkish rule and the restoration of an Arab caliphate.[65] The two projects become fused in al-Kawākibī's use of a ḥadīth that the caliph can only be from the Prophet's own tribe of Quraysh.[66] The ḥadīth would also factor into the discourse of Rashid Riḍā and other Arab nationalists, for whom it served to grant pan-Arab nationalism and anti-Ottoman sentiment an Islamic legitimacy.[67] In a reading of history that was both Sunnī revivalist and Arab nationalist, al-Kawākibī and Riḍā viewed the Ottoman caliphate as a forceful usurpation of the Arabs' historical and religious entitlement to rule.[68] Riḍā, like al-Kawākibī, associated the golden age of early Islam with Arab power and held that Arab revival was the key to Islamic revival.[69] He imagined a future pan-Arab state as headed by a caliph who managed only the state's religious affairs, and a president, selected by the caliph, who managed the state. The caliphate was to be centered in Mecca, while the president's administration would be headquartered in Damascus.[70]

Around the turn of the twentieth century, Syria's proto-Salafīs were often tagged with accusations of affiliating with the "Wahhābī" menace of the Arabian Peninsula. The movement, which had emerged roughly a century earlier and was named for scholar Ibn 'Abd al-Wahhāb, was not concerned with reconciling Islam to scientific rationality, nor with Muslim revival as an answer to European domination. Ibn 'Abd al-Wahhāb's project was simply to restore Islamic monotheism, which he regarded as having been corrupted through innovated practices such as veneration of tombs and trees. His followers did not call themselves "Wahhābīs" but rather Muwāhiddūn, "Monotheists." Following the so-called Wahhābīs' capture of Riyadh in 1902, Ottoman officials grew terrified of alliances between a possible Wahhābī state and Syria's anti-taqlīd reformists who rejected the authority of the clerical establishment. Conservative 'ulama subsequently found in the *Wahhābī* label a powerful means of defaming their reformist rivals.[71] As government and clerical forces exerted increasing pressure and intimidation upon the proto-Salafīs, Egypt became more attractive as a safe haven. In 1903, al-Bīṭār and al-Qāsimī traveled to Egypt, encountering a lively scene of religious reformists. In Egypt, these thinkers were not seen by the British as threats to their power; the British even suspected that they could play 'Abduh and his opposition against each other.[72] As a consequence, figures such as 'Abduh enjoyed intellectual freedom that was not possible in Syria, where discourses that undermined clerical religious authority and the legitimacy of Ṣūfī orders threatened the very structures on which the Ottoman Empire rested its claims to the caliphate.[73]

Upon arrival in Cairo, al-Bīṭār and al-Qāsimī met Muḥammad 'Abduh, engaging him in conversations on ijtiḥād and attending his lessons on Qur'ānic interpretation.[74] Soon after, they met Rashīd Riḍā. When the pair returned to Syria, knowledge of a developing Cairo-Damascus reformist network caused increasing alarm for the Ottoman government. Between 'Abduh's positive relationship to the British government and the rising Wahhābī menace, it was feared that the Syrian reformists were plotting to carve Syria out of the Ottoman Empire.[75]

Meanwhile, the members of al-Jazā'irī's salons in Damascus had matured. Upon graduation in 1906, most of the junior circle members continued their studies in Istanbul, where they were disappointed to find numerous Arab students who had abandoned their own heritage to assimilate into Turkish culture.[76] With the aim of restoring Arab identity, they formed the Arab Renaissance Society (Jam'iyyat al-nahḍa al-'arabiyya) and held weekly meetings to discuss classic Arab literature.[77] In 1907, following al-Khaṭīb's suggestion, Ṣalāḥ al-Dīn al-Qāsimī (Jamāl's brother) and Luṭfī al-Ḥaffār established a Damascus chapter of the group. During their summer vacation that year, al-Khaṭīb and the other Istanbul members returned to Damascus and met with the Damascus members, where it was agreed that Damascus would be the headquarters and site of a banquet at which lectures were presented on various topics, including religious and educational reform, Arabic, and science.[78]

For the Ottoman government, the intersection of Arab cultural revivalism and pan-Arab nationalism with rejection of state-sponsored religious establishments, in the shadow of the Wahhābī takeover of Riyadh, signaled nothing less than the looming threat of an Arab caliphate. Al-Jazā'irī and his colleagues were subjected to raids by government authorities, who accused them of contacts with the Young Turks. In 1907, the year that the Arab Renaissance Society formed its Damascus branch, al-Jazā'irī fled Damascus for Cairo, where he found greater freedom of expression and a welcoming audience of his former disciples.[79] One year later, Rashīd Riḍā visited Damascus and nearly incited a riot for his lecture at the Umayyad Mosque, during which he condemned the seeking of human intercession with God as polytheism. Hecklers, including members of the conservative 'ulama, in turn condemned Riḍā and accused him of association with the Wahhābīs. One of Riḍā's critics charged that to oppose tomb visitation and seeking the intercession of holy figures essentially amounted to rebellion against the Sultan.[80]

The circles of Riḍā and al-Jazā'irī intersect at the person of Muḥammad Kurd 'Alī (1876–1953), founder of the Arabic Language Institute in Damascus, who had been a member of al-Jazā'irī's senior circle and was also a follower of Riḍā's mentor, al-Jisr.[81] Kurd 'Alī, who emphasized the Arab role in Islamic civilization and blamed Turks for Arab Muslims' decline on the world stage,[82] inadvertently contributed to antagonism between the reformist scene and the government when he misquoted the Shaykh al-Islam as having stated that the Ottoman Empire was not a legitimate caliphate. The government subsequently shut down Kurd 'Alī's newspaper, *al-Muqtabas*, which had become an important forum for the Arab Renaissance Society, and Kurd 'Alī fled for Beirut and then Paris.[83] Al-Qāsimī and al-Bīṭār were then brought before the central court's interrogation bureau, where the interrogator asked them about the presence of Wahhābism in Damascus and charged that the Arab Renaissance Society was in contact with the rulers in Najd and Yemen. Al-Qāsimī and al-Bīṭār denied any involvement in the Society and insisted that it was simply a literary club.[84]

In 1907, al-Jazā'irī reunited in Cairo with his student al-Khaṭīb, who was en route to Yemen. Through al-Jazā'irī, al-Khaṭīb met 'Abd al-Fattah Qatlan, the cousin of a Damascene shaykh. Two years later, upon al-Khaṭīb's return to Cairo, he and Qatlan decided to print books on religion, science, and other topics and sell them from their own bookstore across from the Ḥusayn mosque. On al-Jazā'irī's suggestion, they named their establishment the Salafiyya Bookstore (al-Maktaba al-Salafiyya).[85]

This could be the moment at which Salafism starts to become a thing, even if no one yet knows what the thing is.

The Salafiyya Bookstore marketed the writings of al-Jazā'irī but also offered a considerable range of literature beyond what we might mark as ideologically "Salafī" today. "In the 1910s," writes Henri Lauzière, "it is clear that when al-Khaṭīb and Qatlan spoke of the 'forefathers,' they were not using the term in its narrower sense of the first three Muslim generations. They had enough business flair to place virtually any medieval *homme de lettres*, including Ibn Sīna [Avicenna], among the *salaf*."[86] *Salafī* was still apparently an amorphous term, as Jamāl al-Dīn al-Qāsimī complained that many people had no idea of what it meant to be a Salafī or who could be counted as one.[87]

Al-Khaṭīb and Qatlan entered into partnership with Rashīd Riḍā in 1912, relocating to join their store to the Manār Bookstore. In 1917, the Salafiyya Bookstore changed its name to the Salafiyya Bookstore and Journal (al-Maktaba wa-l-Majalla al-Salafiyya) upon the start of its own journal, *Salafyyah Review* (*al-Majalla al-Salafiyya*), edited by Qatlan with al-Jazā'irī as consultant.[88] While the company's publications flooded book markets across and beyond the Middle East, the "Salafī" label would remain vague even in the 1920s. If nothing else, as various Sunnī revivalist and reformist currents throughout the transnational umma increasingly engaged each other in conversation, the Salafiyya Bookstore and Journal gave the future a name.

Though the company's publications included polemics against rationalist or modernist works, Lauzière suggests that the journal reaching Europe was a prime catalyst in the construction of an orientalist master narrative of the Salafiyya as a movement for modernist reform.[89] Between 1920 and 1925, Louis Massignon gave a series of explanations for the term, initially locating its rise in colonial India and later prioritizing al-Afghānī and 'Abduh as founder figures.[90] Massignon's narrative of the Salafiyya as a coherent movement of modernist reformers was reified both in Europe and the Middle East. For Massignon's Salafī imaginary to be accepted uncritically by Orientalist scholars and met with no objection by Muslim scholars such as Shakib Arslan, argues Lauzière, demonstrates the "lack of clarity about *salafiyya* in the 1920s, when the notion was being worked out simultaneously in the West and the Muslim world."[91]

Versions of the Salafiyya Bookstore that emerged in Multan in 1921 and Damascus in 1922 revealed no trace of the reformist rationalism that Massignon had designated as the heart of the Salafiyya. The Multan store was founded by a man with links to India's Ahl-e

Ḥadīth movement; the Damascus store's principal owner was the student of a Hanbalī scholar; both stores had connections to networks in what would soon become Saudi Arabia.[92] The label's meaning developed as the proprietors of the Salafiyya Bookstore and their partner, Rashīd Riḍā, became ardent supporters of the nascent Saudi kingdom, which might have appeared to be the Muslim umma's greatest chance after the destruction of the caliphate and the carving of the Ottoman Empire into colonial mandate territories.[93] The Saudis commissioned printing of Ḥanbalī texts from the Salafiyya Bookstore, and in 1929, working with a Hijzī partner, Qatlan established a Mecca branch of the franchise that printed primarily Ḥanbalī materials in line with the new kingdom's needs.[94]

Following his "Wahhābī turn," Riḍā would go so far as to name Ibn 'Abd al-Wahhāb the divinely appointed renewer who had been sent by God for his century.[95] When Riḍā affirms in a 1927 article that "since its inception, *al-Manār* has been preaching *tawhīd* and the *madhab al-salaf* in matters [of] the dogmas and guidance of Islam," the meaning of madhab al-salaf is more clear than it had actually been in *al-Manār's* early years or in al-Qāsimī's self-identification as a Salafī at the turn of the century.[96]

Throughout the 1920s, the Salafiyya Bookstore and Journal served as a meaningful site of discourse on matters of both reforming Muslim tradition internally and defending Muslims against the encroaching West.[97] Al-Khaṭīb additionally became a bridge between the turn-of-the-century Damascene reformist scene and post-caliphate Islamism. In 1926, al-Khaṭīb and his Cairo circle established what has been described as a "combative and polemical" journal, *al-Fath*, which would play a role in the emergence of the Muslim Brothers.[98] Al-Khaṭīb and the leader of the Muslim Brothers, Hasan al-Banna, were friends, and al-Khaṭīb sought to recruit al-Banna on behalf of the Saudi government to teach in the Hijāz.[99] In 1933, the Muslim Brothers started producing a weekly journal, *Jarīdat al-Ikhwān al-Muslimīn*, which was supported and printed by al-Khaṭīb's press until the Muslim Brothers obtained their own license.[100]

Between the Damascus and Cairo reformers, the call to return to the path of the Salaf answered concerns in multiple political contexts. In Damascus, an Ibn Taymiyyan model of Islamic authenticity served to critique the Ottoman regime; in Cairo, where the crisis was European interference, Salafism provided a means by which a cleansed and revived Islam could restore Muslims to their proper place on the world stage, enabling Muslims to unite politically and simultaneously become "modernized" without submitting to blind imitation of Europe. The network would be triangulated with the emergence of the Saudi kingdom, which represented the aspirations of an Islamically driven Arab empire as envisioned by Riḍā much more than the possibilities for Egypt in his own lifetime.

In the religious authority vacuum following the 1923 collapse of the Ottoman Empire, Cairo's al-Azhar University sought to position itself as the modern center of Sunnī knowledge production. As the twentieth century progressed, Saudi Arabia—bolstered by the mid-century oil boom and prestige as host of the holy cities, Mecca and Medina—devoted enormous resources toward rivaling Egypt's institutional prestige with its own educational and media networks. It was a contest that Egypt had no hope of winning, as Saudi funds even flowed into al-Azhar.[101] In the 1960s, the Saudi-Egypt rivalry intensified, as US-supported Saudi Arabia and Soviet-supported Egypt became locked in what was called the "Arab Cold War." Saudi Arabia, having been a kingdom for a few decades but only in the 1964–1975 reign of King Faisal achieving a centralized state, sought to wield transnational influence with a globalizing Muslim mission, while Egypt's Gamel Abdel Nasser became a globally beloved hero of anticolonial and nationalist movements. Abdel Nasser's pan-Arabism and socialism, the 1958 union of Egypt and Syria as the United Arab Republic (UAR), and a successful revolution against monarchy in Iraq terrified the fledgling Saudi kingdom, provoking an intensified investment in transnational religious networks. In an effort to curb the influence of secularist nationalism, pan-Arabism, and communism, Faisal would spend the 1960s and '70s establishing transnational organizations. In 1962, he founded the Muslim World League (Rābiṭat al-'Ālam al-Islāmī) to counter Egypt's Academy of Islamic Research (Majma' al-Buḥūth al-Isāmiyya), which had been established a year earlier and constructed Islam as compatible with socialism.[102] While al-Azhar simultaneously reinvented itself in the mold of modern universities to become a factory for professional academics, influence of the Muslim World League pushed al-Azhar to the neotraditionalist right.[103] Later Faisal projects included the Organization of the Islamic Conference (1972), the World Assembly of Muslim Youth (1972), the International Islamic Relief Organization (1975), and a network of domestic and foreign educational institutions such as the Islamic University in Medina. It was in the 1960s that Faisal gave his support to the construction of a national mosque for the people of Pakistan, which would be completed in 1986 and named after him. The Nasser regime, meanwhile, did everything in its power to crush religious dissent within its borders, particularly including violent suppression of the Muslim Brotherhood.

The policies of these two states drove the questions and answers of Salafism. In Saudi Arabia, where "Wahhābī" Salafism served as the official ideology of the government, adherence to the way of the Salaf meant rigorous maintenance of a particular notion of monotheism, purification of religious practice, and obedience toward one's rulers. In Egypt, where Salafism developed as resistance against a repressive secularist state, to follow the Salaf meant commanding the right and forbidding the wrong, speaking truth to tyrannical power. Though a politically detached Salafism served the Saudi kingdom's preference *within* its borders, the state found Brotherhood-styled Muslim activism to be useful as a foreign policy, undermining the secularist regimes of rival states. The currents sometimes mingled: During the 1960s, Muslim Brothers came to Saudi Arabia as refugees fleeing the persecutions of Nasser's Egypt and Baathist-ruled Syria, which would lead to the emergence of an informal movement, al-Sahwa, the "Awakening," that has been described as a domestic Brotherhood-Wahhābī synthesis.[104] In later decades, "neo-Salafism" would become a voice of critique and sometimes violent uprising against the Saudi government's official Salafism. As neo Salafīs criticized everything from royal hedonism to encroaching secularism to gender issues, the government poured resources into religious institutions to establish its credibility as a committed defender of Islam.

When Malcolm X embarked on the pilgrimage to Mecca in the spring of 1964, this Saudi-Egyptian tension produced the "Muslim world" that waited for him. Reinventing himself in part between opposing players in the Arab Cold War, Malcolm X carefully navigated his relationships with both the Saudi and Egyptian governments. During his first pilgrimage in the spring of 1964, Malcolm received a private audience with Faisal, who subjected him to a quiz concerning basics of Muslim belief, basically measuring Malcolm's comprehension of pamphlet Islam. While in Cairo, Malcolm also underwent religious training with Faisal's Muslim World League—the organization that paid for Betty Shabazz's pilgrimage after Malcolm's assassination and later worked with the Nation of Islam during its post-1975 move toward Sunnism—and simultaneously corresponded with Muslim Brotherhood exiles, while maintaining necessary discretion with the Nasser regime.[105] He additionally received certifications from al-Azhar, while also becoming the US representative of the World Islamic League (which had been established by the Brotherhood's Said Ramadan in exile), and pitched a request for funds to the Saudi government's foreign affairs department so that he could establish his own Sunnī mosque in Harlem.[106] After having his mind under Elijah Muhammad's capture for so many years, Malcolm found some relief in Saudi Arabia, describing the environment as one that facilitated "objective thinking."[107]

My Muslim genealogy must include this Islam to which Malcolm came, his final conversion; but there was also the Islam that Malcolm had come *from*, his first conversion, which had to remain somewhere inside him, as marked by his continued use of the name that Elijah had given him: Malik Shabazz (Shabazz being the name of Elijah's mythic Black nation that had been lost in the American wilderness). After parting ways with Elijah, Malcolm headed straight for Mecca to reinvent himself in "orthodoxy," but only because Elijah had already created such power and value for Islam that Malcolm would not imagine himself as other-than-Muslim. Why Mecca? After leaving the Nation, Malcolm could have studied Buddhism and embarked on a pilgrimage to Tibet, or he could have embraced Yoruba revivalism during his tour of Africa or become an ayahuasca shaman riding divine jaguars in outer space and fighting CIA-backed soldiers in Peru. Continuing his journey as a Muslim, Malcolm sought to become more of what Elijah had already made him into.

Malcolm's Islam, then, has to include the Islam that he left behind: a heritage of figures like Noble Drew Ali in 1920s Chicago, for whom restoring his people to their timeless religious truth was inseparable from their eternal nationhood. Noble Drew Ali taught that slavery was a result of nations abandoning the creeds of their forefathers and conversely that the return to one's origins achieved salvation. Noble Drew Ali spoke of lost history and the need to go back, to restore what had been lost—perhaps expressed most perfectly in the legend of his trip to the White House basement, where he and Woodrow Wilson searched through a safe filled with flags until Drew Ali recovered the red and green banner of his people. Another legend, reported by Peter Lamborn Wilson, suggests that during Drew Ali's childhood, his family had encountered Jamāl ad-Dīn al-Afghānī in New Jersey and accepted initiation into both al-Afghānī's pre-Salafī circle and a group that traced its lineage to the Ikhwān as-Safa, the "Brethren of Purity" society of gnostics and philosophers from tenth-century Iraq.[108] With or without this account being historical, al-Afghānī could appear more than once among the genealogies that make Malcolm.

On July 4, 1930, a stranger appeared among the poorest neighborhoods of Detroit, going from house to house in the guise of a silk peddler, telling black people who opened their doors to him that they were naturally, *originally* Muslims. The search for lost origins was both religious and biological. The stranger explained that they had lost Islam and become "other than their own selves" after being tricked into slavery nine thousand miles from home. The stranger claimed that black people were the first of humanity and belonged to a Nation of Islam that had no "birth record" because it was "older than the sun, moon, and stars."[109] In contrast, white people had a birth record going back only six thousand years, when they were bred in a eugenics regime on the Greek island of Patmos. White people had created nothing of their own and were themselves the creation of a black scientist.

He additionally revealed that the white devil's rule on this planet had expired in 1914 and that Muslims possessed a spaceship—built in Japan with blueprints from Mecca—that went far beyond anything the devil's greatest minds could imagine. With his proclamation "Islam is mathematics," the stranger claimed that rather than pray for an invisible ghost to solve their problems, Muslims recognized the true causes and effects in this world. While those whom the stranger called "blind, deaf, and dumb, slaves to mental death and power" believed that changes in the weather occurred at the whim of this "mystery god," he taught that Muslim scientists made the weather by experimenting with "high explosives."

As for the stranger's own origins, he told people that he had come from Mecca, the "root of civilization," but that they had not yet seen him in his royal robes. He had slicked black hair and olive skin and referred to black people collectively as his "uncle." Beyond an apparent Ahmadiyya connection, it's impossible to definitively name the discourses that influenced the stranger, but this is perhaps unnecessary. He fits easily within his moment and the decades leading up to him. The stranger's narrative of an eternally existing nation that must be restored to its past greatness, his opposition to hierarchical religious institutions (even while establishing one himself), his advocacy for a rational subject who shuns superstition and thinks independently, and his investments in the truth of science and technology resonate with widespread conversations of the period.

After three and a half years, during which his door-to-door preaching evolved into a growing community of followers, the stranger, Master Fard Muhammad, disappeared. His followers briefly split into rival factions until Fard's minister, Elijah Muhammad, ascended as leader of the Nation of Islam. Elijah claimed authority on the basis that Fard, whom he understood to have been Allāh in person, had named Elijah to be his divinely guided messenger. During Fard Muhammad's brief career, he had assigned his followers new names, which signified the return to their original and natural state as "righteous Muslims." After Fard's disappearance, Elijah instead replaced new converts' surnames with *X*, which signified their Muslim names that had been lost in slavery and remained unknown.

Reading the NOI and Salafism as they mingled in Malcolm's life, they seem less like polar opposites and more like reflections of a shared big idea. For Noble Drew Ali in the basement of the White House, and Master Fard Muhammad distributing "original" names, and reformers and revivalists essentially everywhere in the later nineteenth and early twentieth centuries, the truth was found at the origins.

After Malcolm returned home from Mecca, some of his fellow NOI-turned-Sunnī Muslims asked him if he had seen Master Fard Muhammad. That should demonstrate how messy all this gets. Malcolm's *Autobiography* presents his Muslim journey in distinct phases, marked by painful but clean breaks, but I don't know if that's how a human life ever really works; it doesn't even work for me as a *reader* of that life.

YOU'RE LIKE A CHILD WHO WALKS INTO THE MIDDLE OF A MOVIE

The 1980s and '90s saw the rising significance of American Muslim institutions, such as the Muslim Students Association (MSA) that had been founded in the early 1960s and the Islamic Society of North America (ISNA) that branched out of the MSA in the late 1970s, as sites at which Muslim Brother genealogies intersected with Saudi flows of resources. This also followed the post-1975 detonation of the Nation of Islam under Warith Deen Mohammed, who moved the community toward Sunnī orientation and sought greater connections between African American Muslims and global Sunnī networks, including institutions in both Egypt and Saudi, and the growing prominence of American Muslim converts who sought religious training in Saudi Arabia to become leaders at home. These dynamics changed what could have been the meaning of Malcolm X's time on this earth: As Sunnī pamphlets tell the story, the lesson of Malcolm's life has less to do with global freedom struggle than one man's journey from an imposter cult to true Islam.

"Of all the Islamic schools of thought and perspectives that were operating in the United States throughout the 1990s," writes Shadee Elmasry, "it was the Salafiyya—by way of the Saudis and the University of Medina—that had the most funding, and hence established a strong presence, if not a domination, over the religious discourse."[110] Just how much "domination" the Salafiyya enjoyed is hard to measure, since defining an idea, individual, or organization as "Salafī" is so often slippery. People who claim to have statistics revealing the percentage of American Muslims that can be called Salafī, or the percentage of US mosques that have been overrun with "Wahhābī" influence, are liars, but something was definitely in the air. If it was Salafism, its claims seemed normative enough that it didn't even have to disclose itself as Salafism. When the intro books and pamphlets kept telling me that Islam wasn't "only a religion" but a "complete way of life"—indeed they *all* seemed to say this, in more or less identical phrasing—and a comprehensive system of laws to guide and regulate every aspect of society from the family to the state, it never occurred to me that this kind of claim had a history, let alone that it served as a weapon in Muslim power struggles of the twentieth century. The introductions to Islam that I received did not merely address one phantasmic monolith, the West, on behalf of another, Islam; they had arisen during a contest between two Muslim states, both of which were entangled in the global chess game between two Western empires. My fantasy of Islam as resistance against Western godlessness and hegemony actually found much of its shape as a US-supported counter against Soviet-influenced secularism in the Middle East. So much for the "Clash of Civilizations" or "religion

(Islam) versus the modern world" narratives. So much for tradition as my escape hatch, and so much for me as a free-willed seeker who looked inward for personal truth and then found it.

I don't know how Malcolm would have turned out if he survived beyond 1965, how he might have moved through the changing American Muslim scenes or anti-Muslim Afrocentrisms, or whether a living Malcolm could have brought me to my dīn as successfully as the dead Malcolm. It was in 1992, long before the US Salafī scene's implosion at the end of the decade, that a renaissance of interest in Malcolm climaxed with the release of Spike Lee's biopic. As preparation for watching the film, I read Malcolm's *Autobiography*, where I first learned of Saudi Arabia as the land of origins, the place where Malcolm had to go to find the Real. Then I went to the local college library and picked up a translation of the Qur'ān that had been disseminated through Saudi-directed flows of resources, along with an intro-to-Islam book published by the Faisal-founded World Assembly of Muslim Youth, and a pamphlet by Faisal's personal physician arguing that the Qur'ān displays advanced knowledge of embryology and geology and such. Roughly a year later, I was at King Faisal Mosque in Islamabad.

Pakistan had its own history, both as a land and an idea; it was not reducible to a blank slate on which globalizing Salafī discourse came from Arab states to write itself. The flow of influence between South Asia and the Middle East moved in both directions, as seen in Ibn 'Abd al-Wahhāb's teacher from Sindh and also in the twentieth century as Jamaat Islami ideologue Abu'l-A'la Mawdudi (1903–1979) became enormously significant in Egypt as an influence on Muslim

Brotherhood thought. As with Saudi media networks, Pakistan's history forces me to give a second look to what I had imagined as rebellion against my Americanness. The Pakistani government's "Islamization" process in the 1980s came through US support and encouragement, in service of US strategic interests. Islamization served as a religious counter to the Soviet presence in neighboring Afghanistan, and also as a Sunnī counterweight to neighboring Iran's Shī'ī theocracy.

The flight to Pakistan was less than six months after the first time that I stepped foot in a mosque. It also marked the first time that I ever left my hometown without family; it was my first time outside of the United States (not counting Canada), as well as my first time on a plane since I was two years old. There were too many things to be excited about, and I was too intense in my new-convert piety to regard the opportunity as having been caused by anything but the will of Allāh, so it never really occurred to me to ask who paid for my ticket. I guess it was the school, which means the mosque, which could mean the state of Pakistan or whatever outside sources might support the school. Flying over the Atlantic Ocean at night, I kept looking out at the shooting stars and reading Sayyid Quṭb's commentary on the eighty-sixth sūra of the Qur'ān, also published by the World Assembly of Muslim Youth. Twenty years later, I can have a better sense of the various forces that put me on that plane, the institutions and money and bodies and states. No one's religious life takes place as a pure search for truth in an isolated cloud of ideas. I could not have found my way to Pakistan through the ether. Someone, or rather an unfolding historical process, had to put me in the seat and the books in my hands.

Twenty years after that flight, different processes are paying my way, and I can feel the effects of a new institutional remolding upon myself. The weird part is feeling the change as it happens, as if I'm in midtransformation between two creatures. I ask different questions of texts and approach them with different tools. I refuse to have certain conversations. A new set of names and concepts falls out of my mouth. They all come from somewhere too.

Part of the convert experience is being asked a million times for the story of how you came to Islam. I can't give any answer now except to say that I was in the right place at the right time, I rolled some dice and this is what I got. It's like asking someone how s/he was born, which means asking how his/her parents met, and how their parents met, and their parents and so on, and at some point you realize that you're no longer talking about individuals but big movements of history, wars and famines and mass migrations that force little bodies into seemingly random collisions with each other. Dipping into some history to write this chapter, reflecting on a bunch of nineteenth-century intellectuals who are all great-great-grandparents buried deep in my DNA, ancestors that I would never have recognized . . . something cracked. It was a self-estrangement like gazing at my own X-rays, seeing the bones that had always been there but never made themselves knowable to me as *me*. How did I come to Islam, or how did Islam come to me? At the end of the nineteenth century, an Iranian pretending to be from Afghanistan held roundtable discussions at a café in Cairo; in the early decades of the twentieth century, diasporic Africans in the United States rebuilt their destroyed worlds through new narratives of God, sacred histories and futures, prophecy, and scripture; in the second half of the twentieth century, changes in the global economy empowered a kingdom to promote its religious ideology in every language; here I am, and here is a set of choices for what Islam can be.

If I'm a stranger to myself, if I'm a product of unknown ancestors, I can't know my lord. So I stare at the big flowcharts of names and these arrows of influence pointing in all directions, trying to tie my religion together, seeing not an Islam of eternal consistency but only something frail and vulnerable, subject to whatever causes history to move; and it has me wondering about the options for a fundamentalism that looks like apostasy, in which Islam can only come to me as side effects, instabilities, fragments, random molecules, brokenness and rupture and cross-fertilization forever, nothing predictable, nothing staying in place, forever new empires promoting new books.

7

I WAS A TEENAGE ISLAMIST

>>> Does the order of books determine the order of things? What kind of history of oneself and one's times is coded in the collecting of books? <<< —**Homi K. Bhabha**[1]

IN 1966, MARSHALL McLUHAN had predicted that xerography would destroy authorship and readership as we knew them, enabling anyone to "take a book apart, insert parts of other books and other materials of his own interest, and make his own book in a relatively fast time."[2] This is what we do with our books, with or without the physical acts of cutting or reproducing words. We take our books apart and reassemble them into new things.

It's not enough to say that in 1994, I converted to Islam, because I no longer believe that "Islam" exists as a category that can meaningfully explain what happened to me. Instead, I'll put it this way. I gradually absorbed some books into myself, and from this assortment of claims, I pulled something together and called it "Islam." I won my religion in a scratch-off lottery; my books lined up a certain way, producing a particular construction of Islam in their relations to each other. Change the ingredients of my pile—take one book out, put another in—and Islam might not have taken the form in which I came to know it.

My self-awareness as a Muslim began with those books. What does it mean, then, to be a Salafī? Perhaps doing like Yoda says, unlearning what you have learned, even if what you have learned would itself be called "Salafī" in some circles. Recognize the arbitrary and random nature of your own accumulated "Islam" and go about unpacking your library. Once you see what you've been reacting to, maybe you can start over.

Here are twelve books that I read early in the journey, examined in the order that I originally read them, that contributed to this thing that I would name *Islam*. They were not the only books that I read during that time, but they were the ones that I remember providing the most awesome crises and exhilarations of a young mind being ripped up and reassembled. The older you get, the harder it gets for books to do that kind of thing. I am now twenty years older, have read many, many more books, acquired some critical reading skills that no one cared to give me in high school, and can now put up my guard against authors in ways that were impossible for me at fifteen. The younger me had no idea what he was getting into, and I feel for the kid. To retrace my steps as a Muslim, I reread these books. In a few cases, I still have the same copies that I had read as a teenager, and the creases and smells and dated aesthetics almost put me back into an old head.

MALCOLM X (AS TOLD TO ALEX HALEY), *THE AUTOBIOGRAPHY OF MALCOLM X*

In the 1940s, a prisoner named Malcolm Little embraced Islam under the teachings of Elijah Muhammad and was renamed Malcolm X.

The *X* stood in place of his true family name, his origins that had been erased through the enslavement of his ancestors. His accounts of two conversions to Islam—the first, when he joined the Nation of Islam, followed by a second conversion when he left the NOI and became Sunnī—changed my life forever. I can repeat the Spike Lee blurb on the cover of my copy of *The Autobiography of Malcolm X* and say that it was "the most important book I'll ever read." Amid the Malcolm X resurgence driven significantly by the Republican destruction of America's inner cities, the rising star power of Louis Farrakhan, the revolutionary culture of hip-hop, and the work of Spike Lee, sales of this book rose 300 percent between 1989 and 1992.[3] I read it in 1992.

Malcolm did not speak as a theologian or imām. He did not inspire me to become Muslim by testifying to the power of faith or his personal spirituality or the scriptural basis for his dogmas. He doesn't express a ton of concern with eternal salvation; in its critique of Christianity, the Nation of Islam argues that belief in a blissful afterlife contributes to oppression in the present world, and *The Autobiography* does not disavow this position even after Malcolm splits from the NOI to become Sunnī. Malcolm frequently mentions Allāh but appears to be much more interested in what human beings are doing on the ground, in real life. This aspect of Malcolm's thought causes some to regard his Muslimness (and that of the Nation of Islam at large) as more "political" than "religious," or describe his Islam as "politico-religious." I don't want to fall into that trap here. Malcolm understood himself as a religious man and assessed a religion's value primarily in what it did for or against the achievement of a just society.

What sparked my interest in Islam were the scenes of Malcolm chasing after his lost origins in the prison library, reading all the books available to him, straining his eyes to keep reading in his cell after the lights went out. "Once I heard of the 'glorious history of the black man,'" he recalls, "I took special pains to hunt in the library for books that would inform me on details about black history."[4] History had been "so 'whitened' by the white man" that black people appeared to have no meaningful history at all.[5] Malcolm's search for the knowledge of himself was also an Islamic quest. For Malcolm, the two projects were inseparable: As a Muslim in Elijah Muhammad's Nation of Islam, Malcolm had to recover his divine selfhood that had been stripped away by slavery and oppression, the unknown self that had lost its own name and was now represented by the *X*. Malcolm's pursuit of sacred black selfhood was not a mere navel-gazing mission any more than similar discourses had been for various nationalists or religious revivalists. Malcolm saw the rise of historical consciousness as having crucial political consequences; black people coming together to assert themselves on the world stage first required a collective awakening to their reality as "one of the world's great peoples."[6]

At the time that I found this book, I was not on a search for spiritual truth or a closer relationship to any transcendent divinity. As an avowed atheist, I would not have thought twice about Islam if *The Autobiography* had been filled with abstract God-talk. Instead, Malcolm moved me with three main ideas: (1) big chunks of my background through which I might have been defined—Americanness, whiteness, Christianity—were founded upon fabricated histories; (2) if I read enough books, I would recover the lost truths that these lies had buried; (3) in the process of this intellectual liberation, I could radically reinvent myself and perhaps become a force of benevolence in the world. Because of the story through which I absorbed these three points, I soon came to imagine my radically reinvented self as a Muslim self.

For my own context at the time that I read *The Autobiography*, I took special interest in Malcolm's reclaiming of Jesus from both the Christian distortion of his teachings and the Euro-American whitening of his body. Malcolm's long hours in the prison library armed him with the tools to argue that the Bible itself describes Jesus as black, and that Jesus had been a member of the Essenes, which he considers a "brotherhood of Egyptian seers"—a fact which was "already known from Philo, the famous Egyptian historian of Jesus' time."[7] For an angsty white kid at an almost entirely white Catholic school, it was thrilling to know that careful investigation of Christianity's origins would dismantle the white/Catholic complex in which I lived. So I took from Malcolm an appreciation for the power of origins and historical truth, a sense that would become even more explicitly Islamic as I began to digest ideas from other Muslim literatures.

Returning to *The Autobiography* twenty years later to discuss it here, I searched the pages for a reference to Muḥammad. During his hajj narrative, Malcolm might describe Mecca as the land of Muḥammad, but otherwise, I found only this:

> I'll bet that in the parts of the Holy Land that I visited . . . ten million cigarettes must have been smoked. Particularly the Arab Muslims smoked constantly, even on the Hajj

> pilgrimage itself. The smoking evil wasn't invented in Prophet Muhammad's days—if it had been, I believe he would have banned it.[8]

The Prophet would have probably disapproved of cigarettes; this is the only commentary on Muḥammad that *The Autobiography* offers, even when Malcolm describes his experience of hajj and rebirth as a Sunnī Muslim. It's worth noting that American Islam's definitive conversion narrative, the story that inspired countless thousands of Americans to become Muslims, presents a Muḥammad-less Islam; but I can understand. Muḥammad was not the issue for us. Just as I read *The Autobiography* as an atheist with no concern for God, I had even less interest in the Prophet. Malcolm presents Islam chiefly as a technology of selfhood, a means of knowing, disciplining, and ultimately perfecting the mind, body, family, and nation. The prophets who are sent by Allāh to deliver that technology are not themselves the points of interest. Perhaps in the aftermath of his painful break from Elijah Muhammad, Malcolm was not going to immediately surrender his heart to another man, even one who had been dead for fourteen centuries. Or maybe, while performing hajj as an official guest of the Saudi state, studying Islam in Cairo under the secretary-general of the Muslim World League, and building with Muslim Brothers, Malcolm learned the concept of sunna primarily as a code of legal norms or foundation for political action. Perceiving what he called "orthodox Islam" through the prism of the 1960s Arab Cold War, Malcolm learned about Muḥammad within the constrictions of the time. *The Autobiography*, in turn, offered similar choices, while giving Malcolm's posthumous endorsement to Saudi Arabia as the natural center, the site at which real Islam could be found.

WILL DURANT, *OUR ORIENTAL HERITAGE*

Because Malcolm had mentioned the Durants' *Story of Civilization* (Will's wife, Ariel, collaborated with him throughout the process and is credited as co-author in the later volumes) among the books that he read in prison, I made the vow in my sophomore year of high school to read the entire eleven-volume set before graduation. Malcolm was plowing through the prison library in an effort to retrieve the Asiatic Black Man's history that had been lost or erased; in a kind of racial Salafism, he sought a recovery of the pristine origins. *The Story of Civilization* affirms the white devil's version of history in its structure: "Civilization" is treated with ten volumes for European history, one volume for the rest of the world. Despite the obvious marginalization of everything that's not white, however, *Our Oriental Heritage* is also the *first* volume of the series, confirming the big reveal of Malcolm's reading project: Civilization does not begin with white people.

I read the 938-page opening volume and eventually the rest of the series as an imitation of the "Saved" chapter in Malcolm's *Autobiography* in which Malcolm goes on about all the mind-blowing details of history that he had unearthed. The *Story of Civilization* books were also heavy, musty old hardcovers that felt personally empowering as I walked around with them in high school. Reading about Sumeria, pharaonic Egypt, the Persian Empire, India, and China might not seem immediately relevant to a path toward Islam, but *Our Oriental Heritage* was an early step in rebuilding my view of the world, while also adhering to my only template for what a conversion to Islam was supposed to look like.

ABDULLAH YUSUF ALI, *THE MEANINGS OF THE HOLY QUR'ĀN*

Just as saying simply that I "converted to Islam" fails to describe what really happened, I can't say that at fifteen, I "read the Qur'ān." All I can say is that it felt like the Qur'ān in my hands. In the 1990s, the most popular and established English translation of the Qur'ān was that of Yusuf Ali, which he had completed in the 1930s. Prior to my encounter with his translation, I heard him acknowledged in the "Blax Thanx" tracks from my Professor Griff and the Last Asiatic Disciples tapes.

Yusuf Ali was an English literature scholar and something of a philosopher, nothing close to an imām or madrassa-trained cleric. As such, he serves as a prime representative for the supposed crisis of authority that has afflicted the entire global umma. While not exactly a revivalist—over the course of the twentieth century, his work would increasingly fall out of favor with neotraditionalist crowds—Ali nonetheless had to answer the same questions that would give rise to revivalist projects. Ali produced his translation in the time of British colonial rule in South Asia and wrote under pressure to demonstrate Islam's full compability with reason, science, modern statecraft, and liberal Protestantism. Most of this demonstration takes place within Ali's extensive verse-by-verse commentary and various appendices throughout the book.

Ali's commentaries provided me with my first meaningful glimpse of Muḥammad. True to his own vision of Islam, Ali presents Muḥammad as an empirical philosopher who pursued knowledge of

God through observations of nature and who sought the acheivement of a perfectly just society in which human beings lived in accordance with reason. Yusuf Ali's Muḥammad was also a regular human being and entirely mortal, completely lacking in special superhuman properties and performing no miracles except for the Qur'ān itself. This is a significant departure from how Muslims have historically conceptualized Muḥammad. The canonical ḥadīth collections abound with stories of Muḥammad as a shaman-type who goes around healing people with his touch and providing streams of water from his fingertips. Yusuf Ali doesn't want a Muḥammad who shows off his super powers, engages in conversation with dead prophets in outer space, or wages war and kills unbelievers at Allāh's command, but rather a Muḥammad who can speak to Emerson and Thoreau, or a philosopher-king Muḥammad who uplifts the Arab peoples and builds a new state with wisdom and sound judgment. Again, encountering Yusuf Ali's Muḥammad within my Catholic context, Islam seemed so perfectly rational and enlightened compared to what I had been fed. Ali argues that the Trinity is "opposed to all reason," Catholic veneration of Mary verges on "idolatry," and the doctrines of papal infalliblity and "worship of saints" are reduced to "superstition,"[9] but Islam's conception of divinity remains free of the nonsense that left European intellectuals with no choice but secularism.[10] For Ali, Christian theology is not only irrational, it has also proved socially destructive, as creeds became narrower and more aggressively divisive, and overly speculative metaphysicians broke into "jarring sectarian irrational religions," leading to the fall of the Byzantine Empire before Islam, the "triumphant religion of Unity and Brotherhood."[11]

Arguing for Islam's intellectual maturity and potential as a force for human progress, Ali writes with a conflicted relationship to Ṣūfism. He likes the Ṣūfī capacity for thinking allegorically about verses of the Qur'ān, but repeatedly condemns what he sees as Ṣūfīs' extreme ascetisicm and withdrawal from worldly affairs. Islam as he presents it within a Protestant regime of sense has no room for monasticism, priestly hierarchy, or worship of saints.

Since its initial publication, Ali's translation had been published in numerous editions, and close readings of these successive editions reveal an evolving censorship and rewriting of Ali's commentary. Starting in the 1980s, Ali's editors manipulated his work to match changing trends in Muslim thought. When Ali's work became the preferred English translation for the Saudi government, the authorities performed their own round of cuts and rewrites on Ali's notes, reshaping his thought to meet their criterion for Islamic authenticity. Ali's appendix on the afterlife, in which he treats the explicitly material descriptions of paradise as mere allegories for higher spiritual states, had to go. His critical assaults on Ṣūfism could stay, but his discussion of the mystical meanings of letters was expunged altogether. Years after my first read of Yusuf Ali's translation, I would learn from Five Percenters that their movement's founder, a man named Allah (formerly Clarence 13X), had preferred it for Five Percenters interested in the Qur'ān. I had no idea why until realizing that the former Clarence 13X, living in the 1960s, would have read Ali prior to the purging of dangerous ideas from his text.

The first time that I read anything that could be remotely called "Qur'ān," it was the "New Fourth Edition" of Yusuf Ali's project. The

New Fourth Edition had been released in 1989 by Amana Publications, with assistance from the International Institute of Islamic Thought (IIIT), a Muslim nonprofit group established in 1981 by Anwar Ibrahim and Ismā'īl al-Farūqī. Most of the revisions in the New Fourth Edition are marked by an *R*, but no further information is provided regarding what exactly had been changed. In 1993, neither the revisions nor their ideological consequences could have meant anything to me. When the Amana edition removed Ali's description of the Prophet's grandsons, Ḥasan and Ḥusayn, as martyrs, replacing their names with that of the Prophet's uncle Hamza, I could not have known the implications of this change for Sunnī/Shī'ī polemics.[12] The Salafized version of Ali's Protestantized Islam worked for me.

Besides his revised commentaries, Ali's translation includes an index through which I can find all the verses relating to specific topics. It's the kind of thing that I notice now. Like the very fact of the Qur'ān's translation into my mother tongue, the presence of an index told me that the Qur'ān was chiefly a document to be understood, rather than an aural experience as I would later know it in the mosque, or a script to recite during prayer, or a material artifact that could work as a talisman. Apart from the text, however, I remember my sensory encounter with the book: The pretty gold ornamentation on the sturdy green cover. The weight of the book in my hand and the devout seriousness with which I carried it. The sun coming through the window as I sat in a quiet corner of the library at Hobart and William Smith College to read. The holiness that this goofy junior Orientalist immediately projected onto the mysterious Arabic text. The confidence that in the parallel English text I would unlock the same ancient power that had turned Malcolm Little into Malcolm X. It can sometimes be difficult to pinpoint the exact moment at which someone converts, when disbelief switches to belief. I do not remember having that moment. I was not yet a Muslim when I picked up Yusuf Ali's *The Meanings of the Holy Qur'an*, but I had already stopped being a non-Muslim.

HAMMUDAH ABDALATI, *ISLAM IN FOCUS*

Islam in Focus was published by the World Assembly of Muslim Youth (WAMY), the Saudi government agency that named among its objectives the task of "introducing Islam to the world using all available means."[13] Abdalati explains that the book was "first conceived in response to certain urgent needs of both Muslim and non-Muslim readers in North America."[14] He writes with the twin aims of (a) giving support to Muslim youths in a hostile culture and (b) attracting new converts to Islam. In the case of the latter, I was one of Abdalati's successes, because *Islam in Focus* had me sold.

I remember that the copy of *Islam in Focus* at the local college library had been personally signed by Abdalati himself, which had me mystified. Had Abdalati ever stepped foot in my rotten hometown in the Finger Lakes? I imagined him lecturing to big rooms filled with stupid American college kids, gracefully but firmly representing Islam if only they were sober enough to hear him. For this teenager living in a fantasy world of heavy East/West essentialism, a special fascination came in knowing that a wise sage from the distant, exotic "Muslim world" had touched this copy with his own hands. I imagined that the book had been waiting there just for *my* hands and that I shared a special bond with Abdalati that he would have somehow sensed if we met.

Islam in Focus concretized the vague image of Muslimness that I had found in Malcolm's autobiography. Abdalati speaks of Islam in terms that would have worked for Malcolm, presenting Islam as entirely rational, systematic, the flawless divine blueprint for a just and productive nation, full of physical and mental discipline, respectful of the innate differences between men and women, and calling for human beings to actively resist oppression during this earthly life. Because Malcolm was my only frame of reference for anything relating to Islam, Abdalati worked for me.

Providing Muslim youths in North America with the means to defend their beliefs and practices against hostile criticisms, and appealing to non-Muslims to take Islam seriously, Abdalati presents Islam as a sophisticated and airtight system that answers all the psychological and social challenges that come with being human. He argues that Muslims do not simply hold on to inherited beliefs and traditions without clear proofs for their value; everything in Islam is fully supported by evidence and reason. For example, on the prohibition of alcohol, he writes that to "appreciate the viewpoint of Islam in this respect, one has only to check any news medium, read any medical report, visit any social service agency, or watch any court proceedings."[15]

I used to compare Abdalati's rationalizations to the religious spookiness of my daily environment at the time, DeSales Catholic High School, in which nothing was meaningfully explained. We were supposed to eat the god-bread, drink the blood-wine, get the ashes on our foreheads, and pray to a deep roster of dead bodies, while accepting the absolute infalliblity of the Pope—and by extension, the clerical hierarchy under him. None of it made sense to me, and our teachers only answered questions with reference to "mystery." They made *mystery* sound like an advanced concept that I was too immature to grasp. In contrast, Islam as presented by Abdalati looked like a religion that had been brilliantly designed just for scientists and philosophers, with no room for the spooky. The Catholic Church had historically opposed scientific progress, but Abdalati promises that the Qur'ān was the first book in history to treat nature and the universe as "rich sources of knowledge."[16] "Open any chapter of the Qur'ān," he writes, "and you will find the warmest appeal to search for knowledge through the infinite sources of nature."[17] It seemed as though the Islam of *Islam in Focus* and the Catholicism of my immediate surroundings could not even be placed in the same category; how could two traditions so radically removed from each other both fall under the umbrella of "religion"?

Abdalati's answer: Islam is not just a religion, but a complete way of life.

Abdalati likes to describe Islam as *saying* and *doing* lots of things. There are enough sentences in which *Islam* is immediately followed by a verb for me to picture Islam as some dude that Abdalati regularly hangs out with. Islam, Abdalati tells us, "demands sound convictions and opposes blind imitation"[18] and "always warns against superficial concepts and rituals."[19] Islam "extends its sense of organization to all walks of life," including industry, economics, and politics; but we should be aware that "Islam does not recognize 'secularism' or separation of religion from man's daily transactions."[20] However, Islam's not too overbearing when it comes to the rules—"Islam is very sensitive to the manners of clothing and ornaments."[21] Also, "Islam deals with the very personal life of man in such a way as to insure his purity and cleanliness."[22] In case you were wondering how this Islam guy treats the ladies, Abdalati affirms that his buddy Islam "considers marriage a very serious commitment."[23] Also, "Islam has given woman rights and privileges which she has never enjoyed under other religious or constitutional systems."[24] On the other hand, "Islam does not let woman go loose or wander unrestricted"; rather, Islam "allows her the things which suit her nature and, at the same time, cautions her against anything that might abuse or upset that nature."[25] Islam always has an eye out for you.

If Islam is the one demanding and allowing and teaching, who's *not* doing or speaking? *People*. There is no recognition of interpretation or context: Islam already has the answers and has spoken with the same clear voice throughout all of history. Islam for Abdalati holds itself together as a *system*, delivered fully self-contained with neatly defined boundaries, rather than a *tradition* that might have accumulated over time and in an immeasurable variety of ideas, practices, and communities. The scholars who preserved and transmitted Islam did not make creative contributions of their own; they only received Islam from the previous generation and passed it to the next. Islam says and does things as Islam has always said and done them, throughout all times and places. Islam as a *way of life*, a complete system for perfectly fulfilling all of society's needs and elevating humanity to the utmost that it can achieve in this world, had emerged fully formed in Muḥammad's own lifetime. Moreover, Islam had been the consistent message of all the prophets, going all the way back to Adam. In its final presentation through Muḥammad, Islam appeared in seventh-century Arabia as it had always been. The primordial religion shared by Adam, Noah, Abraham, and Muḥammad even comes with a fully articulated theory of the Islamic State for the political structures of the modern world. For Islam to be universally applicable for all historical settings was proof of its divine origin. If a theological, legal, and political system that emerged in the seventh century could answer all our anguish today, there was no way that it could have come from a human mind, let alone an illiterate orphan who worked the trading caravans. Right?

If Abdalati speaks for Islam, then he must be speaking for all Muslims. In my adolescent Orientalism, I believed that reading *Islam in Focus* was like opening the head of every Muslim on the planet and looking inside, grasping perfectly how the Muslim Mind worked. As far as I understood, Abdalati wasn't theorizing; this was *really* how life in Muslim-majority societies looked. I became like any other small-town kid who dreamed of escaping his/her dump of a town after high school graduation, but with added conviction that a better world was waiting for me wherever I could find Muslims.

Islam in Focus was the text that I used to learn how to perform my five daily prayers. Abdalati includes the Arabic text, Roman transliteration, English translation, and illustrations of the various positions. I photocopied those pages and held them while practicing prayers on a towel that I pretended was a "real" prayer rug. I had not yet met a flesh-and-blood Muslim; my essentialist image of Muslims was still driven by Malcolm, full of discipline and seriousness and self-mastery. Though Malcolm had gone to Mecca without knowing the prayers, the Malcolm image had me sure that I had better perfect this stuff before ever stepping foot in a mosque, or no one would take me seriously as a potential Muslim. I knew that I was saying the words wrong but at least hoped that memorizing the phrases and movements would impress my future brothers. Turns out that I was right; people at the Islamic Center of Rochester were stunned that this kid had taught himself the prayers.

In his how-to-pray section, Abdalati never acknowledges that what he calls "Islamic prayer" is specifically "Sunnī prayer," and that Shī'ī prayer would come with a few modifications. Nor does he indicate which of the four surviving Sunnī schools informed his tutorial, for the standing position, he remarks that the positioning of the hands that he teaches is "in accordance with one school of law," but does not specify.[26] For years, I prayed as *Islam in Focus* had taught me, with no idea as to whether this made me a Hanafi, Maliki, Shafi'i, or Hanbalī (it turns out that Abdalati's guide can be described as "Hanafi ish").

But why did I pray? How had I moved from my earlier atheism to memorizing prayers in Arabic? Abdalati treats prayer like it's all business, offering a ten-point argument for what he calls a "matchless and unprecedented formula of intellectual meditation and spiritual devotion, of moral elevation and physical exercise, all combined."[27] First on the list: prayer is a "lesson in discipline and willpower."[28] Abdalati also says that prayer provides a "demonstration of true equality, solid unity, and brotherhood," as well as an "abundant source of patience and courage, of hope and confidence," which all seemed attractive to me and resonant with what Malcolm would have said. God is mentioned in three of Abdalati's ten points, but what really matters is the prayer's potential to make personal and social change. Even wudhu, the washing that Muslims perform prior to prayer, is explained as "the best hygienic formula which no other spiritual doctrine or medical prescription had anticipated."[29]

Taking a second look at *Islam in Focus* some twenty years after my first encounter, I try to forgive the fifteen-year-old me for having failed as a reader. When Abdalati told me that Islam stood for intellectual inquiry, I never thought of questioning Abdalati himself. It could not have occurred to me that maybe the timeless, transhistorical Islam presented by Abdalati was at least partly a *new* Islam. People who think that Islam needs to experience its own "Reformation" or "Enlightenment" or become "modern," or that Islamic Tradition offers us an escape from modernity, should try this experiment: Search for anything close to Abdalati's articulation of Islam in Muslim texts written within the span of centuries between the Prophet's lifetime and, say, the final quarter of the nineteenth century. Thinkers such as Abdalati reveal (perhaps against their own intentions) that the so-called modernization has already happened and there's no going back.

HUSTON SMITH, *THE RELIGIONS OF MAN*

When I outed myself as a Muslim to my high school religion teacher, he told me that Islam had not yet reached its Enlightenment period, and then suggested that I read this book. He promised that I would be amazed by the way in which Smith summarizes each of the world's great religions as though he is a member of that religion: When he writes about Hinduism, he sounds like a believing Hindu. There's a reason for this: Though Smith doesn't acknowledge it here, he's a disciple of Frithjof Schuon. As head of his own Ṣūfī order, Schuon taught his followers to regard all religious traditions as expressions of the same *sophia perennis*, the "perennial wisdom" by which he could contrast romanticized, capitalized, premodern "Tradition" against our wretched modern world that lacks both divinity and humanity.

Smith basically delivers a pamphlet on behalf of Islam. He starts by repeating the popular narrative of Muḥammad's life and prophetic mission, then explains the Qur'ān and basic dogma, and follows with the Five Pillars and discussion of the "Brotherhood of Islam." I'm not sure what my crusty old Catholic religion teacher thought that this book would do to me, but to read such apologetic, essentialist pap coming from a scholar who wasn't Muslim—at least not in his exoteric profile—only confirmed Islam's truth for me. He repeats the familiar "not just a religion, but a way of life" argument: "Compared with other religions, Islam spells out the way of life it proposes; it pinpoints it, nailing it down through explicit injunctions."[30] He then runs through all of Pamphlet Islam's big points: Islam regulates economic affairs to create a more just society; contrary to Western misconceptions, Islam elevated the status of women; "Islam stresses absolute racial equality," demonstrated by Muḥammad (whom Smith describes as "probably of the same skin coloring as Jesus—a sun-tanned white"[31]) taking part in antiracism's "ultimate test . . . the willingness to intermarry";[32] and Islam's true perspective on peace, violence, and religious tolerance. Smith concludes his treatment of Islam by regurgitating the narrative of

Muslims having once been the great empire-builders and scientists and philosophers of the world, only to have fallen so far, but then drops his jaw at Islam's apparent resurgence in the modern world, attracting converts everywhere, putting up incredible numbers, and awakening the dormant Muslim Mind.

AYATOLLAH KHOMEINI, *ISLAMIC GOVERNMENT*

The cover proclaimed this work to be "Ayatollah Khomeini's *Mein Kampf*" in bigger text than the book's actual title, with a depiction of meta-Khomeini bursting out from behind a giant portrait of himself, ripping through his own face. This was "the official United States Government translation of the Ayatollah Khomeini's plan for Islamic government," accompanied by the publisher's disclaimer on the first page: "Understanding the intentions and tactics of an enemy is the first defense against him. In that spirit we offer this volume."[33] The back cover shows a photo of him in black turban and black cloak, hands open, praying with a bunch of other badass-looking men in turbans and cloaks, captioned with the warning: "Ten years ago Ayatollah Khomeini outlined his plan for Islamic dominance . . . accused the United States of conspiracy and crimes against the Iranian people . . . maligned Israel and the Jewish faith . . . dubbed Christians the lackeys of colonialism . . . and exhorted his countrymen to rebellion in order to establish a theocratic state of Islam. Here is his blueprint, his plan, his strategy."[34] The cover and disclaimer had the opposite affect on me that the publishers intended: I'd gaze at the pictures while vibing out to my Public Enemy tapes and wonder where I could sign up for the revolution.

Following analysis by a *New York Post* journalist (which I processed through the lens of Public Enemy's "Letter to the New York Post"), we get Khomeini's argument for the necessity of Islamic government. "Islam," he explains, "is the religion of the strugglers who want right and justice, the religion of those demanding freedom and independence and those who do not want to allow the infidels to dominate the believers."[35] However, the colonial powers sought to undermine Islam's capacity for resisting injustice by separating religion from politics and reducing Islam to "a bunch of rules on menstruation and childbirth."[36] Khomeini asserts that the Qur'ān and prophetic traditions comprehensively discuss all aspects of the human experience, including economics and human rights, even providing a divine conception of the state, which Khomeini calls a "clear scientific idea."[37] He defends Islamic criminal law against the charges that it is inhumane by pointing to Western laws. Islamic law is considered harsh for whipping the drinker of alcohol with eighty lashes, but Western laws can sentence someone to death for smuggling ten grams of heroin? Alcohol poses a much greater threat to society than heroin, says Khomeini, but the West allows it. Otherwise, he suggests, we could compare the harshness of whipping a drinker eighty times with the harshness of the United States massacring people in Vietnam for a decade and a half.[38] With that argument, Khomeini clicked for me, as I found him speaking to what I saw as Malcolm's global vision. I embraced the Khomeini of 1979 as representating the same Islam that I found in my Malcolm of 1964, an Islam that stood for all the oppressed peoples of the world against their white, Western, Christian, secularist, Crusader, colonialist oppressors. Their voices blended together into one critique: When Khomeini asserts that Islam emerged on the world scene with a perfect system of government, law, and ethics "at a time when darkness prevailed over the Western countries,"[39] I read him through Malcolm's statement, "The black man, original man, built great empires and civilizations and cultures while the white man was still living on all fours in caves."[40]

And like Malcolm, Khomeini was undeniably photogenic. The photos in my copy of *Islamic Government* were supposed to make him look like a deranged temple priest who crawled out of a pyramid, but the Ayatollah's determined glare gave me a new Malcolm, a fearless revolutionary who could stare the devil in the face. Before anyone told me that making pictures of living things was Islamically prohibited, I took a Sharpie marker and drew Khomeini's portrait on my bedroom wall.

It may seem strange to include the twentieth century's most prominent Shī'ī cleric in my Salafī lineage, as Salafīs tend to be vehemently anti-Shī'ī and I've even seen Salafī writers call Khomeini a pagan. As with the Sunnī authors that I read, however, Khomeini doesn't present his interpretation as informed by sectarian or other concerns; it's not to be understood within the context of Twelver Shī'īsm, or Iranian tradition, or the twentieth century. It's not even an "interpretation," but simply the way of Islam. Occasionally Khomeini makes reference to 'Alī and Ḥusayn, but not in any sense that would have struck me as polemical against Sunnī Muslims or even unbearably Shī'ī. Nor would I have seen Khomeini's political theory of vilayat-e-faqīh (rule of the jurist) as formulated within a specifically Shī'ī framework. Maybe I just saw what I saw.

M TARIQ QURAISHI (ED), *SOME ASPECTS OF PROPHET MUHAMMAD'S LIFE*

The imām at the Islamic Center of Rochester gave me this book on the day that I declared shahadah and marked myself as a member of the community. Just a few minutes earlier, he and some other brothers in the mosque office had suggested that I change my name to Mikail Muhammad. Mikail was the Arabic version of my birth name, and the virtues of naming myself Muhammad should have been obvious. So I renamed myself after the best of men and then went home with this book to learn about him.

Some Aspects of Prophet Muhammad's Life was published by American Trust Publications, which had been founded in 1976 by the Saudi-funded North American Islamic Trust (NAIT), which itself had been established in 1973 by the Muslim Students' Association in Plainfield, Indiana. American Trust Publications also put out its own edition of Abdalati's *Islam in Focus*. The contributors to *Some Aspects of Prophet Muhammad's Life* pretty much give me the Muḥammad that I was prepared to see, with no surprises. Quraishi's introduction emphasizes that Muhammad was a "reformer, a revolutionary, and a builder"; he never called for his own deification with statues, he did not preach an ethnic mission but united all peoples, and he opposed monasticism.[41] "Religion, before him, was monastic, for it sought to isolate the individual from society so that he could attain self-purification. Celibacy was glorified." This kind of religiosity was not purely self-effacement, argues Quraishi; it's actually self-*indulgence*, because it focuses entirely on the individual and only harms the society. To correct this problem, Muḥammad brought a "sweeping vision which grasps life in entirety," more successfully integrating all aspects of life and creating both "a new society and a new man."[42]

In his discussion of Muḥammad's Sunna, Mustapha al-Azami asserts that we must "look on the personality and conduct of the Prophet from different angles." These angles are as follows: (1) "Statesman"; (2) "Supreme Commander"; (3) "Head of the State"; (4) "Supreme Judge"; (5) "the most lovable person on the earth for his people"; (6) "the only hope for the salvation of all mankind, including the universe."[43]

Defending the uncorrupted historicity of the prophetic tradition, al-Azami's chapter proclaims, "Purity and genuineness of valuable goods are the hallmark of civilization."[44] Just as governments guard their currency against counterfeiters and artwork is closely examined to prevent forgery, "different sectors of society pay attention to the purity, preservation, and authenticity of what they think to be of importance to them."[45] For Muslims, the precious items to be protected are the sayings and deeds of our Prophet.

If I look back on my home life in the 1990s, I'm guessing that the chapter that hit me hardest was Ahmed Elkadi's "Muhammad as a Family Man." Elkadi opens with a big statement:

> With the increasing rate of broken homes and disintegrated family structures, and the resultant social ills and complications, there has never been a greater need for the Islamic teachings and guidelines related to family and social life.[46]

He backs it up with a bunch of statistics on divorce and crime, followed by the assertion that "if we are serious" about defending the family structure against this new crisis, our solution must come from "a source other than contemporary secular science."[47]

Reading Alkadi's discussion of the Prophet's childhood—"There was a separation of sorts between him and the surrounding corruption of the society"—and the conclusion that he draws from it—"The lesson is to provide the means to protect our children from indiscriminate mixing with the non-Islamic surroundings"[48]—I consider the time in which *Some Aspects* materialized. The book was published in 1983, nearly two decades following the 1965 Immigration Act that had led to massive influxes of Muslim immigration into the United States. By 1983, the question of how parents from Muslim-majority countries should raise children in an overwhelmingly non-Muslim environment would have been a growing concern for immigrant Muslim communities. As a Muslim teenager without the benefit of Muslim parents, I tried to parent myself in accordance with Alkadi's argument, keeping the drunken, fornicating football players and cheerleaders of DeSales Catholic High School at arm's length.

GHULAM SARWAR, *ISLAM: BELIEFS AND TEACHINGS*

An intro-level guide to Islam in the same genre as *Islam in Focus*, this volume was published by the Daw'ah Academy of the International Islamic University in Islamabad, Pakistan, where I spent two months of my senior year of high school. My copy had been given to me by one of my dearest early mentors, who signed the inside cover and dated it August 18, 1994.

The book opens with an explanation of Islam as reflecting the "superb harmony and perfect order" evident in the universe; Islam is the "Religion of Nature" (Dinul Fiṭrah).[49] Sarwar gives brief explanations of concepts like Islamic monotheism (tawhīd) and prophethood and offers a how-to-pray manual like that offered by Abdalati. Also like Abdalati, the virtues of Islamic prayer are explained in a numbered list. Some items appear on both lists with identical wording; both mention "discipline and willpower" and describe prayer as demonstrating "true equality, solid unity, and brotherhood" (for Sarwar, it's "*universal* brotherhood").[50] Sarwar describes prayer as a "training program" and tells the reader, "If your Ṣalāh does not improve your conduct you must think seriously and find out where you are going wrong."[51]

Some parts of this book seemed more immediately salient to my life than others. In his explanation of zakat, Sarwar provides a handy table to help teenagers know the rates that they would pay in charity based on their ownership of precious minerals, agricultural produce, trading goods, cows, buffaloes, goats, sheep, and camels.[52] Sarwar also gives some coverage to the "Economic System of Islam" and "Political System of Islam," reminding his adolescent readers that "Islam views life as a compact whole and does not divide it into many separate and conflicting parts."[53] According to Sarwar, Islam not only teaches us about rituals, but "also teaches us how to run a state, form a government, elect councillors and members of parliament, make treaties and conduct business and commerce."[54] Reconsidering his discussion of the ideal Islamic state, I see a few basic principles, such as consultation (shūra), the accountability of rulers, and equality before the law, rather than an actual theory of government. But in 1994, it was enough for me.

As one should expect in the "intro to Islam" genre, Sarwar devotes a special section to explaining what Islam says about women. Here's how he starts:

> Women have a very important place in Islamic society. Unlike a number of other religions, Islam holds a woman in high esteem. Her importance as a mother and a wife has been clearly stated by the Prophet Muhammad (pbuh).[55]

Sarwar goes on to describe misogynistic attitudes among ancient Greeks and Romans, early Christians, Hindus (who "until recently considered their women worse than death, pests, serpents or even hell"[56]), pre-Islamic Arabs, and even the modern West. In my copy, an asterisk has been penciled next to the mention of a meeting held in France in 587 CE to determine whether women were human beings; I might have been the one who put it there, noting this factoid as a potential weapon in future arguments. "If we keep this picture in mind and look into the position of the women in Islam," Sarwar asserts, "we must conclude that Islam liberated women from the dark age of obscurity, fourteen hundred years ago!"[57] Sarwar argues that Islam's liberatory power does not mean that Islam treats women and men as entirely equal; to do so, he claims, "would destroy the social balance" with the disintegration of family life.[58] Rather, Islam views women and men as complementary opposites, who together form the unit that contributes to a "sound and prosperous society."[59]

If you're wondering what Sarwar means by women and men being "complementary," here's his explanation: "Women tend to be sensitive, emotional and tender while men are comparatively less emotional and more practical."[60] Like men, Islam is also described by Sarwar as practical; Islam, therefore, is a manly thing.[61] When I read this book, I was sixteen years old, fatherless, a virgin, searching for my manhood in the empowering sexism of Malcolm X, and had been recently introduced to a twelve-year-old Muslimah for the purposes of an arranged marriage. Sarwar gave me some tools for both defending Islam on gender issues and rationalizing an insecure boy's need to flex like a patriarch.

Sarwar concludes with a section of maps and statistics to show the distribution of Muslims around the world. He tells us that Muslims form one nation (millah), which is determined not by geography, color, race, or language, but faith. "In the course of history," he writes, "Muslims lost their essential unity, but it should be restored once again for the greater good of all mankind."[62] He asks us to imagine a world in which Muslims achieve this unity. What if Muslim-majority states were able to pool their resources and work together? If we were to add up the numbers for all the world's Muslim-majority countries, we'd end up with a massive chunk of the world's humanity. Additionally, Sarwar reminds us of the vast wealth of oil, rubber, jute, spices, palm oil, phosphate, tin, cotton, tea, coffee, wool, uranium, manganese, cobalt, and natural gas under Muslim control.[63] We could be the new superpower.

Sarwar ends with the kind of argument that I encountered frequently in those days, repeating the basic gist of the nineteenth-century revivalists:

> Muslims who once contributed tremendously to the science and civilization of the world could once again do so if they

> truly get united on the basis of Islam. Real human progress can only be achieved by the faithful observance of the teaching of Islam . . . The Muslim Millah has the potential and the need is for faithful practice of the teachings of Islam.[64]

It wasn't original, but it had power. Whenever I encountered Muslims talking like this—especially older men addressing me personally—it had me believing that *my* generation would be the one to recognize our important mission and most perfectly carry it out. It seemed that I had walked into Islam at exactly the right moment in history, when the tide of civilizational momentum was about to shift.

MUHAMMED SHAFIQ, *GROWTH OF ISLAMIC THOUGHT IN NORTH AMERICA: FOCUS ON ISMA'IL RAJI AL-FARUQI*

Dr. Shafiq was imām at the Islamic Center of Rochester, New York, witness to my shahādah, and my primary mentor and hero figure in those early years. The book was published by Amana, the same press that produced the intensely revised Yusuf Ali translation. *Growth of Islamic Thought in North America* came out in 1994, after I had converted and spent an entire summer at the Islamic Center. It was at the end of the mosque's summer camp program that someone announced the publication and brought out boxes of copies. Before that day, I had not heard of al-Faruqi, but Dr. Shafiq explained to me that al-Faruqi had been his advisor and close friend at Temple University. I processed this to mean that al-Faruqi had been to Dr. Shafiq what Dr. Shafiq was to me, and that this made me one of al-Faruqi's intellectual grandchildren. I took a signed copy home as proof of my lineage, determined to learn about al-Faruqi and better appreciate the family tree.

Dr. Shafiq charts the development of al-Faruqi's thought. Early in his career, al-Faruqi espoused what he called "Arabism," which was not the same as Western-styled nationalism. Al-Faruqi conceptualized Arabism, Dr. Shafiq explains, as relating to "archetypal categories of consciousness" that made for an "Arab stream of being." Though al-Faruqi seemed to have believed that "Arabs" existed as a distinct racial category, he considered Arabness to be universal—as universal as Islam, in fact, because Islam itself was an expression of Arabness. All Muslims throughout the world, regardless of their ancestry or native language, were participants in the Arab stream of being.[65] After al-Faruqi came to the United States and made connections with the Muslim Students Association, he moved from Arabism to Islamism, calling for the world map to be redrawn on religious lines by a transnational Muslim superstate.[66]

True to the revivalist critique, al-Faruqi believed that the closing of ijtihād and flourishing of Ṣūfī orders killed the Muslim intellect,[67] Islam sees no conflict between reason and revelation, and Muslims must obtain mastery of modern scientific knowledge without losing touch with Islam. Al-Faruqi placed special hope in what he called "Islamic Muslim Youth," young Muslims with superior university educations who remained grounded in Islamic knowledge, embraced democracy, and sought a modernist expression of classical Islam.[68]

Thoughts after my second reading: I've had the same signed copy in my possession since 1994, but I'm not sure how closely I ever read it. In all likelihood, my first journey with this book did not go from cover to cover. There are some passing mentions of the Salafiyya, but I have no memory of encountering the term in reference to a modern movement until years later; either I skipped those pages, or the references blew by me. Much of Dr. Shafiq's content would have gone over my head, but I appreciated this book mostly for its symbolic power. Al-Faruqi was the teacher of my teacher, the hero of my hero, so I naturally imagined holding a stake in his legacy.

AHMED DEEDAT, BOX OF PAMPHLETS

In the 1970s and '80s, as evangelical Christian missionaries stormed Africa with booklets and tapes, South African scholar Ahmed Deedat rose to global fame as Islam's great defender. Deedat's Islamic Propagation Centre International (IPCI) pumped out a series of pamphlets that sought to expose the errors and inconsistencies of the Bible and defeat Christian evangelists on their own field of mastery. The IPCI distributed Deedat's writings free of charge, so I wrote them a letter and a few months later received a box stuffed with small booklets bearing titles like *Is the Bible God's Word?* and *Crucifixion or Cruci-Fiction?* Deedat knew the Bible better than his Christian opponents and freely drew from secular biblical criticism to humanize what they viewed as a divine revelation.

Some of the Muslims whom I regarded as personal mentors did not share my interest in Ahmed Deedat. In response to my quoting of his pamphlets, they answered that there was no need to spend our lives studying another religion's scripture to defend Islam; Islam stands firm on its own integrity. But my path to becoming Muslim had been sparked by Malcolm's search for clear proofs—which included exposing the white man's lies about nearly everything, including the true nature and mission of Jesus Christ. Eating up Deedat's literature was just my extension of an Islam driven by Malcolm's *Autobiography*.

Deedat's position isn't that the Bible is entirely *non*-divine, but rather that it contains a mix of divine revelation and human distortion. Sometimes, the divine parts can shine through; though Deedat focuses almost exclusively on proving the Bible wrong, he also makes use of the Bible to prove Islam right. In works such as *Muhummed: The Natural Successor to Christ*, Deedat argues for Muḥammad on biblical terms, interpreting Deuteronomy 18:18 as a promise of Muḥammad's future arrival.

Apart from the Bible, Deedat also quotes from Western intellectual luminaries such as George Bernard Shaw, Thomas Carlyle, and A. J. Arberry, providing their favorable statements on Muḥammad's character and prophetic career.[69] He reprinted a section from Michael Hart's *The 100*, which ranked the most influential people in history, because Hart had ranked Muḥammad as the individual with the single greatest impact. Hart's analysis of Muḥammad resonated with Muslim writers that I had read: As both prophet and political leader, Muḥammad was "the only man in history who was supremely successful on both the religious and secular levels."[70] Moreover, Hart shared in Deedat's critique of Christian origins, claiming that Muḥammad had been much more directly influential on Islam than Jesus had been on Christianity. Muḥammad was the sole founder of Islam, while Jesus had to share credit with St. Paul.

As Brian Larkin has pointed out, our ideas of clear boundaries between religions, or even between religion and secularism, quickly break down with a figure like Deedat. What we see as self-evidently separate territories of "Islam" and "Christianity" become porous, blending into each other, even when Deedat treats them as representing entirely isolated, oppositional, and irreconcilable claims. Deedat was not an "Islamic" scholar in the sense of having formally trained in Muslim institutions, learning traditional texts or methodologies; the scripture over which he claimed expertise was not the Qur'ān but the Bible. While his theology and practice were sufficiently Sunnī for the IPCI to establish branches in, and receive funding from, Saudi Arabia and the Gulf states, he nonetheless derived his rhetorical style, exegetical registers, methods, evidences, assumptions, organizational structures, and publishing strategies from evangelical Christians. What are the consequences for Deedat's Islam, which is supposed to be hermetically sealed and standing in clear truth against all false systems, if it preserves the fingerprints of his evangelical Christian opponents?[71] As a fresh convert who assessed every detail of Islam in comparison to my pre-Muslim life, I wasn't prepared to ask such a question. The way that these books framed it for me, religions were solid things in the world and existed in clear distinction from one another. Otherwise, how could you have a book like *The Religions of Man*? Looking at it this way, Deedat was on *my* team, and he trounced the other team using their own sources. Deedat scored points for the good guys.

Deedat's polemics gave me the thrill of scientific certainty: Islam wasn't a matter of "faith" or "mystery" but possessed a truth that could be empirically proven. At the time, I would have argued that the West became godless and secular because it had outgrown a faith tradition that was antireason, antiscience, antihistorical, and completely unprepared to defend itself against a maturing intellect. The West's problem, as I saw it, was assuming these Christian problems to be problems for all religions. If only they were able to shed their prejudices and give Islam a serious look, I was sure, they could finally have a religion that engages and satisfies the modern mind.

Deedat did give me a mystery buzz, though. One of his booklets, *What Is His Name?* mentions Atnatu, an entity worshiped in Australian aboriginal cultures. According to Deedat, the name *Atnatu* meant "He Who Has No Anus" and represented essentially Islamic concepts about the perfection of divinity and rejection of anthropomorphism. Apart from Deedat's racist condescensions about how amazing it was for this primitive naked savage, photographed climbing a tree, to have a more advanced idea of God than many people in the modern civilized world, his reflection on Atnatu offered something powerful. For Deedat, the aboriginals' abstract, transcendent, disembodied, and anus-less god proved that Islam was something innate and natural to the human essence—that deep down, at our cores, we were *all* Muslims. As the Prophet had said, we were all born in a perfect state of Islam but turned into Christians or polytheists or whatever only by our parents. For me to embrace Islam as my religion meant only that I was cutting through my misguided cultural background to recover my truest and natural self. At some point I'd encounter Muslims who preferred to use the term *revert* rather than *convert* for this very reason. My understanding of reversion might have been a reprocessing of Malcolm X: By rejecting the tradition in which I had been raised and learning to pray in an unfamiliar language, I actually found my home.

SAYYID QUṬB, *IN THE SHADE OF THE QUR'ĀN*

This book was actually the thirtieth volume of Quṭb's epic Qur'ānic commentary, *In the Shade of the Qur'ān*, but the first volume to be made available in English. It was published with support from the World Assembly of Muslim Youth (WAMY), the same Riyadh-based organization that offered *Islam in Focus*. As a Muslim youth myself, it had me wondering how WAMY operated; I imagined a big room with stadium-style seating, like a United Nations for Muslim teenagers, all of them incredible prodigies—brilliant scholars, scientists, historians, and Qur'ān-memorizers who weren't any older than me but had been blessed with Muslim parents and Muslim educations—coming from all over the globe to strategize about our welfare. It seemed pretty awesome.

Someone gave me this book prior to my journey to Pakistan, and I read it on the long transatlantic flight. I had no prior knowledge of twentieth-century Egyptian history or the Muslim Brotherhood. All that I knew of Quṭb came through the brief introduction by his brother: Quṭb had written most of his Qur'ānic commentary during his years of imprisonment. He had been imprisoned and ultimately martyred for his "vigorous struggle" to "achieve the implementation of Islam in the shape of a community which practices Islam in its life and preaches the need for its realisation until it becomes the actual code of practice for the society as a whole."[72]

Quṭb's brother makes a statement in his introduction that might have prepared me to criticize what I would soon find in Pakistan (basically, women not covering their hair properly): "The Muslims, for their part, are now far removed in their practical life from the true nature of Islam." The true nature of Islam, he says, is reflected in the earliest Muslim generations, who "established truth and justice on earth and raised for mankind an inimitable civilization which builds up its structure in the material and spiritual worlds at the same time."[73] Similar to what I had read elsewhere, true Islam is seen as achieving perfect "harmony between body and soul, religion and politics, faith and science, the present life and the hereafter, the practical and the ideal."[74] What was new for me came in the suggestion that Muslims are not actually living out Islam in its true nature; modern Muslims have been intellectually and spiritually poisoned and remain out of touch with their religion. I would understand this through Khomeini's critique of the West and also Malcolm's analysis of the ways in which African Americans had been made to forget their own glorious past. In Pakistan, I attributed what looked to me like a "watering down" of Islam to British colonialism, but also to the effects of Muslims living alongside Hindus for centuries. The survival of Islam (especially if Islam was a comprehensive system for every aspect of life, as all these authors told me) required the establishment of Islamic states.

The introduction by Quṭb's brother did not exactly set me up for a heartwarming experience with the Qur'ān. What the Qur'ān has to offer, more than anything else, is a *constitution*:

> The Qur'an is the constitution revealed by Allah to regulate and govern human life. It is the book which educated the Islamic nation . . . Light should, therefore, be thrown on it from two angles. The first is the angle of education; this shows how the Qur'an, at the levels of the individual, the family,

> the community and the nation, leads man to achieve the highest degree of moral and spiritual nobility possible in this life. The other angle is that of the practical code which regulate human life in its noblest form and in all its spheres political, economic, social, intellectual and moral; that is, a life which is befitting to man whom Allah has ennobled and raised above all species of His creation and entrusted with the task the heavens, the earth and the mountains have all dreaded to shoulder.[75]

Once I moved past his brother's intro and got into the meat of the book, however, Sayyid Quṭb moved me in unexpected ways. The thirtieth volume of *In the Shade of the Qur'ān* corresponded to the thirtieth para of the Qur'ān, in which the sūras were short but emotionally charged. The sūras in this portion are like "continuous loud and violent knocks, or like shouts addressed to people who are fast asleep," writes Quṭb.[76] "This is how I feel when I read this part of the Qur'an."[77] The thirtieth portion "puts strong emphasis on a small number of highly important facts and strikes certain notes which touch men's hearts."[78] These aren't the sūras dealing with inheritance laws or dietary restrictions. They are generally held to have been revealed during the earlier, Meccan years of Muḥammad's career, when he was more street preacher than legislator, and the prophetic mission served more as a call to individual consciences than a new mode of legislation.

I took special interest in the eighty-sixth sura, *aṭ-Ṭariq*, the title of which Quṭb translates as "the Night Visitor," and which the sūra itself then defines as "the star of piercing brightness." The sūra assures us that every soul has a guardian watching over it and asks us to consider our own creation from "gushing water." I tried to recall how Quṭb's commentary might have struck me the first time that I read it, as a small-town white boy who had never even been on a plane but had somehow morphed into this new character of Mikail Muhammad and found himself flying over the Atlantic Ocean to live in a mosque in Pakistan and learn to live in accordance with the will of the Creator of the Universe, Lord of All the Worlds. It all seemed so random, but nothing was random:

> Let man consider his origins and what has become of him. It is a very wide gulf which divides the origins from the final product . . . there is a power beyond the province of man which moves that shapeless and powerless fluid along its remarkable and impressive journey until it is shaped into its magnificent ultimate form . . . there is a guardian appointed by Allah to look after that moist germ, and to guide it through its remarkable journey, which is full of wonders much greater than those met by man throughout his life.[79]

Quṭb goes on to describe the development of cells into a fetus and the amazing miracle of our transformation from "the gushing water into the communicative human being."[80] His commentary then follows the next verses in the sūra, which refer to the Day of Resurrection, when human beings will be helpless and their consciences will be placed on trial. These verses, Quṭb writes, "suggest that that part of the human soul where secrets are safely deposited will be thrown open, searched and exposed in the same way as the night visitor penetrates the covering darkness of the night."[81] I remember that it was night over the Atlantic when I read this chapter. Above the clouds, our night sky was filled with stars, and I could even see more shooting stars.

The sūra describes the rain falling from heaven and the earth splitting open with vegetation. Quṭb weaves these images together with the mention of the "gushing water" from which we are made—"It is the same life, the same scene, the same movement"[82]—and also the earlier image of the star piercing the night's darkness and our own consciences being examined. *Aṭ-Ṭāriq* is one of the Qur'ān's "oath" sūras, in which Allāh makes a vow; in this case, Allāh swears by the star that this Qur'ān is no frivolity and assures the Prophet that the opposition he faces is only temporary: "They try and scheme against you, but I too have my schemes."

Muḥammad's tormentors were only people, Quṭb writes. They had been made from the same gushing water, "brought forth without any strength, ability, or will of their own, guided along their long journey by the Divine power," and now they challenged that very power, the same power that "made the sky, the night visitor, the gushing water and man."[83]

In line with the rest of my early readings, *In the Shade of the Qur'ān* does go heavy on the rationalism. Discussing the Qur'ān's 113th sūra, which provides protection against witchcraft, Quṭb presents witchcraft as chiefly a deceitful manipulation of delicate human psyches, rather than an assault with genuine supernatural weaponry.[84] Quṭb frequently refers to science, but more as an emotional provocation than an authoritative proof. Sitting alone in his prison cell, he finds everything from the entirety of the universe down to the zygote to be filled with signs of Allāh.

In my initial attempt at reading the Qur'ān, I had opened Yusuf Ali's translation to the first page and tried plodding through the second and by far the longest sūra, *al-Baqara*, which was filled with discussion of the Children of Israel and legislation regarding fasting, allowed and prohibited foods, rites of pilgrimage, new moons, jihād, drinking and gambling, treatment of orphans, menstruation, marriage, and divorce. Apart from the mystical buzz that I got from the aesthetics of the book and the fact that I was holding a Qur'ān for the first time, neither the content nor Yusuf Ali's notes were able to profoundly touch me. Quṭb's treatment of the short sūras in the back of the Qur'ān, the loud knocks, had me feeling something. Reading him might have been part of my transition from treating Islam as a rational system for discipline and self-improvement to wanting a new awareness of Allāh, a change in my *heart*. Qutb helped me grow into a real believer. During the flight, I also had a Walkman and a tape of the *Star Wars* soundtrack, and I kept rewinding and replaying Yoda's theme because the Force was with me that night.

MUHAMMAD ABDUL-RAUF, *BILAL IBN RABĀH: A LEADING COMPANION OF THE PROPHET MUHAMMAD*

Which Companions become pamphlets, and why? Someone had given me this short American Trust Publications book at the Islamic Center of Rochester, and years later I'd buy another copy from the Islamic Center of Washington, D.C. Reading it this time, I was less interested in the content than the process by which it came to exist.

Bilāl was an Ethiopian convert who rose from slave status to become, as the book's title says, one of Muḥammad's leading

Companions. In the early twentieth century, non-Muslim authors such as J. A. Rogers wrote about Bilāl in Black newspapers, hailing him as an example of what Black men could achieve in the more equitable world that existed beyond Europe and America. The coverage of Bilāl became a glowing representation of Islam as promoting a genuine brotherhood that white Christians had never achieved nor desired. As the Ahmadiyya movement in the United States increasingly directed its proselytization efforts toward African American communities, Bilāl found coverage in its publication, *Moslem Sunrise*, as embodied proof that Islam solves the problems of racism and oppression.

In the second half of the 1970s, as Warith Deen Mohammed moved the Nation of Islam toward Sunnī Islam, he employed the figure of Bilāl as symbolic of Muslim antiracism and of his own community's trajectory. He renamed the Nation's newspaper, *Muhammad Speaks*, as *Bilalian News* and even offered *Bilalian* as a term not only for the Muslims under his leadership, but also for African Americans at large, all of whom represented the spirit of Bilāl. This 1989 work is a product of polycultural hybridity. The Ahmadiyya, NOI, and even non-Muslims collaborated to make what now appears in the dressing of Sunnī tradition: Bilāl-as-symbol, Bilāl-as-evidence. Bilāl-as-pamphlet. The thin book doesn't take much space on my old bookshelf, but Bilāl remains the only Companion there. In the 1990s, I wasn't walking around with an 'Alī-as-pamphlet or Abū-Bakr-as-pamphlet. For my own Islam and the questions that it had to answer, I ended up with far more biographical knowledge of Bilāl than of any other Companion.

Bilāl's Ethiopian ancestry and dark complexion could not have been mere details of his body, but had to contribute to a divine teaching moment, a hyperracialized and color-conscious proof of Islam's transracial color-blindness. This stack of books gave me Islam as a complete system in which *everything* became a text to be analyzed and understood. Bilāl's black body had to provide us with a symbol, just as rituals and rules could not exist simply as what they were, but required acts of decoding and rationalization. Muslims did not make pilgrimage to Mecca for its own sake, but rather to demonstrate our transnational, transracial solidarity, with the white iḥrām garb erasing all differences of nation, culture, or economic status. The fast in Ramaḍān was not just a divinely ordered abstinence from food, but an exercise in self-discipline and the cultivation of empathy for those who starved without a choice. The headscarf couldn't have been reduced to a garment that women wore because Allāh said so; it had to become an overloaded expression of inner ideals, whether representing a woman's modesty, empowerment, balance of tradition and modernity, or spirituality. This was the Islam of rationalization that books and pamphlets wrote on everything, including Bilāl's skin.

My rereading of old books confronts me with Islam's reality as a product: what I understood to be a Muslim state of being had emerged in part through the relationships between various human endeavors. My Islam was produced by these books, interacting with each other as well as with my human conversation partners. If a knowledge of God also appeared to me through these collisions, God emerging as a *product* of my readings and conversations, to whom had I surrendered?

Marx had compared the imaginary unity of a nation to that of a sack of potatoes, an artificial coherence. The way that it looks to me, religions operate the same way. You throw a bunch of texts, concepts, personages, methods, institutions, and lineages into a sack, and they are no longer things on their own, because we instead perceive unity in the sack, the system, the tradition, the "Islamic worldview," Islam as a distinct and self-defined ideology. I believed with all my heart that the sack of potatoes that I called "Islam" was really a singular object, intact in itself, and that this sack must be either accepted or rejected wholesale. Reviewing my bookshelf, the fantasy of unity has been lost; the potatoes revealed themselves to be mere potatoes in no order at all.

Because the unity of the archival sack is imaginary, each text offers a break from that unity: Every act of reading has the potential to push out other texts or invite new ones in. Even if *The Autobiography of Malcolm X* reads as a polemic against Elijah Muhammad, the book also planted Elijah into my consciousness; my later investments in Elijah's legacy and meanings came as a side effect of loving the Messenger's disciple who rejected him. Some relocations of texts might require greater shocks to the sack than others. Twenty years later, many books that constituted Islam for me have been either switched out for new materials or forced to share space with them. What I am now willing to count as Islam could make little sense to the teen convert reading Yusuf Ali's Qur'ān in the 1990s, though I still claim the Qur'ān and Prophet and continue to repeat the acts of prayer that I first learned in *Islam in Focus*—and Malcolm keeps his place in my heart, even if his meanings for me have changed numerous times. Throughout my time as a Muslim, the same external forms have given shelter to a variety of beliefs and commitments that many would find to be irreconcilable. Even a concept as seemingly straightforward and simple as tawhīd,

Islamic monotheism, has contained so many ideas and meanings for me at various times that it becomes its own unstable sack. This is how the external forms survive for me as the structure for my dīn, and also how my dīn persists even when I change.

8

JOURNEY TO THE END OF COHERENCE: MANHAJ OF NO MANHAJ

>>> And once a thing is put in writing, the composition, whatever it may be, drifts all over the place, getting into the hands not only of those who understand it, but equally of those who have no business with it; it doesn't know how to address the right people, and not address the wrong. And when it is ill-treated and unfairly abused it always needs its parent to come to its aid, being unable to defend itself or attend to its own needs. <<< —Socrates, in Plato's *The Phaedrus*[1]

MODERN SALAFISM CAME to represent a call to textually grounded purification. For the Salafiyya, going back to the origins centered on a renewed interest in ḥadīths; but because we keep making up the sacred past as we go along, we always have choices as to where the origins should be recovered. In the late nineteenth and early twentieth centuries, as many Muslim intellectuals went diving into ḥadīth collections in search of their authenticity, others invested such power in the Qur'ān that they were willing to throw out the ḥadīth corpus altogether.

Like the ḥadīth-based revivalists, these "Qur'ān-only" or "Qur'ānist" Muslims promised that they were cutting away human corruptions of Islam and restoring the pure message that God intended. Both the ḥadīth-centered and Qur'ān-exclusive thinkers saw their back-to-the-source approaches as offering liberation from taqlīd to the established legal schools. Both trends can be understood as expressing a reassertion of the individual reader in ways that could only be possible through modern flows of information.

Both trends were products of their settings. The trend of ḥadīth-based revivalists wanting to humanize Muḥammad—sweep his miracle stories under the rug, marginalize his ascent through the heavens, deny the Ṣūfī doctrines of a cosmic "Muḥammadī light" that preexisted the world, and reinvent the Messenger of Allāh as primarily an ethical teacher, ideal husband/father, wise elder statesman, and template for improvement of the modern individual self—appeared amid the same historical shifts as Qur'ān-only reformists who saw the divine text as a thesis fundamentally in harmony with modern ideas of reason and progress. The nineteenth-century pressures and opportunities that made a movement such as the Ahl al-Ḥadīth possible simultaneously created openings for a countermovement: the Ahl al-Qur'ān, "People of the Qur'ān."

Modern arguments for Qur'ān-only Islam emerged through the colonial encounter, when Muslims faced challenges from Christian missionaries operating on Protestant discourses of *sola scriptura*, as well as the new truth-making power of scientific rationality. The nineteenth century also happened to be a time of growing anxiety over Muḥammad, as new quests to uncover the "historical Jesus" and "historical Buddha" were paralleled by scholarly interrogations of Muḥammad's life and character. Missionary and academic literatures (and the two genres were not always clearly separate) confronted Muslims with scholarly attacks upon Muḥammad, which were accompanied by questions of the sources: Did the Prophet really say and do what had been attributed to him in the ḥadīth literature? Had the traditional sciences of ḥadīth evaluation successfully weeded out inauthentic reports as it seemed to promise? Could the traditional ḥadīth sciences hold up against modern methods of analysis? By the end of the nineteenth century, Muslim modernists had developed anxieties concerning ḥadīth, which in part owed to engagements with Orientalist scholarship. The ḥadīth corpus and sīra literature were cast into serious doubt by missionary-scholar William Muir (1819–1905), who applied contemporary Western historiographical methods to the Prophet's biography in his work, *Life of Mahomet* (published in parts from 1858 to 1861). Muir does not discount the possibility of *some* ḥadīth reports being authentic but regards the corpus overall as having been largely fabricated to meet the legal and political needs of later Muslims or to "glorify" Muḥammad with tales of miracles and supernatural powers.[2] Muir critically dissects narrations of Muḥammad's life, pointing out that the companions who offered anecdotes of Muḥammad's childhood had not actually known him as a child, that companions could enhance their own prestige by forging stories of Muḥammad, and that Muḥammad's rise to power meant that we would never hear his opponents' side of the story.[3] In contrast to the ḥadīth collections, Muir does hold confidence in the Qur'ān as a reliable source from Muḥammad's lifetime. His support for the Qur'ān's authenticity, however, does not read as a compliment; in Muir's judgment, the Qur'ān was such an incoherent, inconsistent mess that it could not possibly have been subjected to a careful editorial process.[4]

Muir's biography of Muḥammad, produced for a Christian missionary agenda,[5] posed a formidable challenge to Muslim intellectuals such as Sayyid Ahmad Khan (1817–1898), who offered his response in 1870. Seeking to renew Muḥammad's legacy for modern Muslims, Sayyid Ahmad sought to cleanse the Prophet of the mythic elaborations that had been attached to his person, avoid or reinterpret stories of miracles such as the angelic intervention in Muḥammad's battles, and give prophethood an Avicennan reimagination as the perfection of an innate human faculty. Sayyid Ahmad was so troubled by Muir's work that he gradually developed a near-absolute opposition to ḥadīth and remained careful to stress the primacy of the Qur'ān over the prophetic Sunna.[6] Some of Sayyid Ahmad's contemporaries were moving in similar directions. Syed Ameer Ali's (1849–1928) work, *The Life and Teachings of Muhammad* (1873), treats Muḥammad not as a mystical being, but rather a normal human with perfected character. *The Life and Teachings* additionally emphasizes the prophetic model less as instruction for how one should dress or eat but rather for the development of one's own compassion, humility, patience, and modesty.[7] Shortly after Sayyid Ahmad's death, Shaykh M. H. Kidwai would call for a reorientation of Muḥammad's miraculous nature away from supernatural acts such as the splitting of the moon. In his view, a far more impressive miracle was the emergence of a noble and refined Islamic civilization from the rough nomads of Arabia, and Muḥammad's greatest miracle was of course the Qur'ān.[8]

In the South Asian context, Muslim debates over ḥadīth authenticity and renewed emphasis on the Qur'ān's supremacy mirrored similar conversations taking place within other communities. As British colonial policy, Orientalist scholarship, and Christian missionaries contributed to the image of a monolithic "Hinduism," and this construction became meaningful for those who were labeled "Hindus," nineteenth-century Hindu reformists sought to differentiate their ideas about genuine Hinduism from what they regarded as embarrassing cultural practices, folk beliefs, and superstition. To this end, it proved useful to restrict the sources of legitimate Hinduism to a core set of sacred texts. The Brahmo Samaj and Arya Samaj located pure Hinduism—defined by inherent monotheism, a universalist message, and claims to a higher truth beyond popular rituals—in the Vedas. A reconstructed, Vedas-centered Hinduism would be seen by its proponents not as a modern creation, but rather the recovery of Hinduism's timeless, original essence.

Limiting Hinduism to what could be supported by the Vedas helped groups such as the Brahmo Samaj and Arya Samaj deflect attacks from Christian missionaries. Troublesome concepts or customs were dismissed as non-Vedic innovations, and difficult content *within* the Vedas simply needed to be reinterpreted.[9] This new scripturalism also encouraged standardization: By insisting on a single, shared scripture, the immeasurable diversity of Indic traditions could be brought under control within a monolithic presentation of Hinduism, the doctrines and practices of Hinduism could be stabilized, and Hindus could more effectively unite on the basis of stable Hindu religious identity. Because diversity potentially signified inconsistency, which could then indicate irrationality, asserting the central authority of the Vedas bolstered the image of Hinduism as a rational system that could compete with other systems in rigorous intellectual debate.

At a time when Western-styled, government-run educational institutions in colonial India promoted empirical rationality as the ultimate measure of truth, and Protestant missionaries offered translations of their scripture (proclaimed as supremely authoritative over the imposter scriptures of "lower" religions) in Urdu, Hindi, and Punjabi,[10] religious debate became largely a contest between scriptures. With western Europeans naming the rules, this meant that sacred texts had to prove themselves as (1) compatible with modern ideas of reason, (2) comprehensive, and (3) historically authentic. It was amid this competitive scripturalism that groups such as the Brahmo Samaj and Arya Samaj advocated the translation of Hindu scriptures into local vernaculars. In their call for a Vedas-only Hinduism, reformists and revivalists defined themselves in part against Muslims ("kuranis") and sought to prove the truth of the Vedas through assaults upon the Qur'ān, which Muslim scholars answered in their own criticisms of the Vedas.[11] One of the more prominent defenders of Islam in pamphlet wars against the Arya Samaj was Mirza Ghulam Ahmad (1835–1908), leader of the Ahmadiyya movement, who became controversial within Muslim communities for his messianic and prophetic self-image. While not denying the ḥadīths' authority entirely, Ahmad did take care to subordinate ḥadīths to the Qur'ān.[12]

Sayyid Ahmad Khan's supporter Chiragh 'Ali (1844–1895) offered a more explicit rejection of the ḥadīth corpus, declaring the "vast flood of traditions" in the generations following Muḥammad to have formed a "chaotic sea" in which "Truth and error, fact and fable, mingled together in indistinguishable confusion" and "all manner of lies and absurdities" were attached to Muḥammad's name.[13] According to Chiragh 'Ali, many of these fictions were crafted for political reasons; others reflect the interest of later generations to endow Muḥammad with "supernatural powers." By the time that Muslims sought to develop methods by which an authentic core of traditions could be retrieved from this sea of fabrications, Chiragh 'Ali charged, it was too late. The canonical Six Books did not arrive until the third century after Muḥammad, and their compilers' "sifting was not based on any critical, historical, or rational principles."[14] In contrast, he argued that the integrity of the Qur'ān could not be questioned.

Restricting Islam to the Qur'ān also placed restrictions on Muslim politics. Writing to depoliticize the Qur'ān in his colonial environment, Chiragh 'Ali insisted that the revelation did not offer a system of civil law or theories of the state, limiting its own authority instead to matters of religion and morality. The Qur'ān's few legal interventions, he asserted, amounted to condemnations of certain social institutions and practices among the "pagan and barbarous Arabs"—or, when a full correction of the Arabs was not possible, at least a reform or reasonable accommodation "owing to their weakness and immaturity" that would expire when they attained higher levels of civilization.[15]

At the start of the twentieth century, Maulwi 'Abdullah Chakralawi (d. 1930), a former member of the Ahle-Hadīth in Lahore, publicly denounced the authority of the ḥadīth corpus and initiated what would become known as the Ahl al-Qur'ān movement. The Qur'ān, he asserted, was trustworthier as a source than the ḥadīth corpus; it was also absolutely comprehensive, providing all the necessary information for life as a Muslim, offering a truth that was rational and resonant with innate human knowledge and universal, natural law.[16] Another Ahl al-Qur'ān group was established in Amritsar by Khwaja Ahmad-ud-Din Amritsari (1861–1936), also a former Ahle-Hadith advocate, who abandoned his reliance on ḥadīths after hearing a report in which Moses slaps Azreal, the angel of death, for attempting to take his life.[17] For Amritsari, the Qur'ān offered a perfect expression of the truth that could be found in all religions, and as such was uniquely qualified to teach this universal truth to the entirety of humankind. In contrast to the Qur'ān's universalism, he argued that excessive attachments to specific prophets only caused divisions among the communities to whom those prophets had been sent.

The Qur'ān, Amritsari insisted, was inherently a call to use rational thought. Confident that God would not—and *did* not—demand acceptance of counterintuitive fables, Amritsari reinterpreted the Qur'ān's miracle stories. Rejecting the ḥadīth literature's elaborate accounts of Muḥammad's ascent into the heavens and instead relying on the scant, vague references to his ascent in the Qur'ān, Amritsari stripped the Prophet's mi'rāj of its supernaturalism and insisted that the event had taken place entirely within the city limits of Mecca.[18]

To assert that the Qur'ān was sufficient to answer every meaningful question was to profoundly alter what counted as meaningful, and thus offered a statement on what did *not* count as essential to Islam. This recalibration of Islam's priorities happened to have greater compatibility with liberal Protestantism's rules about what made for good religion: Reformists argued that a Qur'ān-only Islam would save

Muslims from superstitions, unbelievable fables, exploitation of religion by the state, sectarian divisions, abuse of the ignorant masses by greedy clerics or charlatans posing as mystical masters, and emphasis on the precise details of ritual acts. As most of the details concerning embodied practice came from ḥadīth reports rather than the Qur'ān, Ahl al-Qur'ān Muslims discarded the bulk of the ritual and legal tradition as unnecessary human elaborations upon God's commands. Some Qur'ānists were willing to uphold established modes of prayer as having been so universally transmitted that they must have represented authentic Muslim practice; others chose to design unrecognizable new prayers based exclusively on whatever scant details they found within the text of the Qur'ān.

Though the wholesale denial of ḥadīth characterized by the Punjab's Ahl al-Qur'ān movements did not find the same kind of advocacy in Egypt, proto-Salafī modernists did offer challenges to the ḥadīth tradition. Sayyid Ahmad Khan's Egyptian contemporary, Muḥammad 'Abduh, questioned the corpus. Like Sayyid Ahmad Khan, 'Abduh's ḥadīth skepticism seems to have been related to his networking with European scholars. German Orientalist Ignaz Goldziher (1850–1921) revolutionized ḥadīth studies through the borrowing of methods from modern biblical criticism and also traveled in the same Muslim intellectual currents as 'Abduh.[19] Goldziher, who charged that the ḥadīths were mostly fabricated by later Muslims to impose their political and legal positions backward onto the Prophet, did not produce his work in an isolated "Western" bubble: He studied at al-Azhar for four months and even performed Muslim salāt in mosques. Goldziher's scholarly contributions and social circles embedded him within the "global public sphere" that connected the Western study of Islam with Muslim reformist intellectuals, including 'Abduh's network. While in Cairo, he regularly met with Jamāl ad-Dīn al-Afghānī; in Damascus, he befriended Ṭāhir al-Jazā'irī; Kurd Alī would visit him in Budapest.[20]

'Abduh's ḥadīth skepticism emerged somewhat parallel to that of Sayyid Aḥmad Khān, writes Daniel W. Brown, though 'Abduh had to express his skepticism "much more cautiously."[21] In harmony with classical ḥadīth criticism, 'Abduh held that widely transmitted (mutawātir) ḥadīth reports possess more binding authority than those with less widespread narration (termed *āḥad*, "singular"). He also argued that someone who questions the authenticity of an āḥad ḥadīth cannot be called an unbeliever for his or her doubt. This subdued statement potentially makes an explosive implication, Brown explains, as "'Abduh thus opened the door to personal judgment in deciding what traditions to accept or reject."[22] In 1906, around the same time that British-ruled India saw the birth of anti-ḥadīth movements, Rashīd Riḍā's *al-Manār* journal in British-ruled Egypt published a controversial article that called for a Qur'ān-only understanding of Islam. True to the Salafī project if not its typical method, the article's author, Tawfiq Ṣidqī, linked the rejection of ḥadīth reports with freedom from taqlīd, the unquestioned surrender to classical schools.[23]

Qur'ān-only/anti-ḥadīth arguments continued to circulate throughout the twentieth century, most notoriously in the case of Rashād Khalīfa (1935–1990). Born in Egypt, Khalīfa relocated to the United States in 1959, where he obtained a PhD in biochemistry. Dissatisfied with English translations of the Qur'ān, he endeavored to produce his own, and soon after became preoccupied with the seemingly random "mystery letters" that appear at the start of some sūras in the Qur'ān. It was during his investigation of these letters that Khalīfa experimented with computer analysis of the Qur'ān, leading to his alleged discovery of a mathematical pattern running throughout the text. This "Qur'ān code," according to Khalīfa, provided undeniable empirical proof that the Qur'ān was authored by God.[24] Throughout the 1970s, Khalīfa's findings earned him international fame; he was endorsed by al-Azhar's Academy of Islamic Research, as well as by popular leaders such as Ahmed Deedat and Warith Deen Mohammed. In the 1980s, however, Khalīfa took to issuing virulent denials of prophetic precedent, denouncing the ḥadīth and Sunna as "Satanic inventions" and "100% conjecture," and condemning Muslims who followed ḥadīths as "idol worshipers" for exalting Muḥammad's words and compromising the absolute power of God's word.[25] Khalīfa was reviled by the Muslim audiences that had once embraced him, judged an apostate in 1989 by Saudi Arabia's Islamic Legal Council, and assassinated one year later. His successors have continued to promote his message.

The first source that Qur'ān-only Muslims cite for evidence, as one would expect, is the Qur'ān itself. Verses such as 18:54, in which the Qur'ān asserts that it provides every example for the benefit of people, are taken as the Qur'ān's argument for its own status as self-sufficient and exclusive. Even while rejecting the authority of the prophetic example, however, Qur'ān-only Muslims also make claims upon Muḥammad, arguing that Muḥammad himself was a Qur'ān-only Muslim who did not claim to offer any transcendent knowledge or binding commands outside of the revealed text. Muḥammad's own Islam is presented as having been a Muḥammad-less Islam: His name is invoked to authorize his erasure. Qur'ān-only arguments challenge the ḥadīth corpus from within: While dismissing the ḥadīth corpus as unreliable, they confidently make ḥadīth-based arguments that Muḥammad's Companions were averse to writing ḥadīths.[26] Such reports empower Qur'ān-only Muslims by locating their opposition to ḥadīths at the very origins of Islam, resting on the prestige of prominent and revered companions of the Prophet, most notably 'Umar, as transmitters of the Prophet's words. This means that (1) some anti-ḥadīth Muslims ironically rely on the authority of ḥadīths to argue that we should not regard ḥadīths as authoritative, and (2) while treating skepticism toward ḥadīths as the more critical and intellectually mature approach, they uncritically accept ḥadīths that happen to work for them.

In her work *Ḥadīth as Scripture: Discussions on the Authority of Prophetic Statements in Islam*, Aisha Musa pushes hard to establish traditional credentials for modern opponents of ḥadīth authority, both on Islamic (showing that opposition to ḥadīth cannot be reduced to a "modern-day heresy") and postcolonial (showing that rejecters of ḥadīth authority are not "'Westerners' who are seeking to 'Westernize' Islam to fit their culture") grounds.[27] Seeking to demonstrate that Qur'ān-only Islam is not a product of European influence, but instead an "essentially Muslim"[28] and "indigenous Muslim"[29] response to the problem of the ḥadīth corpus, however, brings a new problem: the assumption that *anything* can be considered "essentially" or "indigenously" Muslim in such an interconnected world. Musa also seems to expect that if she can show Qur'ān-only Islam to have come entirely from *within* Muslim intellectual tradition, completely free of

European influence and "innovation" from outside, that the Qur'ānist argument instantly achieves some precious authenticity—an opposition to ḥadīth-based Salafism through Salafism's own gimmicks. Just like the Salafiyya, Qur'ān-only Muslims reinvent the past to inscribe themselves at its center, insisting that what they advocate is not a reformation, but a revival of the original Islam.

UNIVERSAL FLAGS

Even for modern Muslim intellectuals who did not entirely reject the ḥadīths, the Qur'ān would take on a life that could have been conceivable only in modernity, as enhanced possibilities for reading the Qur'ān would transform the experience of the text. Comparable to the addition of dots and vowel marks to 'Uthmān's codex, the Qur'ān experienced another revolution of accessibility and standardization in 1925, with the establishment of a mass-printed "standard Egyptian edition." Apart from the fact of mass printing, the edition was innovative in a number of ways. Though sūras of the Qur'ān were not originally titled, this edition included the popularly known names for each sūra (such as *al-Fātiḥā* for the first sūra), which would lead many readers to consider the titles as having always been a natural part of the Qur'ān. The standard Egyptian edition also specified each sūra as having been revealed to Muḥammad either in Mecca or Medina. Of the multiple acceptable vowelizations recognized by Sunnī Muslims, the standard Egyptian edition favored the voweling of Hafs. As the standard Egyptian edition became the template for modern reproductions of the Qur'ānic text, the Hafs reading would become *the* Qur'ān for most of the world.[30]

The standard Egyptian edition, which would be printed in factories for use in government-controled schools and mosques, emerged at a critical moment, the early hints of an Egypt-Saudi rivalry over political and religious power in the region. As this rivalry escalated in the later Arab Cold War, the Qur'ān would play an important role, as the Saudi government responded to international rising literacy and needs for reliably printed texts by establishing the King Fahd Holy Qur'ān Printing Complex, which printed over 135 million copies between 1984 and 1996 alone.[31] Along with the Qur'ān itself, Saudi institutions disseminated government-approved translations and commentaries.

Though various technologies of interpretation, whether classical Greek philosophical tradition, visionary mysticism, or modern literary theories, are avoided as threatening innovation and even exegetical violence upon the clear message of the Qur'ān, technologies of reproducing and disseminating the Qur'ān—such as mass printing, audio/visual recording, and digital media—are perceived as ideologically neutral, assumed to make no impact on how the revelation is understood. But this new capacity for the entire Qur'ānic text to become available for widespread public consumption would necessarily express assumptions about the Qur'ān's purpose and meaning, which may not have been fathomable prior to the technological advances that enabled it. The triumph of mass printing meant that for the first time in history, it could be commonplace for Muslims to possess their own personal copies of the Qur'ān, and for Muslims who did not speak Arabic to access the Qur'ān's message in translation. Unprecedented accessibility came with big consequences: The idea that regular Muslims could/should attempt to engage and *comprehend* the Qur'ān's text as individual readers, rather than simply recite the text as a devotional act or receive interpretation from imāms in Friday sermons, became relevant in ways that were never before possible. It should also be said that printing technology appeared at a time when interpretation of the Qur'ān was affected by another modern pressure: the devastating impact of European colonialism upon Muslim educational structures. All this would have an enormous impact on the ways that Muslims worked with the Qur'ān—and the question of *who* could do that work.

Some of the most influential Muslim writers of the twentieth century offered commentaries on the Qur'ān without having been trained as religious scholars, including Yusuf Ali (1872–1953), Sayyid Quṭb (1906–1966), and Abū al-A'la Mawdūdī (1903–1979). Ali was a Western-educated student of English literature; Quṭb was a novelist and journalist; Mawdūdī was a newspaper editor. All three men had received some religious education in their childhoods, but none could lay claim to advanced Islamic scholarship. Approaching the tradition as autodidacts, these non-'ulama Muslim intellectuals differed from each other in their chosen materials. Ali's Qur'ān commentary, for example, draws from the Prophet's biography but makes little use of specific ḥadīth reports; Mawdūdī's Qur'ān commentary relies extensively on ḥadīths. Despite such differences, the Qur'ān was consistently privileged as the key site on which calls for reform or revival of Islamic thought must be made.

This modern centrality of the Qur'ān changed the way in which it was read, as the Qur'ān's sūras became increasingly analyzed as rhetorical wholes. Treating each sūra as a self-contained message is not entirely an invention of modernity, as we can find it in the commentaries of important premodern scholars such as Zarakshī (1344–1391) and Suyūṭī (d. 1505); but in the twentieth century, this approach became largely standard. It has been suggested that the shift away from atomistic, verse-by-verse interpretation toward more holistic and thematic methods emerged with the need among numerous twentieth-century thinkers for the Qur'ān to be repositioned as the foremost site of Islamic knowledge. With non-Qur'ānic sources such as ḥadīth and accumulated tradition falling under new methods of critical scrutiny, the Qur'ān itself needed to enable a broader potential for meaning than a verse-by-verse reading seemed to allow. The unity of each sūra as its own discursive artifact thus became increasingly attractive.[32]

Zooming out further, movement away from verse-by-verse reading encouraged greater considerations of thematic coherence in the Qur'ān at large, along with the potential for this thematic unity to generate new meanings in the text. This approach is exemplified in the twentieth century by modernist intellectual Fazlur Rahman (1919–1988). Rahman saw the Qur'ān as the central source of Islamic ethics. Echoing Salafī complaints of Islam's corruption from outside forces, he complained that his view was not the historical Muslim norm: "One cannot point to a single work of ethics squarely based upon the Qur'ān," he wrote, "although there are numerous works based upon Greek philosophy, Persian tradition and Ṣūfī piety."[33] Rahman sought to fill this gap with the development of a new Qur'ānic hermeneutics.[34] His emphasis on the Qur'ān did not mean that he wished to discard Muḥammad; on the contrary, informed by Avicennan theories of prophethood, he called attention to Muḥammad's heart as the locus of divine revelation to such an extent that he seemed to call the Qur'ān's divine "otherness" into question.[35]

Rahman developed his Qur'ānic hermeneutics at a time in which historical context was increasingly hailed as the key to unlocking a text's meaning; this view remained popular in broader literary theory through the 1970s. For Rahman, historical context served as a means of determining the Qur'ān's ethics that could take the reader beyond a literalist cherrypicking of isolated verses. Using issues of context to address the Qur'ān's apparent acceptance of polygamy and slavery, for example, Rahman argued that in both cases, the Qur'ān worked within the limits of its time and place. Without making a clear stand to abolish slavery and polygamy immediately, as this would not have been feasible, the Qur'ān instead issues sanctions and recommendations that demonstrate a "moral ideal towards which the society was expected to move."[36] Rahman suggested that through analysis of what the Qur'ān was trying to achieve within the bounds of its own context, we could successfully distinguish between the Qur'ān's *universal* message and its *historically contingent* rulings. This method would allow for the possibility of a modern Islamic humanism that could adhere to the Qur'ān's big-picture themes (i.e., "justice," "mercy") even while departing from the details of specific verses.

Arguing that comprehension of the Qur'ān would be largely impossible without looking at Muḥammad's life and the times in which he lived, Rahman did not advocate a wholesale rejection of the ḥadīth corpus. He did remain cautious in his use of ḥadīths, as he regarded many traditions as later fictions (including the Prophet's ascent through the heavens). If a ḥadīth came into apparent conflict with the Qur'ān, for Rahman there was no question that the Qur'ān would overrule the ḥadīth. Rahman valued the Sunna but drew a distinction between what he called the "prophetic Sunna" and the "living Sunna": the former being the normative customs of Muḥammad, while the latter was the Muslim community's ongoing redefinition and reinterpretation of Muḥammad's behavior for new contexts. What went wrong, in Rahman's view, was that the ninth-century ḥadīth movement petrified the Sunna as a fixed collection of texts, and that the details of an isolated ḥadīth report could be assumed to represent the comprehensive Sunna. In similar fashion to his moves with the Qur'ān, Rahman sought to understand Muḥammad's sunna without treating every detail as authoritative. The living Sunna could not be reduced to the letter of the text, but instead reflected a dynamic, ongoing process of living by Muḥammad's example amid changing times and circumstances.

For a variety of reasons, many of the great scholars and thinkers who have contributed to the "Progressive Muslim" scene—whether or not they self-identify as "progressive Muslims"—have chosen the Qur'ān as the chief terrain on which battles over issues such as gender equality are to be fought. While the Qur'ān is placed at the center of progressive arguments, progressive Muslims often position the ḥadīth corpus and/or its primary advocates as Islam's greatest obstacle against gender justice. It remains a popular sentiment among progressive Muslims that if we can push away the historically accumulated ḥadīth and tafsīr that have concealed the Qur'ān's true meaning, finding our way to a new and "direct" encounter with the text, we will successfully find Islam—defined here entirely within the eternal message of the Qur'ān—to be wholly resonant with ideals of modern feminism. Like the science-obsessed modernist Muslims who sought to prove that the Qur'ān displays miraculously advanced knowledge of natural phenomena, some progressive Muslims would claim that the Qur'ān's original message included a call for gender equality that could only be fully comprehended fourteen centuries later.

The Qur'ān-centered nature of progressive Muslim arguments could be situated within the same intellectual trends and historical shifts that made Qur'ān-centered Islam appealing to so many Muslims from the nineteenth century onward. There is also a question of the particular training that progressive Muslim intellectuals bring to their sources. Equipped with Western literary theory and modern hermeneutics, which had first developed through the attempts of Christian scholars to investigate the Bible, progressive Muslim thinkers perhaps find their toolboxes more intuitively applicable to reinterpreting divine scripture than sorting through the unique problems of ḥadīth studies. Meanwhile, for many progressive Muslims, the mere mention of ḥadīths evokes nightmares of puritanical religiosity, unsophisticated textual literalism, repressive legalism, superstitious ritualism, sectarian intolerance, and the vaguely defined boogeyman of "Wahhābism," often racialized as an ethnocentric "Arab Islam" and caricatured with references to the beards and clothing choices of its adherents. Finally, the status of the Qur'ān as God's word means that people can theoretically conceive of it as free from the constraints of earthly patriarchy; while the revelation was delivered through a man, this man does not own the words as their "author." In contrast, the ḥadīth corpus remains bound to this earth and is inescapably the work of men who were products of their historical setting, with all the limitations that it imposed on them.[37] Again, we must recognize that even when we read narrations attributed to 'Ā'isha or any other woman of the Salaf, we do not have direct access to her voice, but rather her voice as represented by male-dominated scholarly networks and institutions of knowledge.[38] The ḥadīth corpus can therefore be exposed to varieties of critique from which the Qur'ān would be protected.

To get into progressive "Qur'ānic hermeneutics" projects, we must work with a few assumptions: (1) that we have access to the Qur'ān in its original and eternal form, its integrity perfectly preserved, absolutely innocent of any human interventions to add or redact content; (2) that the Qur'ān can speak in "universals" such as universal justice, universal equality, universal *anything*; (3) that the Qur'ān's "universal" messages represent broader themes of the text, even if they do not necessarily find harmony with the specific content of every verse; (4) that the relationship of any particular verse to the Qur'ān's universal or thematic truth provides a measure by which we should weigh its value against other verses; (5) because the Qur'ān's universal themes are what really matters, any isolated verse of the Qur'ān can be overruled by what we have named as the Qur'ān's true heart. By the logic of this approach, if the Qur'ān's universal message calls us to greater mercy and justice, but domestic violence betrays what *we* recognize as mercy and justice, then domestic violence cannot possibly be endorsed by the Qur'ān, no matter what a specific verse appears to be saying.

Maybe the Qur'ān's statements of spiritual equality between women and men should erase verses articulating their legal inequality, and maybe the Qur'ān's monotheism is betrayed by hierarchical relationships between human beings. I don't know. This all rests on what you personally assume about the Qur'ān's ultimate purpose and how this text is supposed to work. Maybe the Qur'ān's references to God with male pronouns occur *only* due to the limitations of Arabic grammar, and maybe the divine "he" doesn't relate to any broader gender logic running throughout the text. Again, this isn't simply the self-evident truth of the Qur'ān, but a conclusion that you might reach with the preexisting values that you bring to your reading. For the Qur'ān to express an obvious opposition to patriarchy, I have to decide that this is what I want to see. Even if I reject the traditionalists' verse-by-verse reading method that progressive Muslims disdain, choosing instead to read "thematically" with an eye for the Qur'ān's broader message, there's still a reasonable chance that I can find patriarchy fully endorsed by the Qur'ān, even as one of the Qur'ān's "universal" themes. Contrary to the notion of a god so absolutely transcendent and wholly *other* that this god could never be contained within human constructions of gender, I can also read the Qur'ān as speaking for a he-god who assumes men's domination of women to be the natural, normative order of the universe. This reading, after all, does not seem to have experienced meaningful challenge prior to the modern interest in gender equality.

Gender-sensitive Qur'ān hermeneutics works like a shell game in which the shells are pushed around to make us miss where the hetero-sexist pea has been hidden. Ebrahim Moosa describes this privileging of our favorite verses to control the meaning of less charming ones as "hermeneutical acrobatics or a hermeneutics of wishful thinking."[39] Though I personally agree with Amina Wadud's response to Moosa (that such disparagement from privileged, self-identified "progressive" male scholars provides nothing useful and can only be destructive[40]), this doesn't make the problem go away. What hermeneutics offers seems to be less a critical method than a critical-sounding means of affirming, "The text says whatever I want it to say."

I would ask what gives us the eyes to claim our universals, especially when the concepts that we hold as universal, such as gender egalitarianism, lead us to radical breaks from the ways in which the Qur'ān has been comprehended for nearly fifteen centuries. Isn't our interest in the Qur'ān's gender egalitarianism itself the product of historical forces that asked new questions of the text? Don't we also read from within the bounds of a time and place, or have our sophisticated methods enabled us to step out of the world that gave us those very methods? We defend our universal Qur'ānic ethics, while exiling other readers to their particular contexts, through our use of modern (and postmodern) Western literary theories; and we forget that these theories themselves, rather than universalize our voices, only locate us within particular intellectual genealogies and our own narrow *context*. While accusing other thinkers of misreading the Qur'ān through the filters of their cultural backgrounds, Western-educated scholars find the Qur'ān's "universal" truth with tools developed by nineteenth-century European Christians who had sought new understandings of their Bible, or mid-twentieth-century European Marxists and Marxist-inspired thinkers who examined the importance of power and context in our constructions of reality.

Like a liberal mirror of Salafism, progressive Muslim hermeneutics confidently tells us which methods of interpretation transcend interpretation and which ones have strayed from the pure origins. Like the Salafiyya, progressivists plant their flag on the origins of Islam, present themselves as heirs to the Qur'ān's truest spirit, and condemn various traditional authorities as innovators and corruptors. While calling our attention to the Qur'ān's multiplicity of meanings and the subjectivity of interpretation, progressivists nonetheless tend to make proclamations against those whom they accuse of having read the Qur'ān wrong. Even when celebrating the individual reader as the true locus of meaning, these emancipators of texts can be as hegemonic and authoritarian as the most rigid literalists, and their flexing of Western academic training and literary theories can execute power plays just as much as mystical hierarchies or appeals to capitalized "Tradition."

There's a political stake here, as the progressivist reform project cannot be neutral in matters of empire. Progressive Muslim hermeneutics happens to share some overlap with the agendas of forces such as the RAND Corporation, the conservative think-tank that associated close observation of Muslim rituals (such as prayer and fasting) and behavioral codes (such as ḥijāb) with "backwardness and underdevelopment, which in turn are the breeding ground for social and political problems of all sorts."[41] The RAND Corporation has advocated for Muslims to be retrained in their approach to the Qur'ān, namely, to be fed new methods of reading that would disenfranchise traditional institutions and modes of authority, creating a new kind of Muslim.[42] Because the Qur'ān says much less in terms of rituals and embodied practices than the ḥadīth corpus, Qur'ān-only Islam (particularly when the Qur'ān is read with what Sabah Mahmood has called "secular hermeneutics"[43]) can more effectively produce the kind of liberal, rational, autonomous, Protestantized Muslim that the RAND Corporation wants to see.

Considering progressive Muslim attempts to control the Qur'ān's meaning, I recall al-Ghazālī's polemics against the Ismā'īlī Shī'īs. Constructing arguments to discredit the Ismā'īlīs, al-Ghazālī worked in the service of a Sunnī empire against a Shī'ī empire, but that's not the immediate issue. At the heart of the Ismā'īlī claim to power was an argument for authoritative teaching (ta'līm) in the hands of the Imām, who alone possessed knowledge of the "hidden" (bāṭin) meanings of verses that could overrule their plain-sense "manifest" (zāhir) meanings. With privileged and infallible access to the inner nature of the Qur'ān, the Ismā'īlī Imām's presentation of a verse's "truest" meaning required no reasoned argument: The Imām claimed textual authority over the Muslim masses by virtue of interpretations that he would never have to explain or defend. Taking on the Ismā'īlī Imāmate, al-Ghazālī sought to disarm this mode of authority (without throwing out the possibility of mystical insights or intuitive interpretation altogether). In doing so, he had to advocate for a tradition of fallible human scholars against those who would claim to supersede that tradition by virtue of their supreme esoteric truths. While recognizing al-Ghazālī for what he was—a state-employed propagandist—and having sympathy for the Isma'īliyya in my own present amid widespread Sunnī antagonism, I can recognize al-Ghazālī as offering an important critique. Mocking the attempts at symbolic arguments furthered by the Isma'īliyya, al-Ghazālī remarks, "The drowning man clings to anything."[44] Like many in the progressive Muslim scene, I have felt the desperation of a drowning person when it came to my Qur'ān. In my drowning, I have clung to a number of interpretive quick-fixes, such as historical context and universal themes, that could not sustain me.

What happens when our alternative readings fail us? Amina Wadud, after wrestling with 4:34, the Qur'ān's "wife-beating" verse for two decades, finally threw up her hands and confessed, "There is no getting around this one."[45] Refusing to accept any circumstance in which men might strike their wives with God's approval, Wadud says no to the verse's literal application, while continuing to emphasize that even if rewriting the Qur'an is not an option, human beings are the makers of its meaning.[46]

There are scholars who brush off modern concern regarding 4:34 with assurances that the "classical interpretive tradition" has made every effort to regulate spousal violence and empower women with legal recourses when the limits are transgressed. These arguments might help to complicate the picture but will not satisfy everyone; they don't go far enough for me. Against this romanticism of the tradition, Ayesha Chaudhry's recent work on 4:34 argues that premodern Muslim interpretive traditions provide no useful resources for asserting that it is *always* and *absolutely* wrong for a man to commit violence against his wife.[47]

Chaudhry maintains hope in what modern progressive interpreters, operating on their own "idealized cosmologies" and releasing themselves from the authority of premodern scholarly traditions, can do with the words. For Chaudhry, the Qur'ān remains innocent and open; the Qur'ān's problems remain the fault of its readers. Against

Chaudhry's optimism, Aysha Hidayatullah's work offers a word of caution. Hidayatullah writes from the place that she calls the "edge" of the Qur'ān, when "we have reached and exceeded the limits of clear-cut Qur'ānic support for our ideals."[48] In *Feminist Edges of the Qur'an*, Hidayatullah carefully examines the approaches used by exegetes who hold commitments both to gender justice and the Qur'ān's status as a divine revelation, and she reflects on the possibility that the former will not always have the latter on its side. She identifies the problems but doesn't try to produce easy pamphlet answers. While asking us to consider new ways of thinking about the Qur'ān when our particular notions of justice no longer live in its text, she refrains from offering a new hermeneutical saccharine to make the words sweet again. So now what?

Various parties make claims that the Qur'ān is *inherently* liberatory or oppressive or progressive or violent. The lived reality of language says that the Qur'ān is inherently nothing but uncontrollable. The Honorable Elijah Muhammad promised a future book that would arrive someday: "There is coming another Islam. You will get another holy Qur'ān."[49] I might imagine it as the *musḥaf Fāṭima*, a lost text from the Prophet's daughter, since the divine force of my dimethyltryptamine vision spoke to me in her form. The revelation of this future scripture can come *every* day; I never know what's going to happen when I read. And I must still decide what I can do with the present Qur'ān. Without a dream of faithfully retrieving the Qur'ān's innermost essence, witnessing this essence as entirely in harmony with my own values, and rescuing my Muslim sisters and brothers from whatever went wrong with human readers outside the text, the urgency of clearly distinguishing what's "inside" the Qur'ān from what's "outside" starts to break down. I still have a Qur'ān and ḥadīth corpus, both of which offer me bottomless reserves of beauty and horror, and neither of which are going away. For me to be a Muslim does not mean that I have sorted out the Qur'ān's thousands of verses and our much larger ḥadīth corpus into a system that can sustain enlightened "Islamic" positions on gender or pluralism or whatever it is that troubles us. I only have the reflections of these words in my present Muslim self.

I have given up hope that we can force a community's twenty-three-year experience of divine communication into a thesis or rulebook by squeezing it between two covers, and I am no longer invested in the hermeneutical authoritarianism, whether progressive or conservative, feminist or antifeminist, that assumes the Qur'ān to possess a perfect unity. A key weakness of hermeneutics as described by Terry Eagleton—its general failure/refusal to "consider the possibility that literary works may be diffuse, incomplete and internally contradictory"[50]—seems to be a more compelling point of departure, though this would hit some readers with theological challenges and probably offer little of value to activists (progressive and conservative alike). Even if we surrender our need for the text to offer a singular, stable platform through the clear univocality of its Author-Father-Lord, maybe there's still something for us in the Qur'ān.

If progressive Muslim hermeneutics is just intuitive esotericism disguised as a critical method, maybe we should go ahead and be mystics. I say this with full seriousness. Mysticism can uphold the power of divine revelation even while releasing you from its words.

The most peace that I have felt with the content of the Qur'ān in recent memory came during my ayahuasca vision. The vision both released me from constraints of the text and bound me to it, since release came only through permission of the text's author. The morning after the ayahuasca ceremony, I recited the Qur'ān in prayer, loving both the text and the author, with no sense of tension or contradiction.

We can find a space for mystical interpretation cracking open in Wadud's *Inside the Gender Jihad*. Wadud takes care to demonstrate that her "No" to the Qur'ān is not reducible to a disavowal of the revelation, but reflects everything around the Qur'ān that interacts with it: No one arrives at knowledge of God through the claims of a text alone, but through various means by which that person interacts with the text, such as prayer, reflection, and observation. She holds stock in these modes of encounter with the Qur'ān: "The text is not the only representative of the divine," she tells us.[51] What I take from Wadud here is an affirmation of *experiential* knowledge that expands the limiting window of a seventh-century revelation. Perhaps what I'm calling "mysticism" here is simply a trust in experiential knowledge: It might be all that I have left. When someone believes in the Qur'ān as the revealed word of God, and *knows* in her heart that God *cannot* be homophobic, then her Qur'ān does not contain a homophobic word. This approach, of course, would have mortified al-Ghazālī, who upheld the prohibition of *tafsīr bi'l ra'y* (tafsīr by opinion) when applied to the reader who would find revelation speaking in accordance with his own opinion (*ra'y*) and inclination or desire (*hawā*), arguing that "if he did not have that opinion and inclination, that meaning would not have appeared to him from the Qur'ān."[52] According to scholars such as Ibn Taymiyya, however, al-Ghazālī himself had transgressed the bounds of personal subjectivity.

Personal mysticism isn't the most useful tool if you care about reforming Islamic legal traditions or establishing a new normative interpretation for 4:34, but those aren't my projects. I do not work with Islamic law, nor do I believe that spousal violence can be defeated by new strategies for reading scripture; I say this as the son of a violent Christian man who would not have been dissuaded from beating his wife by a feminist hermeneutics of the Bible. Nor do I assume that mysticism can solve all social problems, because my wife-beating father was also a mystic of sorts and justified his violence by citing visions and dreams. I'm not interested in mysticism as a device for achieving authority over scriptures or other people; there's no claim to elite classes of knowers or unveilings of hidden secrets here. I want only a way to cling to the Qur'ān for my personal health, even at times that I give up on reading it.

Mysticism can supplement the text, sometimes by producing entire new texts. The mystical theologian (and scourge of both Ibn Taymiyya and modern Salafīs) Ibn al-'Arabī claimed to have received entire texts of Qur'ānic exegesis from Muḥammad in visions, blowing apart our distinction between mystical knowledge and reliance on the Prophet's teachings. Critics of Ibn al-'Arabī accused his mystical texts of straying from (and sometimes outright denying) what they guarded as the clear messages of the Qur'ān. Mystical knowledge might smooth out the problem of upholding origins in a world that changes, since Muḥammad never stops speaking: What

Muḥammad says can no longer be limited to what particular generations preserved or invented of the historical person. For its explosion of the origins, a mystical investment makes for a definitively anti-Salafī move: Personal mysticism affirms inexhaustible multiplicities of meanings without even the flimsy restraints of logical argument or the communal coherence offered by an authoritative imām, let alone the Salafī anchor of transmitted knowledge. Of course, this creates as many problems as it solves. I can anticipate the possible critiques here and agree with them, but I'm still more interested in heading for the Qur'ān's baraka energy fields than seeking nourishment from jurists.

Mysticism can be its own Salafism, since Ṣūfī orders trace their genealogies of masters back to Muḥammad in somewhat Salafī-ish ways—usually through 'Alī, but Abū Bakr has also been represented as an initiatic master. And depending on what the term means to you, Ibn Ḥanbal, the compilers of the Six Books, and Ibn Taymiyya were mystics—certainly not the kinds of mystics who would consider liberation from religious law through drug-induced visions to be legitimate, but mystics nonetheless. Not all their information came from books or transmitted reports; they also received personal communication from Muḥammad himself, centuries after the Prophet's death. It was after seeing Muḥammad in a dream that Bukhārī embarked on his grand *Ṣaḥīḥ* project: In the dream, Bukhārī was swatting flies away from Muḥammad, which he understood to mean that he would rescue the Prophet from fabricated ḥadīths. Dreams in which Muḥammad vouched for the soundness of specific ḥadīth scholars and their transmissions also played a role in arguments for or against them. The legal tradition safeguards against relying on dreams and visions as sources of binding evidence, and interpretations of scriptural exegesis have sought to regulate esoteric interpretation and preserve the authority of exoteric meanings, but the mystical might also loosen the grip of dominant tradition. Ibn Taymiyya once scolded a woman who had attempted to preach at a mosque's pulpit, as this act defied what he understood to be Islamic gender norms; that night, Muḥammad showed up in Ibn Taymiyya's dream and corrected him, declaring that she was a pious woman and that he had behaved unjustly toward her.[53]

Thinking about Elijah Muhammad's promise of a new Qur'ān while reading Elijah Muhammad's FBI file, I began to think of our present Qur'ān as a file that had been edited by an agency to become acceptable for release. In this sanitized public version that we access, wide streaks of black marker run over the important secrets, but mysticism offers one way of running through the archive without an institutional chaperone and accessing the file without redactions. People who need their religion to prove its rationality might say that there's nothing scientific about mysticism, but there's nothing scientific about any of this; we're arguing over what the mystery god intended to say in his address to a mystic in a cave some fifteen centuries ago. When the tradition falls apart and the origins are long gone, my last resort is to drink the vine and dive deeper into my own self. If we can find the authors of divine revelations somewhere in our intestines, they might let us read with them, or give us permission to keep it moving. Either way, the classical interpretive traditions and contemporary literary theories would both lose their urgency.

THE SENSIBLE QUR'ĀN

> . . . while they are dancing, even the most perfect tango performers cannot fully grasp the semantic complexity of tango lyrics.
>
> —HANS ULRICH GUMBRECHT[54]

Without trusting in my own self and the reactions of my body, I wouldn't have an attachment to the Qur'ān. When I first opened the Qur'ān at fifteen years old, I did not yet *believe* in it as divinely revealed, but at least *sensed* a certain power in the book's intimidating weight as it rested in my hands, its beautifully decorated green and gold cover, the gold illuminated by a sunbeam coming through the window, the delicate thin pages. I remember the Arabic script appearing alongside the English translation, establishing both its authenticity and ancient mystery, at least to the exoticizing eyes of an adolescent Orientalist. The content of what I read in translation was actually kind of boring, since I had expected the text to offer a linear narrative. As many first-time readers are frustrated to discover, this is not how the Qur'ān was organized. I do not recall any mind-blowing information from the translator's extensive commentary, but I can still remember the sublime quiet of that college library and how it felt to step back out into the street after returning the artifact to the shelf, energized and disoriented. Before ever registering the Qur'ān for what might be its message, I experienced the Qur'ān as a material object and processed the Qur'ān through my senses.

Is that the start of interpretation? Is it the start of faith? Can someone register the Qur'ān as God's word before actually believing in God?

Our tradition tells stories of Companions who were initially sworn enemies of Muḥammad's prophetic mission, only to then have their hearts transformed by encounters with the Qur'ān. We often conceptualize their (and our) encounters with the Qur'ān strictly as engagements of the rhetorical content, forgetting that our bodies mediate between the words and ourselves—whatever those *selves* might be, if they're not entirely our bodies. The Companions read or heard the Qur'ān while remaining within their bodies, receiving the Qur'ān alongside the constant bombardment of sensory stimulation that goes with the typical experience of being human. The conversion story of 'Umar, for example, centers on his *hearing* discussion of the Qur'ān, followed by his *seeing* the written verses with his eyes, but also refers to other sensory information: the sight of blood after he strikes his sister in the face, the sound of his sister's voice as she speaks to him, the sword that he holds in his hand, his washing with water prior to handling the verses on whatever material they might have been inscribed. We can also imagine the bodily effects of 'Umar's violent rage, the quickening of his breath and pounding of his heart, and perhaps physical panic when he sees what he has done to his sister, after which he regains his composure. Maybe washing himself and then reading the Qur'ān has a calming effect, slowing his breath and centering him; or the power of its words might send an electrifying rush through his body. For every second of that episode, 'Umar's central nervous system was processing two million pieces of sensory information. This did not take place in isolation from 'Umar's effort to grasp the Qur'ān's discourse through his abstract, disembodied, immaterial "mind"; he reflected upon the Qur'ān with a brain that was part of his body. His acceptance of the Qur'ān's truth was a neurobiological event.

'Umar and I both had sensory encounters with the Qur'ān, but it could not have been the same Qur'ān. The mass-printed masḥaf that I held at fifteen would have been unrecognizable to 'Umar, not only for the medium of printed books or an English translation appearing alongside the Arabic, but even for the Arabic script itself, elaborately dotted and voweled. He could not read my Qur'ān any more than I could read his. The culture around the Qur'ān has changed: Though 'Umar's sister tells him to wash before touching the verses, we also have reason to consider that the material production of the Qur'ān was not given the same reverence in their time that it receives in ours. Nor are our bodies the same; if I were magically transported to seventh-century Arabia, simply breathing the air would ravage my modern immune system and kill me within an hour. Just as importantly, the ways in which we understand our bodies are distant from each other.

The question of whether selfhood is biologically or socially formed is not helpful here: We are made of corporeal matter that could be called "natural," but upon entry into the world, this natural body is immediately subjected to the training of learned behaviors and language. Our bodies are not purely biological but also social, since the "body" is a concept that we learn from other people, and this concept varies across societies. My surrounding culture tells me what it means to have a body: Society teaches me about my body through modern categories such as "race," "sexual orientation," and "mental illness." None of these categories are universal: In different times and places, they would be imagined differently and thus construct different bodies.

Even "sight" is a concept that changes throughout history: Premodern science explained sight through theories of extramission (in which the eyes emanate a kind of fire beam that apprehends the perceived object) or intromission (in which the perceived object replicates itself and becomes imprinted upon the perceiver's brain). In the ocular science of another day, questions of whether Allāh can be perceived with human eyes came with added consequences; to see Allāh could mean not only locating Allāh in time and space, but even *touching* him with your eye lasers. My eyes cannot be natural, because it is not only nature that decides their possibilities and limitations.

My eyes are not 'Umar's eyes, so our dreams and visions will not be the same. There's a popular cultural expectation that if you find yourself on the verge of death, you might see your life flashing before you as a montage of scenes. This would have been inconceivable in 'Umar's world, since people did not have the "life-flashing" experience prior to the invention of film: "In 1900," writes media scholar Friedrich Kittler, "the soul suddenly stopped being a memory in the form of wax slates or books, as Plato describes it, rather, it was technically advanced and transformed into a motion picture."[55]

My ears are not 'Umar's ears. In her book on radio, Susan J. Douglas describes a "major perceptual and cognitive shift" and "revolution in our aural environment" brought on by the advent of sonic media.[56] I access the Qur'ān as an mp3 archive, from which hundreds of human voices—some that belong to the living, others to the dead—can be retrieved and made to recite my selected sūras through a computer or car or smartphone. Is it reasonable to expect that sonic media and the transformation of recorded sounds into digital files simply provide new tools to preserve an eternal text, without meaningful interference in the process of interpretation? Or should we ask what *isn't* changed? Should radically different ear cultures produce identical responses to the Qur'ān?

As cultures make the body, bodies in turn make culture: It is only through my body that I can receive and process information from the world and send an understanding from myself back to the world. Knowledge and belief are always embodied and thus remain vulnerable to changes within the body. This had me thinking about Muḥammad's body and the ways in which the Qur'ān authorized itself through effects on his flesh. Muḥammad was not a philosopher reading the Qur'ān strictly as a set of theoretical prepositions; the Qur'ān was a sensory phenomenon as much as an intellectual one. When he first experienced an alien power seizing his body and commanding him to recite words, what could any words have meant in that moment?

The Qur'ān does not provide much clear information about its own process of delivery. The verses of the Qur'ān that discuss revelation appear to be more concerned with the (im)possibility of humans encountering Allāh—that is, how Allāh can or cannot be perceived with human senses, discussed with reference to veils and angelic intermediaries—than the human side of that encounter, how revelation looked, sounded, and felt for Muḥammad. This is an aspect of the Qur'ān that I can find only in literature *about* the Qur'ān, that is, discussions of the Qur'ān in ḥadīths. In the corpus of literatures covering Muḥammad's life, the event of revelation (which is described as tanzīl, "descending") is represented as a physical trauma. The bodily effects upon the Prophet were observable to those around him:

Muḥammad was said to sweat profusely during these experiences, and his face would change. Muḥammad's body increased in heaviness to the point that if he was leaning on a Companion when the revelation hit, the Companion would fear that his own body was about to be crushed. Anti-Islamic polemicists have attempted to use the physical symptoms of revelation as proof that Muḥammad was an epileptic. Scholars who wish to find the "god part of the brain" and examine mystical experience entirely through neuroscience have also sought to understand Muḥammad through these accounts. Both endeavors are weakened by our lack of direct access to Muḥammad's body. To the "Muḥammad was an epileptic" theory, I would suggest that perhaps it's clinically unprofessional to diagnose a patient that cannot be observed (even if these ḥadīths are flawlessly preserved reports from eyewitnesses, which is not guaranteed). To the "neurotheology" people, I say that it's bad scholarship to treat textual reports about Muḥammad as equivalent to having scans of Muḥammad's brain.

What I do find compelling in the ḥadīth accounts of revelation is an idea of the Qur'ān as a shock to the body, an experience of transcendent ecstasy and anguish. The Qur'ān refers to the impact of its recitation on the Companions' bodies: "The skins shiver of those who fear their Lord; then their skins and hearts settle to the remembrance of Allāh" (39:23). After the death of the Prophet, his surviving Companions are said to have discussed the limits of the Qur'ān as an embodied experience. Communal memory records that the Companions were troubled by rumors of Muslims who fainted at the sound of the Qur'ān's recitation. Crying was deemed acceptable, but not the loss of consciousness. 'Ā'isha is reported to have used 39:23 in argument against those who might faint, insisting that the Qur'ān is "nobler than to have people lose their minds from it." For the Companions and/or the custodians of their memory, the integrity of reading had to be maintained. Despite their efforts to protect the Qur'ān's sobriety, later literatures would continue to report of Muslims who became ecstatic or fainted at the sound of beautiful recitation; in the eleventh century, a Shāfi'ī scholar even compiled a book on individuals who had died upon hearing the Qur'ān.[57] I am not dead, but my body has been shocked and disturbed (in the right way) by listening to the Qur'ān. I could share in the crying and trembling with my sisters and brothers, even if we did not share the same understanding of the words. Which mattered more?

I recognize the Qur'ān as something that happened first in Muḥammad's body, then in the bodies of his Companions—who saw and heard and touched him, even as the revelation was taking place—and then in the bodies of the Followers, who could sit at the Companions' feet and inherit from them. And then in the bodies of the Followers of the Followers, and so on. Some Muslims, consumed with the imperative to make Islam rational and "modern" and/or define their religion in contrast to the Christian deification of Jesus, often seem embarrassed by ḥadīth reports in which Muḥammad's body is depicted as having miraculous powers. Such stories, they argue, constitute departures from the pure monotheism of the Qur'ān. Trying to imagine what the Qur'ān might have represented in the age of the Companions, and the significance of Muḥammad's body as the site of Allāh's textual disclosure to the world, it becomes less of a problem for me. Perhaps our efforts to keep the Qur'ān entirely a collection of textual statements for critical analysis reflect the more dramatic departure.

Sometimes the revealed discourse can come alive for me, but I also find myself moving away from the Qur'ān as an intellectual quest. The Qur'ān's significance might come when I recognize my eyes, ears, mouth, and nose as orifices of arousal, penetration, and perhaps even comprehension. For the Qur'ān to make sense, I need it to be sensual. I don't just *read* the Qur'ān; I also *see* it with my eyes. To see the Qur'ān provokes a physical response, with or without reading and comprehension. The Qur'ān can be written in calligraphy so elaborate that it seems to have been designed to render the text unreadable. Like an abstract painting, this Qur'ān might empty itself of content to deny all interpretation, demanding that it be received in the immediacy of its being, not the consequences of its argument.

I *hear* the Qur'ān. Like calligraphers who beautify the divine text as an act of devotion, reciters can beautify the Qur'ān with their voices. This is an experience of the Qur'ān that remains with the original Arabic; the rhythms and rhymes defy translation and must be taken as they are. Listening to the Qur'ān, or moving my own mouth to reproduce the Qur'ān, has caused a tingling through my body even at times that I could not capture the content; I have been floored by Allāh's speech even when the *sounds* could not function as meaningful *words*. The mode of delivery matters; something can happen to verses that are used to justify violence, communal intolerance, and sexism, or even verses on mundane matters such as inheritance laws or the prohibition of incest, when recited in a manner that softens the hearts. On the other side, verses that are usually read to emphasize mercy and compassion could produce new meanings if someone were to scream the verses as though in torture. Because most of the world's

Muslims are not native Arabic speakers, and I went through much of my Muslim life without seriously studying Arabic, I remain mindful of contexts in which the Qur'ān as an aural experience potentially conveys meanings that cannot be located in dictionaries or grammar textbooks, just as a song does not communicate exclusively or even primarily through its lyrics.

I have a copy of the Qur'ān that its previous owner had heavily scented with oils. After almost twenty years, this Qur'ān still has a distinct *smell*, which forever attaches what I read in this Qur'ān to him and the time in my life when I had known him. The Qur'ān also proves itself on my skin, as I *touch* the Qur'ān; my lips kiss the revelation. I can even taste and ingest the Qur'ān: Healing practices such as writing verses of the Qur'ān on material, washing off the ink, and then swallowing the rinsings as medicine find endorsement in the opinions of early Salafī-approved figures such as Ibn Ḥanbal.

The Qur'ān's power extends beyond its ability to make convincing arguments or dazzle listeners with eloquent speech. Whether actualized with sound or sight, the Qur'ān's very presence intervenes in its surroundings: The Qur'ān's recitation or inscription of verses on amulets and talismans repels the Shayṭān. In some contexts, a Qur'ānic amulet was called ḥijāb, the same term used to describe a woman's headscarf, for its function of "covering" or protecting the wearer from evil.[58] Even coins bearing Allāh's name can become carriers of the sacred. With or without sharing the conception of reality in which these practices operate, I can say that my embodied experience of the Qur'ān brings its own power. Sensual encounters with the Qur'ān activate a mental archive of images and stories, myths and memories, to achieve changes in my condition with or without deliberate effort at interpretation.

I am not so naive to think that we can escape the problems of interpretation through our flesh, but perhaps "meaning" isn't the only meaning. My body is the site at which narratives meet neurons. Some of my most powerful experiences in Muslim prayer have come not through intellectual reflections on the words that I recited, but sensory overload: praying eighty dizzy rakats at a mountaintop mosque outside Damascus after running up the mountain through Syria-in-July heat with no water, or quietly reciting the Qur'ān while gazing upon the graves of Ibn Taymiyya and Ibn al-'Arabī, or losing myself in the mosh pit around the Ka'ba in Mecca, buzzing out in a jumble of sweaty pilgrims' bodies. Or my slow and clumsy prayer at the Islamic Center of Los Angeles after a mujāhidīn ayahuasca trip. The ayahuasca vision was not reducible to chemical effects; the chemicals worked in negotiation with my socially acquired knowledge. My body processed ayahuasca through a storehouse of ideas that had become significant for me, causing the dimethyltryptamine to produce/become Fāṭima. The Prophet's daughter as I witnessed her was formed from a collaboration between texts and drugs, language and flesh, and our conversation in my blood became a new text for me to read.

This retreat into my body cannot offer a new interpretive system with the appearance of critical rigor. It only allows me to keep my love for the Qur'ān, which might have more to do with physical responses than philosophical harmony or linguistic coherence. This means that I remain bewildered by the Qur'ān and can love it even when I am troubled by what it seems to be saying. I can love the Qur'ān for more than the truth of its words, and with more of me than my literacy.

Even if I have lost much of my desire for a Qur'ān that can be translated or interpreted, the words have not disappeared. I experience a Qur'ān that simultaneously demands and rejects its interpretation. My Qur'ān can still say things, but its messages appear to me less as building blocks of a comprehensive thesis than as bits and pieces of overheard conversation, or screen captures of text messages sent from an unknowable author to an unknowable reader. The statements are not meaningless, but I am missing most of the story and can comment only on how they read to me. I'm not interested in pushing my own ideas about ethics or justice onto the Qur'ān and calling it the real "Qur'ānic ethics" or "Qur'ānic justice." Rather, I have a preexisting notion of justice that I bring to the Qur'ān. This is a lesson that I take in part from Malcolm X, who said that he believed in a religion that believed in freedom, and that if a religion kept him from fighting for his people's freedom, he would say, "To hell with that religion." Whether surrendering himself to the intellectual custodianship of Elijah Muhammad or the scholars at al-Azhar and the Muslim World League, Malcolm trusted his inner ethical compass as an authentic source of Islam.

My own sense of justice can be awakened not only by scholarly argument with sound theoretical framework and proper citations, but also a slam poet whose words come with a booming voice and swinging hands, and I receive the Qur'ān more as slam poetry than an academic journal article. For the Qur'ān to present a legal system is not the only way that it can help to make a better world. Recognizing the Qur'ān as a twenty-three-year event that took place nearly fifteen hundred years ago, I am drawn to those who witnessed the event and participated in it: the Prophet and his Companions, who *lived* the Qur'ān as a collective brain-melting mystical experience. That's just me. This does not decipher the Qur'ān's "true" meaning or bring me back to the origins, nor does it solve the basic problems of interpreting a text, but highlights supplementary texts that ultimately pose the same problems. Muḥammad's life, I am told, was an embodied Qur'ān, and I attempt to read him as such through the mediation of his Companions' memories. My encounter with the Companions is in turn mediated by their companions, the Followers. And so on, and so on, forever, until now we end up with a faceless, nameless cloud, "The Scholars," whose mediation is supposed to transcend mediation and give us the real thing. What I end up taking from the Qur'ān's expanded universe is only more alienation, a deepening sadness that our pious predecessors are gone forever, because Salafism calls me to place utmost value on the Salaf but cannot actually deliver them.

I do what I can to work with the materials, mindful of their limitations and mine, defenseless against the Salafī charge that I am hopelessly separated from the event of the Qur'ān. Before I can construct an idea of the Qur'ān's eternal message on anything, my own perverse Salafism has deconstructed it, putting me back in my place. I was led to attempt moves away from textual interpretation and toward sensual engagements of the Qur'ān, strangely enough, by my fixation on a word that I sought to interpret: that challenging word from 53:2, *ṣāḥibukum*. This mention of "your companion" inspired me to think about bodies and risk abandoning words. The Qur'ān is more than literature and can be experienced in ways that do not place discourse at the center. Without confidence that literal translation, rational interpretation, or textual representations of the Salaf can transcend my constraints as a reader, I withdraw into a fleshy mysticism that transcends nothing, that seeks to go *in* rather than *up*. While this actually has precedents in the lived tradition, my sensory encounters nonetheless represent deviations from the Salaf, both because of the artifact that is encountered and the senses with which I encounter it. The Qur'ān that I register with my senses is not the Qur'ān of the Salaf. The world in which I was made produces a different Qur'ān, and also different bodies, than was imaginable in the Salaf's time. Unable to transcend my flesh, I cannot claim the ways of the Salaf, because my very skin is nothing but heretical innovation.

In whatever avenue I take to the Qur'ān, I arrive only at my own lack, defined by the pathetic limits that my humanity forces upon the eternal. There is no reading the Qur'ān "as it is," even if I see this as the ideal, even if my Salafī urge requires it. The Qur'ān creates needs that it cannot satisfy and issues commands that I cannot obey. The Qur'ān points me to supreme absence because its author leaves meanings beyond my reach, the heroes who could pin down its words for me are long dead there is no one alive who can show me how to imitate the dead, and no text that can actualize the law of the ancients exactly as they would apply it to the bodies of my world. The Qur'ān becomes a kind of graveyard, which I mean in the most reverential and loving way, since the Qur'ān's own words could be interpreted to say that graves show us our true condition.

To be a Muslim (as far as I grasp what it means to be a Muslim), I allow the Qur'ān to actually hold a power over me, while accepting that what it gives me will not be its truest meaning that must be embraced by everyone. This is where the body again comes into play: If my encounter with the Qur'ān is embodied, it will, at some point, situate me in regard to bodies other than my own. Because my reading relates me not only to a book but also to communities, what I *do* with the Qur'ān in physical space matters as much to me as what I *think* about the Qur'ān in private contemplation. The Qur'ān of my body must undergo translation into a Qur'ān for the mosque. This is where I am thankful for the communities that do want the Qur'ān to clearly tell them things and who simultaneously pad the Qur'ān with elaborate interpretive traditions. They keep their prayer rows straight, and their various modes of knowledge provide me with reliable Muslim scripts at times that I need them.

I am taken back to my post-ayahuasca prayer at the Islamic Center of Los Angeles, when my unspeakable inner blasphemies were transmuted into outward conformity. Standing together in prayer, shoulder-to-shoulder and feet-to-feet in straight lines; facing the same qiblah; and following the same imām was enough to fill the gaps between our interpretations of verses. It is not valuing what the Qur'ān says that makes me a Muslim, but rather seeking the effects that the Qur'ān produces. For the Qur'ān's effects to direct my movement in harmony with my sisters and brothers, however, I actually need more than the Qur'ān. Performing my love for the people of the mosque, I draw from both our shared revelation and our shared language of inherited bodily practices, which at least presents itself as derived from the Salaf. With this in mind, imagining the Qur'ān and the tradition of the Salaf as two separate entities does not strike me as useful: Their intersection produces the body of text through which we produce our Muslim bodies.

The Qur'ān is like the Ka'ba: When you view the Ka'ba from far away, it is impossible to read the gold Qur'ānic calligraphy that ornaments the structure's black veil, the kiswa, let alone recognize that in fact every inch of the kiswa bears calligraphy as well. I do not know the discursive content of the Ka'ba's veil, but I don't have to read those words for the Ka'ba to *work* as the Ka'ba, for it to do what the Ka'ba does.

I remember the first time that I stood in front of the Ka'ba. I had walked into the Haram with my gaze lowered, my intention being that I would not first witness the Ka'ba from around a corner or with a column obstructing my view. I looked down until seeing the feet of pilgrims walking their circuits around the Ka'ba. Knowing that I was directly in front of the Ka'ba, I raised my head and saw the blackness of the kiswa against the black night behind it and the piercing whiteness of the stadium-style lights.

There were no words for that moment. My attempt to describe it in a book failed; unable to convey that moment's reality with text, I have become an unreliable narrator for the inner conditions of my own self. I am failing it now too. When I saw the Ka'ba, I did not see the embroidered words that covered the kiswa. Disappearing almost entirely within the blackness of the veil, the words could not function as an attempt from an institution to communicate meanings. Nor could the text of the Qur'ān have defined the Ka'ba for me. I had not memorized specific verses about the Ka'ba to prepare me for that moment and was not running over the Ka'ba's origin story in my mind; did I believe that there was ever an Abraham? I did not know where my personal sense of the Ka'ba had come from, or why it meant so much to stand in front of the Ka'ba. If I were to retrace those steps, walking backward through all of the information that I had ever received about the Ka'ba, cataloguing this whole lifetime's stream of texts and images, how systematic or coherent could my experience of Islam look?

Like me, the Ka'ba had a life; it has moved through time: The Ka'ba took a journey to reach this pilgrim. A particular history provided me with this Ka'ba. Though many Muslims express outrage over radical transformations of the holy sites and surrounding city under the modern Saudi regime, these changes only depart from a Mecca that would have already been unrecognizable to the first Muslims: Over the centuries, the Ka'ba has changed in size, shape, and design. Even the Qur'ān verses that presently appear on the Ka'ba would have been unreadable in Muḥammad's era. But somehow, when the house and the pilgrim faced each other, neither of them possessing historically stable selves, the Ka'ba turned out to be real—and my own self seemed real too, anchored by an illusion of the timeless.

Whether or not I would call my encounter with the Ka'ba "mystical"—and *mysticism*, like everything else, is a term that developed over time and through particular regimes of knowledge—the Ka'ba gave me something that defied or at least temporarily suspended the power of books. This is where I am at with the Qur'ān, which exists as so much more than a text to be quoted or critiqued. If we stop asking how, let go, and allow ourselves those wordless moments, antitheologies or erotic theologies, and perhaps recognize that internal, subjective, antirational encounters with our tradition might be what holds the tradition together, we can lose the urgency of treating textual interpretation as anything close to a science. I don't always find the Qur'ān operating as an instruction manual for my life, but this is no longer what I ask from it. The words carry pilgrims to places where words no longer work.

9

PILGRIMS OF THE PROTO-ISLAMIC

>>> *All that you touch,*
You Change.
All that you Change,
Changes you. <<<
—Octavia E. Butler[1]

WHY DO *STAR WARS* characters speak English? The "long, long ago" and "galaxy far, far away" still has to make itself intelligible to the present in our own galaxy. Species such as Wookiees, Ewoks, Jawas, and Hutts are othered and exoticized in part through their unique indigenous languages, but Luke Skywalker, his friends and family, and most of their key allies and opponents speak my language. Because of the long-ago/far-away thing, they can't call it "English"; they speak English where there is no England. While the movies never actually name Luke's language—just as they never explain why the protagonist in this galaxy far, far away looks like a white boy from our world—the novelizations refer to a *lingua franca* called "Basic" through which characters from different star systems and species can communicate with each other. "Basic" has a unique script but in its spoken form remains an earthling tongue. If it didn't, these movies could make no sense to me.

Existing within the limits of a narrative film series that has been made for an audience on this planet, spoken Basic always becomes the audience's language. Basic, therefore, can be dubbed over the original film as Spanish, or Japanese, or Arabic. In at least one case, the form that Basic takes can potentially change relations between characters: Because the "alien" language spoken by Nien Numb in *Return of the Jedi* is actually Kikuyu, a Kenyan language, watching the films dubbed in Kikuyu would make Nien Numb a speaker of the same Basic as everyone else. Anyway, if Luke Skywalker always speaks in the language of the audience, he never has a language of his own: There's no such thing as "Basic" beyond the viewers' need for coherence. It's impossible for me to ever know how Basic is actually supposed to sound, as if the *Star Wars* universe were real and Luke's words were not always created for our ears. This is also my problem as I try to relate to the Qur'ān and Sunna, which came to me from long, long ago and a galaxy far, far away and must speak in the terms of their audience.

After all this, what did I get? I moved books around on the shelf, retraced my steps, and deconstructed. The origins kept calling me, even though I no longer thought of the origins as attainable. Reexamining my 1994 bookshelf, I picked up Yusuf Ali's Qur'ān translation again, repeating my attempt at fifteen to start at the first page and push through until the end. This time, what struck me as the Qur'ān's big points hinged on the question of pain:

1. God is the owner of all pain in the universe.
2. God is able and willing to inflict pain upon us, both in this life and the next.
3. Those who recognize God's ownership of pain and follow his commands will be rewarded with eternal life in a garden completely free of pain.
4. Those who do not submit to God's exclusive control over pain will be subjected to an existence filled with unbearable pain, primarily through God's agents setting them on fire.
5. God has offered this deal consistently throughout human history and has repeatedly destroyed entire nations for turning him down.

Despite the proliferation of verses that describe God as merciful and forgiving, the Qur'ān's content can sometimes read to me like a knife to my throat. It doesn't help much if the god holding the knife says, "But if you follow my orders, I'll give you endless playtime with magical vaginas instead of cutting you, because I am the Compassionate and the Merciful." I have to confess that these are not the terms by which I live my life. But is it Islam? Is it "what the Qur'ān says," or what my eyes showed me because earlier that week, I had been reading Elaine Scarry's discussion of the Bible from her seminal work, *The Body in Pain*? Or perhaps this representation of God as administrator of pain only disturbs me because I live in what Foucault calls the "age of sobriety in punishment," during which public executions in the name of sovereign monarchs have been replaced by prisons that deprive punishment of its theatricality. Today, whether a state inflicts violence upon its citizens publicly or privately gets treated as the marker between civilization and barbarism. If the body still serves as the site of truth, it does so in different ways.

I do not live in the same logic of the body as the Qur'ān's original audience. When I go to mosques and listen to living people explain what they see in the Qur'ān, however, Islam becomes something else: Verses are weighted differently, changing their relationships and meanings. Some of my sisters and brothers rigorously investigate the Qur'ān and see only God's compassion manifesting in verse after verse. Others filter the Qur'ān's verses of pain, punishment, and fear through the Prophet's assurance beyond the Qur'ān's text that divine mercy overwhelms divine wrath. Others still might intuit God as a god of love and know in their hearts that this is really the Qur'ān's heart, with or without seeking confirmation in the words themselves.

The texts of the Qur'ān and ḥadīth corpus are not exactly at the center of our lives as Muslims. They *can't* be, since this is never how texts actually function in the world. This remains a difficult idea to express not only to the folks who get branded as "fundamentalists" or "literalists" but also to arrogant pop-atheist types, who assume that they can prove religion's stupidity and danger by flipping through scriptures and pointing at the statements that they find displeasing. For all their claims to heightened intellectual sophistication, the pop-atheists end up looking as simplistically textualist as anyone. No religion is ever *just the book*, no matter what the book's most passionate advocates claim, because "meaning" is never just the words: Meaning comes from whatever can act with force upon the words.

ISNĀDS VERSUS RHIZOMES

An alleged statement of Muḥammad is authenticated by its isnād, the chain of transmitters that trace it back to one of his Companions, with faith that Companions possess unquestionable integrity as reporters. *Isnād* comes from *sanad*, meaning "support"; the text's honor is supported by a trustworthy reporter asserting that s/he received it from a trustworthy reporter, who in turn had heard it from a trustworthy reporter, and so on, all the way back to its original reporter, an eyewitness to the Prophet. For the ninth-century ḥadīth scholars who became formative figures of what gets called "proto-Sunnism," the science of the isnād served as a means of self-authorization. Through the promises of isnād criticism to retrieve and preserve the original Islam, the Ḥadīth Folk asserted their truth-making power against the claims of rival groups. To look closely at the field of isnād criticism might undermine the vision that many people hold of early Muslim history, which presents philosophers who advocated science and reason as losing a battle with antirational and "fundamentalist" Ḥadīth Folk. This simplified narrative, a post-Enlightenment reading of the pre-Enlightenment past, gets reproduced in the ways that people talk about contemporary tensions in Muslim thought, as though we must retrieve our "lost" legacy of Muslim rationality and let the philosophers finally win (even philosophers, apparently, need their own Salaf). The developers and champions of isnād evaluation, however, weren't exactly opposed to reason; they just recognized the vulnerable subjectivity of what we construct as truth, relying instead on methods of ḥadīth criticism that they treated as a science. In the eyes of the Ḥadīth Folk, it was the rationalists who lacked scientific rigor: Unlike geographers or mathematicians, rationalist philosophers and speculative theologians could produce no definitive answers, only an endless diversity of personal opinions. The promise of isnād evaluation was that truth could be established by a rigorous evaluation of each ḥadīth's lineage of reporters: In that sense, the Ḥadīth Folk were not antirationalist at all. If the chain of transmission withstood critical scrutiny, a ḥadīth was to be accepted bi-lā kayf. It has been argued that even though master ḥadīth critics did consider textual content (matn) as a means of evaluating alleged statements of Muḥammad, they tended to produce their findings as the result of isnād criticism. If a scholar such as Bukhārī found a ḥadīth to be questionable based on what it said, he would rather base his rejection on the flaws of its transmission rather than his personal discomfort. To openly devalue a ḥadīth report based on its textual content—that is, to say that a ḥadīth is unreasonable or that it contradicts the Qur'ān—would mean surrendering the Ḥadīth Folk's assertion of methodological supremacy upon which the entire claim for their authority was founded.[2]

Isnād criticism reproduces textual history in a "family tree" model: An early chain of transmitters stands as the center, the point of origin, from which later transmitters produce a proliferation of branches. Through comparing the branches, we can examine the ways in which ḥadīths developed variations, potentially identifying outliers and revealing which version of a ḥadīth was the oldest and presumably most authentic. At the ends of these branches we have the compilers of ḥadīth collections, such as Bukhārī, who assembled ḥadīths and their authenticating isnāds into massive archives. As these collections gradually accumulated the power of canon, the collections themselves became authentications. We commonly perceive each collection as a mass, undifferentiated block of authority. Bukhārī's collection, properly titled *Al-Jāmī' al-Ṣaḥīḥ al-Musnad al-Mukhtasār min Rasūl Allāh wa sunanihi wa 'Ayyamihi*, is more popularly called *Ṣaḥīḥ al-Bukhārī*, the "Authentic of Bukhārī." In casual conversation, the title is often reduced to his name, conflating the man with his archive: Instead of defending a ḥadīth by its specific line of transmitters, we say simply, "It's in Bukhārī."

Isnād evaluation can be seductive, especially if you work in the humanities but have an inner math dork who otherwise never gets to come out. The isnād is a genuinely amazing tool. I've spent thousands of hours playing detective with chains of transmission, trying to unlock the secrets in straight lines and construct biographies for snippets of texts, losing whole days and nights in those rabbit holes. It's not always clear what I get out of it; sometimes, isnād evaluation feels like a drug in its own right. I lose all sense of any world beyond these names and lines until the sun comes up, and then I have to slowly reintegrate into the shared reality of living bodies.

Whether or not the isnād reliably provides the data that it claims, I am interested in the structuring consequences of the isnād, the way that building our tradition on isnads produces a way of seeing the tradition itself. The isnād presents human relationships in a particular way: Elder scholars transmit units of data to students, who in turn pass the information to their own students, and so on, producing straight textual lineages that branch out like trees. Just as the ḥadīths themselves often leave out the context—presenting exchanges between the Prophet and his Companions as apparently transpiring in a universe of empty space, their interactions backdropped by an unused green screen—isnāds disembody both the teachers and the students. In the isnād, we have names connected by lines that move unilaterally from teachers to students. The immense body of biographical dictionaries will flesh things out a bit more: In these volumes, we can learn where transmitters lived and died, what schools they followed, the remarks that master ḥadīth critics made about them, and so on. The data preserved in biographical dictionaries is what the compilers regarded as essential for examining an isnād's reliability, so it looks at the parties involved in these teacher-student links with a particular set of eyes. I wonder what might happen if different eyes envisioned the dictionaries.

In what master ḥadīth critics called the "science of men," what made someone a trustworthy reporter? In a word, corroboration. Transmitters whose names were associated with the most strongly corroborated reports were recognized as the most reliable sources.[3] Corroboration had to come from scholars who themselves had been deemed trustworthy by this process, and whose personal integrity and memory had been positively assessed by the network. The master ḥadīth critics declared themselves both the referees and winners of a conformity contest, and their network thus reified its own right to control by a circular process of self-authentication.

Scholar Scott C. Lucas named the isnād-centered methodology of ḥadīth transmitter criticism, along with the developing notion of

Muḥammad's Companions possessing universal probity as ḥadīth reporters, among the communal touchstones that contributed to the emergence of Sunnī Islam. In some circles, this is a radical idea, since we don't ordinarily think of Sunnism as *having* an emergence; we assume that Sunnism was always there. When imagined as the generic, universal, undifferentiated and "orthodox" Islam, Sunnism cannot have an origin: Sunnism is taken for granted as the origin from which everything else deviates. Constructs such as Shī'ism, on the other hand, are imagined to have "emerged" as "offshoots" from a primordial Sunnī norm, and thus receive histories that track their founders and points of departure. The "offshoots" are discredited with attacks upon their origins: Shī'ism is accused of having been founded by a Jewish convert seeking to undermine Islam from within; the founder of the Ahmadiyya is likewise believed by conspiracy theorists to have been an agent of the British Empire; the founder of the Nation of Islam is portrayed as a white con-artist. You can tell the logic of a particular orthodoxy by its mode of attack: Polemical stories about sectarian founders are important for people who believe that there are such things as "founders," that truth and falsehood are measured by the origins. Islamophobes seek to debunk Islam altogether by this same logic, attacking all Muslims through charges that Muḥammad was a warmonger, charlatan, megalomaniacal cult leader, and pedophile.

The "family tree" model is commonly used to draw a linear progression of Judaism → Christianity → Islam, each category delivered intact by its founder, with all three sharing in a common metafounder as "Abrahamic" traditions. This is not how I look at the history of religions. The man formerly known as Clarence 13X, who in 1964 changed his name to Allah and is now remembered as "founder" of the Five Percenters, once held up a plate and said, "Whoever made this plate is the god of this plate." But it's hard for me to imagine plates or traditions as products of a singular will.

The model of the family tree mirrors not only the isnād-centered study of ḥadīths, but also the self-imagination of whichever brand wins the privileged status of "orthodoxy." As Christa Bürger observes, trees "indicate the essence of the enemy."[4] The tree model represents tradition as a natural unity, clearly naming the tradition's center and positioning all of the "branches" in relation to that center. "There is always something genealogical about a tree," write Gilles Deleuze and Felix Guattari; "It is not a method for the people."[5] Presenting our tradition's history as a tree cannot help but establish a hierarchy: one group or coterie of great individuals or schools will have their names inscribed on the trunk, while others find themselves relegated to the branches, or the sub-branches, or the twigs at the outermost extremities. The tree model, presenting orthodoxy and heresy as easily observable facts of nature, maps distance from an imaginary center and thus tells us who to take seriously and who to exclude from the conversation. Throughout my Muslim life, I sought the legitimation that trees could offer: In my teen years, I loved that the imām who witnessed my conversion and became my mentor had been taught by Isma'il al-Faruqi, endowing me with a genealogy. Among the Five Percenters, I justified myself as Azreal Wisdom—my name meaning "Azreal No. 2" in their righteous algebra, Supreme Mathematics—heir to the first Azreal, a Companion to the man that they called Allah.

The first Azreal told me that being Azreal is a lonely thing. Despite the tree structure that Azreal might have granted me with his name, Azreal status remains antistructural, an integration of opposites that defies location in one category. Even when teachers incorporate me into their trees, the tree model is not my only option. Deleuze and Guattari present an alternative to the tree in their image of the rhizome, a subterranean stem such as that found with potatoes. In contrast to roots, the rhizome decentralizes. The roots provide an anchor by which the tree "plots a point, fixes an order";[6] the rhizome has no roots to serve as a point of origin. Instead, every point in the rhizome connects to every other point, allowing for no linear chain, no beginning or end. Because it lacks a center, the rhizome cannot have a margin. The rhizome cannot define or uphold notions of orthodoxy or heresy; trees are the better choice for making judgments.

In the case of the isnād, a rhizome-inspired model can redraw these connections to move in more directions than the tree allows. Rhizome-styled isnāds would not represent the transmission of knowledge as a straight path of teacher → student → student's student: Rather, the rhizome might represent students acting upon teachers, students talking to their peers, and teachers acting in response to other teachers, mapping broader networks in which these relationships took place, and even connecting the ḥadīth networks with everything perceived as lurking outside its boundaries: heretics, fringe groups, rebels, philosophers, and popular storytellers. In the question of Islam at large, abandoning the tree for the rhizome means surrendering the quest for roots, as the rhizome, having no beginning or end, is "antigenealogy. It is a short-term memory or antimemory."[7]

A rhizomatic Islam cannot authorize itself by presenting Abraham's footprints in a gold cage.

This book is a rhizome. I begin each of my chapters with epigraphs, ripping quotes from other authors out of their original contexts. The epigraphs reveal both that I say nothing by myself, since I am always writing in conversation with the books that float around me, and also that in my selective citing of other authors, I manipulate and exploit them. But the diversity of sources that contributed to this work demonstrate the impossibility of locating an author within a straight lineage.

The Qur'ān itself reads as a rhizome more than a tree, though of course the Qur'ān has its own vertical isnād: God → Gabriel → Muḥammad → the Companions. But as has been shown, flows between the various links of this chain moved in more than one direction: Verses would descend in relation to the unstable world in which the first Muslims lived, answering the questions that Muḥammad and his Companions asked. Belief in the Qur'ān as uncreated and eternal, preexisting the universe and all these people and events that it discusses, agrees more with the tree model; but in both its process of delivery and the organization of its verses, the Qur'ān is a rootless rhizome. The verses are not ordered chronologically, so the Qur'ān does not allow for an easy retracing of its steps in history. The verse believed to have been the first revelation appears near the end, in the 96th of 104 sūras; the Qur'ān commands, "Recite!" after we have already recited several thousand verses. What is popularly held to have been the final revelation, the "This day I have perfected for you your dīn" verse, appears very early in the book, in the third sūra.

Whether or not it preexisted our universe, the Qur'ān annihilates its own past.

What happens if you try to read the Qur'ān from beginning to end? The Qur'ān, in flagrant defiance of linearity, can be entered at any point and instantly connect you to any of its other points. Any piece of the Qur'ān can be cut off and regenerate itself as the Qur'ān in essence. The Qur'ān has no self-evident center: No part of the Qur'ān can be less "Qur'ān" than any other part, even if verses abrogate each other and we all choose particular bits and pieces to carry with us (the shorter sūras that we have memorized for prayer, or the verses that defend our opinions, or the verses that encapsulate the heart of Islam however we define it, or perhaps the ones that give us heartache) while ignoring or forgetting others. The Qur'ān does not give you a clear journey of A → B, but a maze with infinite entrances and exits, warp zones and worm holes. The Qur'ān speaks of a straight path but remains a text for wanderers. I have never had the experience of reading the last page, closing the book, and feeling that I had followed a path to its conclusion.

Considering how the history of Islam would look when visualized with the tree model, I try to locate a point on that tree that could have represented Islam as I found it. How close to the roots was the particular Islam that I encountered at fifteen? My point of entry was Malcolm X; on what branch does he belong? Even if the post-NOI, reborn-in-Mecca, "I pray with white people" version of Malcolm is the one that made my entry possible, my image of Malcolm cannot be reduced to his Sunnī turn. I was inspired to pursue knowledge of Islam by Malcolm's first conversion, his rebirth in prison as a follower of the Honorable Elijah Muhammad. My encounter with Malcolm came at a time in which the pop-culture revival of Malcolm's legacy and the rise of Louis Farrakhan's stardom enabled each other. As Zaheer Ali's work has shown, their mutually supported ascents came through a hip-hop culture that promoted both of them without tension, making no theological or sectarian distinction between them (or even between NOI Malcolm and post-Mecca Malcolm).[8] Becoming a Sunnī Muslim through Malcolm's journey in and out of the NOI, owing my image of Malcolm to both Elijah and the Saudi state, could I say that I had embraced the Islam of the trunk, the "mainstream," or the sub-branch of a sub-branch? Where do I locate myself now—how do you position a Muslim for whom both Isma'il al-Faruqi and the former Clarence 13X are righteous ancestors, or a Muslim who was brought back to the mosque by hallucinogens? I have prayed at the bodily remains of both Ibn al-'Arabī and Ibn Taymiyya, prayed at the tomb of Bilāl because the NOI brought me to him, prayed behind Amina Wadud as a son of her thought, and performed an 'umra in Mecca as a Five Percenter on behalf of my teacher Azreal, breaking down the ritual acts with Supreme Mathematics. This is where the tree model fails. Instead of claiming one branch or another, I might envision Islam as fallen leaves that I have raked into a pile: Their relationships are now determined not by the branches from which they came, but the power of my tool and labor to gather them together.

CASE STUDY: PITTSBURGH

During my stint at the First Muslim Mosque of Pittsburgh, I did not know that it was the city's alleged "hotbed of Salafism." Nor did I know its history, or even consider that it had history. I did not yet think of the lives of mosques.

What would become Pittsburgh's Salafī community first emerged in the 1920s as the local center for another movement, Noble Drew Ali's Moorish Science Temple of America (MSTA). The leader of the MSTA's Pittsburgh chapter, Walter Smith Bey, was a former Christian preacher, leading a Moorish congregation comprised entirely of former Christians. In his efforts to provide Islamic instruction to these new Muslims, Bey was assisted by Dr. Muḥammad Yusuf Khan, who had come to the United States from India. Khan, a self-described "Educator, Psychologist, Metaphysician, Divine Medium . . . an authority of Sufi philosophy and the Eastern subjects"[9] had previously attempted to spread Islam in Chicago, where he took out ads in black newspapers calling them to the religion "of your forefathers" and had been accused of selling healing powers.[10] Conversion to Islam, his pamphlets boasted, would "tone down your nervous excitement," "improve temperament," and "teach you how to have the thrill of influencing and controlling people in your personal relations."[11] Bouncing between Chicago, Pittsburgh, Cleveland, and Cincinnati, he seems to have financed his movement through selling lectures and correspondence courses (on "metaphysical science" and Ṣūfism), imported turbans and fezzes, charms, "dust from a prophet's tomb," twenty-five-cent prayers, and mosque membership fees.[12]

Coming to Pittsburgh's Moorish Science chapter in the early 1930s, Khan eventually took over as sole instructor and introduced some radical changes to the group, starting with reliance on the Qur'ān (rather than Noble Drew Ali's text, popularly known as the "Circle 7

Koran") and ḥadīths of the Prophet Muḥammad. He also encouraged Moors, who generally suffixed their birth names with *Bey* or *El*, to adopt what he considered to be fully Islamic names (Walter Smith Bey thus changed his name to Nasir Ahmad). In a major departure from MSTA practice, Khan instituted the five daily prayers. It appears that these moves caused a schism in the group between Moors who followed Khan's reforms and those who insisted on the teachings of Noble Drew Ali. A general assembly of the male members engaged in "heated discussion" and possibly violent altercations. It was even alleged that a "disgruntled brother" bombed the mosque.[13] Khan's supporters followed him into what they conceptualized as more "traditional" or "global" Islam. The split among the Pittsburgh Moors seems to have corresponded to similar schisms in other northeastern cities and a "significant exodus from the MSTA" following Noble Drew Ali's death in 1929, "one that would . . . lead to a change in the direction of the history of Islam in America."[14]

Khan, who had come to the United States bringing "books and Islamic reading material of all kinds," started a school for members to study Arabic, study the Qur'ān and ḥadīths, and hold lectures and discussions on "the implication of Islam in the Western World." He was also a member of the Ahmadiyya, and his work in Chicago had been part of the larger Ahmadiyya missionary project. Khan named Walter Smith Bey/Nasir Ahmad the head of the Ahmadiyya for the Ohio Valley region and, through this camp of attritioned MSTA members, turned Pittsburgh into the "center for a new wave of Ahmadiyya Islam."[15]

Through claims to possess greater knowledge of classical Islam than what Moorish Science offered, Khan had emerged triumphant among the Pittsburgh Moors. By the mid-1930s, however, the same questions of authenticity would force his departure, as Pittsburgh Muslims increasingly came to regard Khan's belief in Mirza Ghulam Ahmad's prophethood as unacceptable. Khan also fell out of favor at his Cleveland base, as his handpicked deputy, Chaudhri Mohammed Ashraf—who had scammed the community with outrageous charges for Urdu lessons and who required Ahmadiyya identification cards, photographs, fingerprints, and legal name changes from his followers—was chased out of town and Khan's own possessions were auctioned off as compensation for the mosque's troubles.[16]

The faction in Pittsburgh's second Muslim schism that drove out Khan for his views on Mirza Ghulam Ahmad would become the founders of the First Muslim Mosque.[17] The Pittsburgh community seems to remember this as a conflict pitting Ahmadiyyas against Sunnīs, though it appears to have been between rival factions *within* the Ahmadiyya: the Qadianis, who upheld Mirza Ghulam Ahmad's prophethood, and the Lahoris, who denied it.[18] Pittsburgh's Lahori faction would eventually leave the Ahmadiyya altogether in the late 1930s to join the Addeynu Allahe-Universal Arabic Association (AAUAA), a Sunnī group founded by Muhammad Ezaldeen. Born James Lomax and widely known as Lomax Bey, Ezaldeen was himself a formerly high-ranking MSTA official in Chicago who had left the MSTA, undergone Sunnī religious training in Egypt, and returned home to teach that Black people were the original Arabs.[19] Robert Dannin writes that Ezaldeen's "principal collaborator" in the AAUAA was none other than Nasir Ahmad, the former Walter Smith Bey.[20]

From the 1940s on, the history of the First Muslim Mosque is entirely Sunnī, which almost makes for an end of history, because it can be difficult to map the mosque's journey from one variety of Sunnism to another. I don't know the moment at which this mosque adopted the mission statement presently found on its website:

> We ascribe to the understanding of Islam upon the pristine way of the pious predecessors, as-Salaf us-Salih, and we do not believe there is any other way to success except upon that.[21]

I have a small booklet by Jameela Hakim, *History of the First Muslim Mosque of Pittsburgh, Pennsylvania*, which was published in 1979. She writes as a member of the community in the decades after its Sunnification, but explicit Salafī language is not yet there. We could question whether the mosque in the 1970s would have been "Sunnī" enough for the Muslims who occupied it during my time there in 1995, or if the 1990s mosque could satisfy the institution as it runs today.

At first glance, we can easily draw a linear trajectory for the mosque's history, as it appears to progressively become more "orthodox" in stages as the decades roll on. But the mosque takes part in several interconnected histories, and none of these shifts could have transpired as sudden flicks of a switch. The transformations from Moorish Science to Ahmadiyya, or from one version of Ahmadiyya to another, or from Ahmadiyya to Sunnī, or between competing versions of Sunnism, came as processes, with the before/after divisions much harder to draw than we might expect. If each new chapter came as a shift in the consciousness of a *community*, an assemblage of bodies moving together, it could not have materialized with a collective born-again moment. These "chapters" cannot be so cleanly divided as chapters in a book. There are weird spaces between them that have no names. The mosque's whole history could be imagined as a sequence of in-between spaces.

Islam as I experienced it at the First Muslim Mosque of Pittsburgh—an Islam described with boasts like "authentic" and "orthodox"—rested on a legacy that its own rules would deem inauthentic and heretical: Moorish Science, different strands of the Aḥmadiyya, and possibly inadequate Sunnīs. The local "hotbed of Salafism" has no history without the followers of two men, one from 1920s Chicago and the other from late-nineteenth-century Punjab, who claimed to be prophets. Praying, eating, sleeping, and learning at that Salafī mosque, I took part in a tradition that was also Moorish Science and Aḥmadī. Even the earliest Sunnism of the mosque was one that had come through former Moorish Science adherents and brought Sunnī knowledge from Egypt into conversation with Black Israelite doctrines.

The mosque's Salafism is in debt to its non-Salafism; for it to have been the city's *First* Muslim Mosque, it has to acknowledge its entire life as a mosque, which includes its pre-Salafī history. The trajectory of the First Muslim Mosque of Pittsburgh illustrates the turn to tradition as a rupture, a break. Tradition arrives not as a comfort but a shock. When it first shows up, tradition unsettles and destabilizes; it can do none of the things that tradition is supposed to do, because it is not yet empowered as "tradition."

On the other hand, tradition has to be expressed in terms that can be understood and accepted. Tradition must sell itself by terms that are already meaningful to its new audience. What is presented as "tradition" must somehow become relatable to that which exists outside tradition; no matter how badly its advocates want to purge their environment of what they deem inauthentic, tradition cannot attain the perfectly receptive "blank slate" on which it writes itself with no interference. Tradition always carries an integrated history.

This has consequences beyond the First Muslim Mosque of Pittsburgh. We like to imagine Mecca's pre-Islamic history as the complete antithesis of what Mecca would become after Muḥammad: The age before Islam is thus called Jahiliyya, "Ignorance." In this narrative, society was overrun with greed, oppression, inequality, cruelty, slavery, misogyny, tribalism, and superstition before the arrival of Islam turned everything into its opposite, like the flipping of a switch. But if Muḥammad's mission was so radically unthinkable to the people of Mecca, how did it succeed? If the Jahiliyya time was so "ignorant," how could people have had the means to recognize Muḥammad's mission as divinely mandated?

The knee-jerk answers would assert that this achievement of the impossible proves the miracle of Islam, or that Islam overcame the Jahilī culture by speaking directly to the innate core of human beings, their *fitrah*. But when we look at the terms in which Islam could be presented, we find that language actually mattered: however "innate" our primordial dispositions towards "truth" might be, truth still has to come through language. The notion of conversion as a dramatic self-transformation informs conversion narratives both of the earliest Muslims and converts in our own world: Imprisoned, addicted, degraded Detroit Red is suddenly saved by exposure to Islam and turns into Malcolm X. But for Islam to have transformed Malcolm (or the Prophet's Companions) so deeply, it could not have been entirely alien; it had to make itself intelligible. Malcolm's jahiliyya could not have been absolute. He had to already know something about truth in order to value and recognize truth when it came; and truth had to speak his language, meeting him within his own field of knowledge, proving itself by the terms that he set. This is why the common assessments of Elijah Muhammad as "syncretic" for having "mixed" Islam with Christianity or black nationalism, or portrayals of the seventh-century Muḥammad "plagiarizing" from Judaism and Christianity to invent a new religion, make no sense to me. We never use terms like *syncretism* to describe an "orthodox" text such as *A Brief Illustrated Guide to Understanding Islam*, though it clearly brings us an Islam that is supplemented with other forces and transformed by them.

There can be no Islam if people don't already have the eyes to see it coming. Popular representations of Islam's origins do allow for truth-knowing power in the Jahiliyya time, with claims that Muḥammad's mission was foretold and confirmed by dreams, physical marvels, and even polytheist soothsayers. No matter how sharp and clear a line we draw between the "before" and "after" stages of Islam's history, Muḥammad's mission required endorsement from Jahiliyya modes of knowledge. Today, the endorsement might come from science, as some Muslims argue that the Qur'ān's discussions of human fetuses display advanced knowledge that Western embryology could only confirm centuries later. Or feminism: Muslims might insist that the Qur'ān spoke of gender equality long before the idea was even conceivable in Europe. Or US civil religion and "interfaith" dialogue:

Muslims dig through the Qur'ān with confidence that they will find all of their cherished principles of pluralism, egalitarianism, social justice, and freedom of personal conscience waiting for them. Or New Age drug shamanism: Drink ayahuasca, see Fāṭima, and get yourself back to the mosque. Or lineages that were already Muslim, but perhaps not Muslim enough for some measures: When Malcolm X stood before the Ka'ba in Mecca, he might have done so as a guest of the Saudi state, but he also stood on the shoulders of the Honorable Elijah Muhammad. At no moment in history—whether in Muḥammad's own lifetime or any of the generations that followed him—have Muslims ever witnessed Islam-in-itself, Islam as it would appear in complete insulation from everything non-Islam.

For a case similar to the First Muslim Mosque of Pittsburgh on a larger scale, consider the Sunnification of the Nation of Islam following the 1975 passing of Elijah Muhammad. After the ascension of Elijah's son, Warith Deen Mohammed, the Nation of Islam moved away from its doctrines of divine scientist-imāms and racialized theodicies, heading toward an Islam that was simultaneously old and new. But the NOI's process of Sunnification was only authorized by the fact that these people were *already* Muslims and cared about their status as Muslims. If the NOI had simply dismissed its entire history as inauthentic, it would have lost its cohesion as a community: Without a profound investment in Elijah Muhammad and what he had given them, there would have been no reason to move toward a different kind of Islam, and Warith Deen would have possessed no justifiable power by which he could lead them to it. Warith Deen's authorization came from his position as the gifted son of a man who had been recognized as a divinely guided messenger, and the designation of Warith Deen for future greatness as an infant by his father's teacher, who had been recognized as Allāh in person.

Conversion to Islam happens as a network of points that connect at the new Muslim, rather than a single line drawn between the convert and whatever had provided the first exposure. Alexander Russell Webb (1846–1916), popularly regarded as America's first Muslim convert and proselytizer, only embraced the appearance of Islam that a variety of intersections made accessible to him. Islam became a possibility for Webb, a member of the Theosophical Society, through his Theosophist belief that at their esoteric cores, all religions expressed the same shared reality. The particular representation of Islam that resonated with him came from modernist reformers in colonial India such as Sayyed Ahmad Khan, Ameer Ali, and Chiragh Ali. Finally, he filtered this brand of Islam through his own Victorian assumptions about race, gender, civilizational progress, Christianity, the wisdom of the "East," rationality, modernity, and the truth-seeking individual. As Webb's biographer, Umar F. Abd-Allah, writes, "In all that he did, Webb was unmistakably Victorian. Even in going against the Victorian mainstream, he proceeded to do so in a Victorian way."[22] The Islam to which Webb converted had to be a Victorian Islam.

I tried to draw a rhizome-modeled map of the things that produced Islam as I found it in the 1990s and soon realized that this wasn't simply "Islam in the 1990s" but Islam *for me*. Starting with Malcolm X, I charted the relationships between figures, movements, powers, and discourses as they fell into each other and became an assemblage that I would name "Islam." Malcolm led me to Yusuf Ali's translation of the Qur'ān, which emerged from the same British colonial milieu to which the Ahmadiyya movement developed as a response. In the 1990s, Yusuf Ali's work (in highly revised form) was still the translation preferred by the Saudi government and connected media networks, leading to a strong likelihood that it would be the first Qur'ān to find my hands. My encounter with Yusuf Ali's Qur'ān, in the rhizome map, stands at an intersection of Malcolm X, late twentieth-century Saudi state power, and early twentieth-century British colonialism. It was also British power that led to the birth of Pakistan, where I would study Islam in a mosque built by Saudi royal money. The Ahmadiyya movement, developing within the web of religious communal relations that took shape under British rule, became highly significant for the modern representation of Islam as inherently antiracist, and its presence in the United States was crucial for the development of the Nation of Islam. The NOI, of course, interacted with other forces to produce Malcolm. Malcolm's criticism of the United States as a global oppressor led me to heroize a man who voiced that same critique and led his people to revolution a decade and a half after Malcolm's assassination: the Ayatollah Khomeini, whose face covered my bedroom wall, despite my staunch Sunnī commitment.

Reconstructing my Islam as a rhizome, the Qur'ān and Prophet could not claim the center, but instead constituted two hubs in a network. My rhizome-Islam had no center, because every point became a center for countless points that also linked to each other and became hubs themselves. By the time that I grew exhausted with this project, the map looked insane but also strangely coherent, as though these disparate items were meant to add up, like they really became a thing together: "Islam" in quotation marks. Throw in stuff like the Gospel of Barnabas, mosque pamphlets, how-to-pray videos, Ahmed Deedat, "scientific proofs for the Qur'ān" arguments, a sizeable body of literature explaining how Islam gave women all the rights that they would ever need, 1990s hip-hop, books from Afrocentric indie presses about the color of Jesus, my Malcolm X T-shirt and Africa medallion, and the Islamic Center of Rochester, New York. This was an Islam that could have made sense for some; I was certainly not the only Sunnī convert in the Clinton years who walked in through those gates.

My real point of entry into this rhizome was not even Malcolm; the seminal group Public Enemy, which consisted partly of NOI members, provided my point of entry into Malcolm X. Professor Griff constructed a global Blackness and global Islam in which Malcolm and Farrakhan both received shout-outs alongside Khomeini and Gaddafi, non-Muslim revolutionaries such as Che Guevara, and Afrocentric scholars such as Ivan van Sertima. Without mentioning Malcolm's name, Arrested Development's "Fishin' 4 Religion" reproduced Malcolm's critique of Black churches. I also owed something to Naughty by Nature. Though they did not identify with Islam or speak of Malcolm, Naughty by Nature's 1991 song "Ghetto Bastard" opened up hip-hop as a safe space for the exploration of my world: The verse "Never knew my dad, motherfuck the fag" spoke to me as though it had been recorded only for my ears. My Public Enemy tapes likewise spoke of the urgency of fatherhood—"Put a man in the house and all the bullshit stops"—in ways that nourished a thirteen-year-old white boy trying to figure himself out. Hip-hop gave an affirmation to my fatherlessness that also informed my reception of fatherless Malcolm.

My exposure to hip-hop culture had come through *Yo! MTV Raps*, which I had initially started watching because I wanted to see MC Hammer. So MC Hammer, not only a pop rapper but also a Christian minister, opened the door for me to accumulate a web of resources that would, in my eyes at least, invent itself as Islam, and then invent me, and allow me to reinvent it in turn. Maybe this kind of thing is more immediately obvious with the convert, since discussion of my Muslim status always turns to how I moved between categories. We have a more difficult time recognizing conversion experiences *within* Islam.

When someone converts, what is the actual change that takes place? What is marked by the recitation of shahāda in front of witnesses? What degree of transformation enables the convert to become an ingredient in the making of Muslim community? How much of a convert's pre-Muslim life really gets erased, and what of Islam does the convert rewrite? What if we asked these questions of converts throughout history, considering the ways in which Islam was filtered through pre-Islamic modes of knowing truth? Contrary to popular "conversion by the sword" narratives, the Islamization of new Muslim territories came gradually and through complex processes of blending and negotiation. Something changes when I think of all conversions as potential acts of violence upon Islam, while also broadening my definition of "convert" to include every Muslim ever. The funny thing is that some don't even accept "convert" as a designation, insisting that you call us "reverts." But I cannot speak for the return that is claimed.

With full confidence in my knowledge and power at fifteen to recognize absolute truth, I judged the Qur'ān to be a genuine revelation from the creator of the universe, and Muḥammad to have been the single greatest human being who had ever lived. I made the decision to become Muslim and defended my choice to others as having resulted from my careful consideration of logical, scriptural, historical, and even scientific evidence; but then I adopted the transcendent guidance of the Qur'ān and the Sunna as my protection against the flimsy subjectivity of human reason and rational proof. I did not see the irony then, and many fail to see it now: Following my prejudices and predispositions, I chose to "surrender" to divinely revealed sources, which in turn empowered me to condemn others who adhered only to their prejudices and predispositions. I became a Muslim through embracing arguments that satisfied my desires and opinions, and *then* decided that desires and opinions were my enemies. The reality is that I was always in charge: Bearing witness to the truth of Islam meant that I perceived my personal assessments of the Qur'ān and Muḥammad to have been divinely guided.

The pamphlets assure me that Islam offers an answer to the supposed extreme individualism and moral relativism that plague godless "Western" modernity. But if Islam's solution is possible only when I *choose* to identify myself as a Muslim, and the field of power relations in which I live enables that decision—and Islam itself, as I understand it within this field, must also affirm my power to decide—the foundations of Western secularism's alleged "anything goes" culture survive unthreatened. Islam becomes another consumer path, the cultivating of individual selfhood through adoption of particular lifestyle brands. Authoritarian religious scholars lack coercive power over us without our consent; so they *ask* us to grant them dominance, and they offer persuasive arguments for why we should make that choice and buy into their brands. In recognizing our power to choose them, the experts admit that they have already lost. Today's 'ulama promote themselves through the same channels as singers and comedians. The most globally influential Sunnī scholar, Yūsuf al-Qaraḍāwī, achieved his worldwide gravitas through hosting a program on Al-Jazeera and founding a website. While endowed with the necessary scholarly credentials, he remains an entertainer in show business and must compete for his audience. While scholar-brands present themselves as custodians of an eternal Tradition and necessary guides for ignorant masses, they must also provide what will make the ignorant masses happy, always negotiating with the needs of the market.

AFTER AUTHENTICITY: DĪN-ENTERTAINMENT

The tradition can only be tied down after it wanders too far, and there's no "too far" until it has already gone there. "Orthodoxy" as a concept represents innovation, an attempt to protect the origins from change by imposing new regulations that inevitably produce more change.

To act as a proper guardian of orthodoxy, one must first define the thing that needs protection. This is often the work of formal creeds. Since the creedal articulation of orthodoxy's terms is provoked by the emergence of troublesome heresies, there is no orthodoxy that can exist before its violation: Rigidly defined orthodoxy itself is the offshoot, the product of historical change. What pamphlets present as the creed of the Salaf, stressing affirmation of Allāh's attributes and the uncreatedness of the Qur'ān, could not have drawn the line between belief and disbelief before they figured into a power struggle. Orthodoxy is created by heretics.

What happens if our greatest protection against innovation, the Sunna, turns out to be a social construction that evolved over time, changing in both its meaning and significance? Or if the ultimate orthodoxy-making mechanism, the dream of scholarly consensus (‘ijma), had originated with efforts to defend accepted local customs *against* the demands for ḥadīth-based proof? What if al-Ash’arī, a foundational figure for "normative" Sunnī theology, was himself a former Mu’tāzila, and had formulated his Sunnī theology in response to the Mu’tāzila challenge? Or if strife between Muslims over the Qur’ān’s status as created or eternal had emerged from debates between Muslim theologians and their Christian opponents?

What if Sunnism began with a sectarian fringe of ḥadīth scholars that eventually won the right to call itself mainstream? What does it mean for the compilers of the Six Books to have been seen as brash and rebellious upstarts for their revolutionary collections, before these collections eventually attained the prestige of "canon" and "tradition?" Bukhārī, the man whose very *name* has become a means of establishing, performing, and policing orthodoxy, was chased out of town more than once for allegedly holding unacceptable views on minute doctrinal points regarding the Qur’ān’s uncreated status. And Bukhārī had also condemned Abū Ḥanīfa, eponym for the largest Sunnī legal school today, with the charge that Abu Ḥanīfa had abandoned the Sunna

What does it mean that heroes of the supposed mainstream, such as Ibn Ḥanbal and Ibn Taymiyya, were imprisoned and persecuted for opposing what was politically privileged in their own lifetimes as true Islam? What does it mean to speak of the "orthodoxy" of al-Ghazālī’s thought if he drew from the ideas of his "heterodox" opponents—Avicenna and even the Ismā'īliyya, who are commonly reviled (or celebrated) as Sunnism's extreme antitheses? What if Ibn Taymiyya, who complained of al-Ghazālī integrating these unwelcome sources into his thought, was himself infected by a conceptual contagion from the Neoplatonism that he despised? "Islamic Tradition," popularly defined, is a house of cards. If we stand too close, our breath sends it crashing down.

When I approached the grave of this Muḥammad whom I love, whose grave was it? I can ask this question in the most literal sense, as the bodies of Muḥammad, Abū Bakr, and 'Umar are buried next to each other, and we can ask which body lies where. Today, one of the graves is identified as that of Muḥammad, but people have not always been so confident. It was during expansions of the Medina mosque, which had been adjacent to Muḥammad's house (in which all three men had been buried), in the reign of al-Walīd (r. 705–715) several decades after Muḥammad's death, that the question was first settled. When workers were repairing a collapsed wall, the discovery of a foot in the rubble caused panic that Muḥammad's remains had been disturbed. 'Ā'isha's nephew, the great scholar 'Urwa ibn al-Zubayr, assured everyone that it had not been Muḥammad's foot. Several centuries later, historian al-Samhūdī (d. 1506) entered the burial chamber after much of the structure had been damaged by fire, and he could not determine the exact site of Muḥammad's grave.[23] Beyond the problem of locating Muḥammad's "real" character in texts, we face the problem of locating his actual body.

The ḥadīth corpus is presented to me with the prevailing assumption that in these collected representations of one man's words and deeds, I have a blueprint to guide my own life. We are pushed to treat Muḥammad as a self-contained body of text that can be interpreted, a source of retrievable themes and meanings. From our projects of swimming in this vast ocean of reports, we are supposed to extract an essence, a consistent "prophetic character," a way of being that actualizes innate Muḥammad-ness. But I wouldn't think of an ocean as coherent, or a jewel that I had retrieved from the ocean floor as representative of the ocean's "essence." The ocean is too big to have an essence.

The more that I make the claim to myself that I love the Prophet, the more I yearn for the origins, and the more I find myself alienated and estranged, living in this exile of post-Islam in which everything points to the Prophet's absence. I simultaneously push back against the reformist constructions of a Muḥammad-less Islam and confess that after Muḥammad's death, *every* Islam is Muḥammad-less. If Islam is exclusively the way of the Prophet and his Companions, Islam cannot exist in our world; I have no choice but to make takfīr on everyone, you're all out. Trying to capture and textually freeze that original moment—which can't even be reduced to a single moment, but twenty-three years containing trillions of moments and contexts, experienced from as many different angles as there were Companions—is like taking a snapshot of a waterfall, and then making a copy of that photo, and then a copy of the copy, and then a copy of the copy of the copy, and so on. If we go back through the generations and trace the genealogy of our degraded image, we don't arrive at the actual waterfall, but only the first *image*; our "original" is only the original attempt at reproduction.

The Companions did not need the innovative structures that later Muslims developed to preserve, interpret, and regulate the early community's legacy. This is a problem that Salafism points out to me, though Salafīs place enough faith in their own methodological assumptions to avoid the problem's full consequences. The age of the pious Salaf ends after the third generation (the Followers of the Followers of the Companions), but post-Salaf scholars are trusted to have preserved and transmitted the Salaf's example and made their imitation attainable for us. As I read the "three generations" model, taking Salafism seriously means going farther with the critique than Salafīs are generally willing to go. The Salafī vision of declining history and ongoing degradation forces me to confront the idealized "way of the Salaf" as an impossibility. If I cannot claim to know the variant of Islam against which all others should be measured (innovation *compared to what*?), my universal takfīr does the opposite of what takfīrs usually intend: The doors are opened to let everyone in.

Something gets deauthorized here, but it's not the eternal message of the Qur'ān, or the sublime example of the Prophet, or the binding precedent of his Companions, or the intellectual tradition that we entrust to speak for them, because none of those constructs had real authority to begin with. We deauthorize ourselves as guardians of the Real, along with the scholars and mystical knowers that we appoint as parental figures. It's both liberating and insecure. There's no new sheriff in town, no one to hold it all together and keep us safe.

What I end up with is not an authentic Islam, but only a choice between inorganic simulations. Each mosque offers portrayal, representation, and the chance to perform in a kind of theater, a live-action roleplaying that can pull me into a fantasy world, tell believable stories, and provide experiences to shape my thoughts outside the world of the game. That's the best that I can do. Whenever I am in the San Francisco Bay Area—the planet of Muslim hipsters—I try to visit not only Master Fard Muhammad's alleged grave, but also the Ta'leef Collective. They create a good experience at Ta'leef, an endearing and inspiring simulation, and I consider Ta'leef head Usama Canon my friend and brother. He calls Ta'leef a "third space" in which Muslims should feel safe and unjudged. "Come as you are to Islam as it is," he says. I show up as one of the misfits needing a suspension of judgment; I participate in their simulation, contribute to it as another body in the room praying and eating with them, listen to the lectures, and then leave. Ta'leef events refresh me as a Muslim, both in terms of my internal attempt at Muslim-ness and my social connection with Muslim communities. If there are any points of potential disagreement between the Ta'leef people and myself, I can check them at the door. I spend some time in their simulation and then go back to my own, or I explore another. Ta'leef's simulation operates on certain assumptions about correct ritual practice and authentic sources, but these aren't the only choices available. I can choose my favorite simulations based on their resonance with my own needs and will not conflate my preferences with a pure Islam that does not exist. I seek what's personally useful, not what's real, because none of it's real. I don't know if this is really Allāh's dīn or just dīn-entertainment.

To experience religion in this way did not come to me from nowhere. It draws from multiple genealogies and lineages, Muslim and non-Muslim, and can be called a product of certain historical forces and power relations. This fact alone does not provide the basis for a critique. A deconstructionist Salafism only bounces that critique back upon itself. My Salafism and my Five Percenterism can agree on one point: We will not find the Absolute, even if we search for trillions of years. For Five Percenters, this would mean that we assert our own agency to actualize the divine with our bodies; for Salafīs, we avoid our own subjectivity by seeking refuge in the limits of the text. The impossibility of both claims leads me to the same place. No universal truths are going to spill out of my body. Literalism and bi-lā kayf remain as personally subjective as any other approach, and there is no way of reading in which only the Author speaks. We must speak for ourselves while denying this as a choice.

I remember the Qur'ān's warnings against treating our own desires as God—verses in which I might interpret the Qur'ān to be forbidding its interpretation. To pick up the book means asserting control over it, no more or less than the refusal to pick it up. If I can call myself any kind of Salafī, it is for my desire, not my faith that the desire can be fulfilled through a rigorous method, a manhaj. I have a Salafī notion that everyone is doing it wrong, but I have no means of protecting myself from that charge.

What makes the simulation real for me is our shared yearning to make it real, to have a simulation that connects us to what's greater than it. Ironically, this loss of absolutes strikes me as deeply Islamic: The refusal to surrender becomes a surrender itself, a recognition of my limits. Because there can be no access to the divine text without our imperfect human interference, and meaning is not simply what a speaker feeds to a passive listener, it no longer matters if the text is divine. The consequences are the same. Boom, done. The words are disarmed. Even if the Qur'ān comes from a divine source, the fact of its speaking in a world makes it human.

Many would say that this expresses a lack of commitment or discipline. A couple of master's theses have been written about me with the critique that I reduce Islam to a matter of individual opinion: Islam is whatever we want it to be, so treat it like a buffet and take what you want. I am presented as a solipsist who advocates loosey-goosey religiosity, the kind of religion that denies itself as religion: a flaky liberal kind-of-Ṣūfism that you might tag as "spiritual, not religious." For me to challenge other humans' claims to power over interpretation apparently means that I have no dīn at all. For the demands that it makes, this response to my work reads like a Ten Percenter move. It does seem strange that a failure to accept the right of other humans to make my religion for me can be treated as a sign of intellectual or moral laziness.

I could say a few things to that charge, but most importantly, the problem is that it reduces my life as a Muslim to my varying interior conditions. It ignores what being Muslim actually means for my body in the world of brick-and-mortar mosques filled with flesh-and-blood sisters and brothers. Critics who suggest that I define Islam entirely by my personal whims neglect the fact that in those same books, I also write about the mosque that I must share. They tend to focus on my reports of snarky, punky internal monologues but not what I actually *do* as a Muslim in relation to Muslim communities: What do my prayers look like? What is my Muslim life as a body among other bodies? What happened at my Muslim wedding? During my pilgrimage to Mecca, did I show up at the Ka'ba wearing a spiked leather jacket and throwing bottles?

I cannot make an "Islam is whatever I say it is" argument unless I'm the only human being in the world. As long as I seek Islam *out there* with other people, my whims have to negotiate. Life in the mosque is never simply a choice between surrender and individualism: My whims get more say in some contexts than in others. My experience of Islam is necessarily determined by what a web of relations makes possible for me, and the terms of negotiation are always changing. The colliding forces involved in these relations include multiple communities, institutions, discourses, and personal networks, both Muslim and non-Muslim, that can pull on me at various times, as well as the variety of significations that I carry: white, male, hetero, convert, American, author, academic, feminist, punk, Five Percenter, alternately "orthodox" or "heterodox," and so on. All of this contributes not only to the answers that I find, but also to the questions that I bother to ask.

Even if I treat Islam like a buffet, I have never seen a buffet in which my freedom of personal choice was truly absolute. My desire negotiates with a limited range of choices that the governing institution, the restaurant, is willing to offer; the patrons ahead of me in line who might take my preferred items for themselves; the patrons behind me, to whom I should be courteous; the spatial limits of my plate; fluctuations in my physical condition, perhaps brought on by what I had just consumed in my previous round at the buffet; and of course the price that I must be able and willing to pay in order to access the buffet in the first place, as well as the process of selection by which my dining companions and I agreed on this particular restaurant. Rather than a simple anarchy of individuals taking whatever they want, the buffet actually represents a complex, collectively shared field of enabling and restraining conditions.

On the other hand, sometimes you know when you're in the wrong place. If eating at a particular restaurant gives me food poisoning, nothing is changed by someone telling me, "But my brother, this is an established restaurant, and these chefs have studied under masters at the most highly regarded culinary institutes in the world, and everyone respects them. Unless you have their level of knowledge, you can't say a word of critique." Even without qualified training in the chefs' methods, I can read the evidence in my body. Trusting the five-star masters isn't worth bloody diarrhea.

I don't want to be the dislocated po-mo individual (and privileged white man) who says that he can do without community institutions, as many of these institutions serve important functions beyond what you might immediately call "religion." Rather, I'll say that while there is no such thing as the capitalized "Muslim Community" as some intact whole, I care about the Muslim Community as people imagine it, and I care about multiple Muslim communities in which I take part. If we no longer maintain hope for perfect authenticity—striving instead for dreams of *postauthentic* Islam—this doesn't have to require the universal takfīr: It could mean treating Islam as a bridge to others, a shared pool of stories and artifacts and actions that connect us, rather than a fenced-off territory from which we must banish our undesirables.

Peace to the Salafī gods. I remember one of my favorite destabilizers: First Born Prince Allah, the Five Percenter elder who was also a disciplined Sunnī Muslim. He would take part in Friday prayers at a Sunnī mosque and then teach Supreme Mathematics at the Five Percenters' headquarters. Many of First Born Prince Allah's Sunnī brothers viewed Five Percenters as the most despicable and outrageous heretics; many of his Five Percenter brothers, meanwhile, condemned his prayers. On top of that, his library included Ahmadiyya thinkers. Firm binaries contrasting a clearly drawn "orthodoxy" to "heterodoxy" do not help us to understand First Born Prince Allah. Like First Born Prince Allah, I have found myself at both Masjid Malcolm Shabazz and the Five Percenters' Allah School, even on the same day. I have also alternated between Friday prayers at Salafī mosques and Shī'ī mosques, which would be unthinkable to many on both sides.

As much as we tout diversity and polyculturalism as hallmarks of the great "American Islam," there's nothing uniquely American about First Born Prince Allah's negotiation. In my travels in Pakistan and Ethiopia, I either experienced or heard about the flow between "Thursday night Islam" and "Friday afternoon Islam." Thursday night, you can hit the local shrines, where there might be chants, drums, and drugs—hashish in Lahore, chaat in Harar. Friday afternoon, you clean up, head to the biggest mosque in town, and present yourself as a respectable member of the mainstream at juma'a prayers. I can love my dīn in both its Thursday-night and Friday-afternoon versions. There are times when I need one more than the other, or one opens my way to the other. In my head, depending on the day, there may or may not be an unspeakable secret to my prayer; but with the acts of my body on Friday afternoon, I contribute to the production of public Islam. Even if the tradition that authorizes a particular community's scripts cannot be everything that the community claims for it, I am usually willing to take the bargain that my communities offer: conformity to the script in exchange for a shared simulatory experience of the Qur'ān and the Prophet.

I embarked on the pilgrimage to Mecca while in my nameless condition, bringing an Islam in which a hodge-podge of materials are all connected to each other, and I didn't stink-palm anyone. The public Islam of the Saudi state, the official Islam of the pilgrimage, also renewed itself as a point in my rhizome. There is additionally the public Islam of the American state. It's important that I recognize the deep American-ness of my Islam without romanticizing the myth of American "religious freedom" or the state's supposed lack of intervention in religion. The forces that come together to make my Islam do allow for flexibility in some respects. Within the field of legal possibilities in which my partner and I live, we can afford to surrender the progressive project of imposing modern gender equality onto the Qur'ān, Sunna, or Muslim legal tradition: If any of our sacred sources are found to support or condemn domestic violence, for example, nothing changes between us or our rights over each other. This is a luxury. I can also cross Sunnī-Shī'ī lines easier in the Bay than in some places and openly make confessions that would violate blasphemy and apostasy laws somewhere in the world. But my American Islam is also what gets me detained at airports, subjects me to long interviews with the FBI, and has me questioning whether I'd feel safe living with my family in North Carolina. Not all of the forces that can apply pressure on our religious lives are themselves obviously "religious." If there has ever been a society in which publicly claiming a religion did *not* situate someone socially or politically, it wasn't the United States, let alone the United States as experienced by Muslims.

Maybe an Islam derived from holy drugs is part of my problem, enabling only a neoliberal authorization of my own intestines. Or it's the last line of defense: What I took from the ayahuasca experiment was not a secure manhaj grounded in established sources or recourse to traditional Muslim institutions of knowledge, but at least Islam as a *sensation* that found its most perfect expression in the mosque, in the embodied language of Muslim prayer, my imitation and simulation of Sunna. The private conditions in my head are unstable, but the memory of what to do with my body in a mosque at least enables a relationship to the people of the mosque. That's not nothing. With my body, I give love to the prayer of my brothers and sisters, even if the secrets of our prayers remain irreconcilable. In part through the ingestion of federally regulated ayahuasca, I locate my home within federally regulated Islam.

I want to defend hypocrites, but my dīn-entertainment is not exactly hypocrisy, and I am not a tourist. I bear witness to the oneness of God and the prophethood of Muḥammad. After that, I require no translation: My dīn no longer has to convince me of itself, and no one can argue me out of it. Inside the mosque, I submit to the soft demands of whatever simulation the mosque offers, and then I'm back to my own world. I indulge in the simulation, playing by its rules while keeping up my guard. When the simulation transgresses the limit of its rights over me, I step out of its game. Once in a while, I need a particular medicine that only the mosque provides. In exchange for my access to this medicine, I try not to be destructive to the mosque or the people of the mosque—whether a Salafī mosque or a Shī'ī mosque or a mosque that separates my brothers and sisters by gender or a progressive congregation in which I pray behind a woman imām.

If I had to name the secret of my prayer, it might be nostalgia, the pained longing for a past that I can desire precisely because it is unattainable. Nostalgia says that the truest Islam is never in my own hands, but always buried in a superior past. I yearn for this past—a past that I have never experienced—without any chance that my yearning can be fulfilled. The commodified simulations produced at "Reviving the Islamic Spirit" conventions aren't going to revive the dead bodies that can make this real for me. Nostalgia is a fantasy that will never hold me accountable: What I desire has never existed, and will never exist, beyond the dreams that I choose to buy into. Neither the perfection of the past, nor the sincerity of my desire for the past, can be thrown into question by the past ever showing up.

Maybe it's not nostalgia for a communal Muslim golden age, but instead a nostalgia for *my* golden age, the feeling of that brand-new-convert glow twenty years ago when all of this was simple, clear, and *really real.* Nostalgia for the mosque is a nostalgia for versions of me that I might have lost: The mosque offers a simulation of what I had seen as my best self. My prayer keeps the memory of that kid alive and leaves the door open for him to stop by and visit.

Nostalgia is neither faith nor faithlessness. Islam is not only a belief that drives action, but sometimes the reverse. When formal aqīda has crumbled, moving my arms and legs by a familiar routine makes me feel my dīn again. The sensations of prayer trigger whatever memory has linked to the prayer: kindness, compassion, ethics, family, community, my smallness and mortality, Allāh's greatness and eternity. The mosque performs a chemical intervention in its own right, and embodied Muslim prayer activates the neural pathways—the memories of a Muslim discipline imprinted on my fleshly matter—to remake me in a believer's body.

Sometimes I can let go of all the hyper-critical academic stuff and invest in my dīn of sensation. I temporarily suspend my questions and join in the prayer with my sisters and brothers, choosing to forget that we could even historicize our ritual scripts as products of power struggle and scholarly mediation. On the best days, this simulation feels real enough to hold me over until the next time. What I get is an Islam of joy and love: I get joy from being a Muslim, and I love my Muslim family. A word, *Allāh*, shows up amid this joy and love, communicating a variety of meanings at different times; and a man, or a blissful vision of a man, appears to me as my phantasmic surrogate father, Muḥammad. When I give the experience my consent, it can produce the kind of tears that clean this devil up, flushing out the poison. This is the technology that I have named Islam.

FUTURE SALAF

We inherit and we are inherited. A white teenager named Mark Hanson became Hamza Yusuf in 1977, the year that I was born. Since I've been called a "Hamza Yusuf for the bad kids," I wonder about Muslims who were born in my year of shahādah, 1994. In 2008, *The New York Times* ran a story about taqwacore and quoted fourteen-year-old Naina Syed as saying that my novel helped her to create her identity. Naina later joined a Ṣūfī order, got a Karbala tattoo, and ended up becoming the first Shī'ī student at Zaytuna College. The same article quoted fifteen-year-old Hanan Arzay as calling the book her "lifeline" and saying that it saved her faith.[24] I don't know how she turned out.

I found (and continue to find) Islam through people, and now I receive feedback from those who found it through me. Apart from the punk-rock novel, my creative nonfiction works also became their points of entry, in no small part through a publishing industry that often elevates personal memoirs and reflections over clerical scholarship as legitimate windows into a religion. This is the same secular marketplace that sold Islam to me through *The Autobiography of Malcolm X* and continues to promote books by ordinary Muslims "speaking for themselves" as products that will help non-Muslims to better understand Islam.[25] Regardless of my intention, my books also contribute to a secular da'wa industry of what scholars have termed "Muslim media chic."[26]

A blogger, naming me as an influence on his early explorations of Islam, credited my books along with various Qur'ān translations, Vali Nasr's *The Shia Revival*, Carol Anway's *Daughters of Another Path*, Karen Armstrong's biography of Muḥammad, and *The Autobiography of Malcolm X* as forming the assemblage that he called "Islam" and to which he converted.[27] What kind of Islam does that sack of potatoes make? To what origin, exactly, can it *revert* him? Is it really Islam? And if not, if it is only a portal that leads to other portals, at what point does that process arrive upon the real thing, the Islam of preexisting coherence and unbroken unity?

Five Percenters also write to me, saying that my books brought them to what they call "knowledge of self." Sometimes they address me by my Five Percenter name, Azreal Wisdom, recognizing me as a student of Azreal, the original white Five Percenter from the 1960s. Just as the third generation of Muslims, the "Followers of the Followers," sought elders who could report from what Companions had told them about the Prophet, Five Percenters ask me what Azreal's teacher, the former Clarence 13X, taught him about particular topics. Their own concerns inform the questions that they ask, which in turn decide the legacy that Azreal can leave behind: In particular, white Five Percenters always want to know what Azreal said about their potential to be devils or gods and what place they can occupy within the culture. I tell them what Azreal told me. Now a link in chains of Five Percenter ḥadīths, I have been appointed a preserver of legacies, which inevitably and problematically means that I take part in their reinvention. To share the past with a new generation, even if my memory is reliable and I remain truthful in what I share, requires that I make something new.

For whatever people say that reading me did to/for them, I can't draw them as branches from my tree. I'm just as much a branch of their trees, because I am affected by them; whatever I write next must respond to them. Giving talks at colleges and universities, I leave transformed by encounters with Muslim Students Association members who were not yet born when I first embarked on conversion. When MSAs invite and engage me, they alter the field of possibilities that I had allowed for myself.

I don't have a tree. I have no idea what I'm saying here. Writers write with intentions, sure, but our intentions alone cannot decide the life of the words. Interpretations that readers give to my work are often more satisfying to me than the meanings that I originally had in mind. We are rhizomes, not roots, and I don't know what songs were playing in the coffee shops as these kids read me.

More than one Muslim has written to say that s/he now hates my books and what they stand for but added that without reading them at the right time, her/his dīn could not have survived. When scholars use the condescending term *proto-Islamic* in reference to the Moorish Science Temple and Nation of Islam—which looks to me like a more polite way of saying *pre-Islamic*, which in turn is a nicer way of saying *Jahiliyya*—I can't help but imagine myself as the proto-Islamic ancestor for someone, illegitimate but necessary, an embarrassment but still in the genealogy. That's the kindest reading that I can give to myself. I wonder about our own places in the isnāds, the ways that we enable access to our heritage for those who come after us, since what we give them cannot claim mint condition. The Ibn Ḥanbal action figure is forever out of its package, its joints loosened by our play.

If restoring the sacred past is our dream, then the past is a future. We are salaf to the Salaf, ancestors to our ancestors. We precede the pious predecessors. We occupy middle-points in other people's journeys: They are heading from somewhere to somewhere and encounter us along the way to becoming Muslims, always *becoming* Muslims. They serve as middle-points for us too, because we are still moving. People who imagine a difference between *Islamic* and *proto-Islamic* are just arbitrarily drawing lines based on their personal tastes. We all draw lines to decide the point at which something is no longer recognizably Islamic for us. I mark my own limits: I pray without hesitation behind female imāms and affirm safe spaces for queer Muslims, but performance of ṣalāt in English is usually too severe a departure for me. I sometimes feel discomfort with visual depictions of Muḥammad, though I have also drawn him myself. My limits can be determined by theological, ethical, or political commitments, but also by aesthetics and presentation.

Nothing can be called *Islamic* if by this you mean an Islam that mixes only with itself, responding only to itself. I am not the Islamic but forever the proto-Islamic, the Seal of Muslim Pseudo in my pyramid-shaped Ka'ba. My body is never purely a Muslim body, but always a contact zone, a border zone, a place where Islam meets something else. On top of that, the thing that I call "Islam" in this meeting is already a mixture before I meet it; I can only find Islam as it emerges out of other contact zones, other bodies. The charge of syncretism loses its punch when we recognize that *everything* is syncretic, blended, a product of encounter, an unending mix tape that is compiled only from other mix tapes.

The Ta'leef Collective has offered workshops in "mindfulness meditation," a practice so well-traveled in the United States that its Buddhist backstory, like yoga's Hindu backstory, has been all but erased. "Mindfulness" as a concept has grown popular in part through the American commodification of Buddhism into a marketable wellness product for mass consumption, but also through its extraction *from* Buddhism, relieving the practice of explicitly "religious" and "foreign" baggage and rewriting it as a secular technology. Translated, universalized, and filtered through American therapy culture, the Buddhist discourse of sati can inform Muslim thinking about niyya (intention), serve as a rationalization of practices ranging from the five daily prayers and meditative zikr to the fast of Ramaḍān, and even become a fully ḥalāl ingredient in an authentically sourced "Islam as it is."[28]

When conceptualizing our traditions as experiences defined by encounter and exchange, we must remain aware that these exchanges do not take place on an even field of power. I take seriously the warnings against molding Islam in conformity to the pressures of empire. While the United States has appropriated feminist themes to justify its invasions of Muslim-majority societies, however, this does not allow us to call every radical Muslim feminist an agent of neocolonialism. And if some would charge that my supposed anything-goes Islam is exactly what the empire wants, I should say that this deregulated, destabilized Islam is also what opened me to Elijah Muhammad declaring the empire's flag to signify "slavery, suffering, and death" and Muhammad Ali citing his faith in Elijah when he refused to join the empire's war.

I restored much of my Muslim self through drinking ayahuasca, which is portrayed by its advocates as dating back several thousand years to an indigenous Amazonian wisdom that predates written history; but I value the medicine for what it achieves in my body, not the imaginary timelessness that people claim for it. Ayahuasca shamanism only emerged in the age of European colonialism, an intersection of indigenous healing practices with missionary Catholicism, West African traditions, the successive terrors of the transatlantic slave trade and the industrial rubber trade, and reached me through Euro-American New Age. Encounter is what we end up with, no matter how far back we go. My dīn (or dīn-entertainment) will always be a hybrid creature, and hybrids can be monstrous or marvelous. I want to imagine my dīn like the Burāq, the weirdo that Muḥammad rode into the heavens, depicted in some traditions as a hybrid with the head of a woman, the body of a horse, big Pegasus wings, and the tail of a peacock. The Burāq sounds disturbing but becomes beautiful in its execution. After my hybrid dīn does its work inside me—or after we work together inside me—I send it back out into the air, and the process of proto-Islamic becoming never ends: If there's no origin, everything is the origin. Achievement of the authentic no longer stands as a thinkable finality: Proto-Islam forever comes together and dissolves and reassembles. A mujaddid might come to restore the dīn every century, but proto-Islam renews the Qur'ān for twenty-five thousand years at a time.

Retreats away from textual interpretation and into the signs of my body do not solve all of my problems, but they at least preserve my openness to hope that a more complete Islam might come—whether that means a future Qur'ān or attainment of the one true manhaj. Meanwhile, the Prophet is not waiting to be discovered in his true form and unburied. He does not even preexist us, but appears with a new body in every point of departure, every break, every disorder, every unacceptable innovation, every hybridization. Islam is what happens tomorrow.

NOTES

1

1 Baudrillard, Jean. "What Are You Doing after the Orgy?" trans. Lisa Liebmann, *Artforum* (October 1983), 43

2 Schubel, Vernon. "Tripping with Allah." *Kirkus Reviews*, Vol. 81, Issue 4 (2/15/2013), 205.

3 Wright, Robin. "Don't Fear All Islamists, Fear Salafis." *New York Times* 20 Aug 2012: A19(L).

4 Ibid.

5 Abou El Fadl, Khaled. "The Ugly Modern and the Modern Ugly: Reclaiming the Beautiful in Islam." In Omid Safi, ed. *Progressive Muslims: On Justice, Gender, and Pluralism*. Oxford: Oneworld, 2003. 33–77.

6 Levy, Joseph M. "Wahabi Rising Adds to Near East Unrest." *New York Times* 8 Apr 1928.

7 Philly, H. St. J.B. "Ibn Saud's five year reign brings firm peace to Arabia," H. St. J. B. *New York Times* 4 Jan 1932, xii.

8 "Arabs in Paris Say 1,000 Joined Seizure of Mosque: Radio, TV and Working Women Truckloads of Arms and Dates Source of Arms a Question." *New York Times* 30 Nov 1979, A18.

9 Middleton, Drew. "Turmoil in Iran Is Breaking Up Patterns in Gulf: Military Analysis Halt to Modernization Defend Sectarian Identity Treaties with Soviet Bloc." *New York Times* 2 Dec 1979, 17.

10 Burns, John F. "Yemen Links to bin Laden Gnaw at FBI in Cole Inquiry." *New York Times* 26 Nov 2000, 6.

11 Andelman, David A. "Analysis: A Salafi Conspiracy in Boston Bombings?" *USA Today*, 28 Apr 2013. http://www.usatoday.com/story/news/world/2013/04/28/boston-bombings-sunni-salafi-russia/2118901/.

12 Ismail, Salwa. "Producing 'Reformed Islam': A Saudi Contribution to the US Projects of Global Governance." In Madawi al-Rasheed, ed. *Kingdom Without Borders: Saudi Arabia's Political, Religious and Media Frontiers*. London: Hurst & Company, 2008. 113–134.

13 Shakir, Zaid. *Scattered Pictures*. Hayward: Zaytuna Institute, 2005. 17.

14 Katz, Jonathan G. *Dreams, Sufism, and Sainthood: The Visionary Career of Muhammad al-Zawawi*. Leiden: Brill, 1996. 170.

15 Ibid, xiii.

16 Hammer, Juliane. *American Muslim Women, Religious Authority, and Activism: More Than a Prayer*. Austin: University of Texas Press, 2013. 34.

17 Sacirbey, Omar. "With a New Imam, a New Outlook." *Boston Globe*. 3 Dec 2011. http://www.bostonglobe.com/metro/2011/12/03/with-new-imam-new-outlook/GcyTn4n4g9ADqIsgV089xH/story.html?s_campaign=sm_fb.

18 Elliott, Andrea, Eric Owles, and Josh Williams. "Yasir Qadhi: An American Cleric." *New York Times* 18 Mar 2011. Web. 11 Jun. 2014. http://www.nytimes.com/interactive/2011/03/18/magazine/american-cleric.html?_r=0.

19 Ibid.

20 Grewal, Zareena. *Islam Is a Foreign Country*. New Haven: Yale University Press, 2013. 165–67.

21 Tourage, Mahdi. "Performing Belief and Reviving Islam: Prominent (White Male) Converts in Muslim Revival Conventions." *Performing Islam*, Vol. 1, No. 2 (2012), 207–26.

2

1 Gordimer, Nadine. *A World of Strangers*. London: A & C Black, 2012. 45.

2 Safi, Omid. "Introduction: The Times They Are A-Changin'—a Muslim Quest for Justice, Gender Equality, and Pluralism." In Omid Safi, ed. *Progressive Muslims: On Justice, Gender, and Pluralism*. Oxford: Oneworld, 2003. 1–29.

3 Ibid.

4 Eberle, Gary. *Dangerous Words: Talking about God in an Age of Fundamentalism*. Boston: Shambhala, 2007. 69–71.

5 Kueny, Kathryn M. *Conceiving Identities: Maternity in Medieval Muslim Discourse and Practice*. Albany: SUNY Press, 2013. 32.

6 Ibid, 28.

7 Ibrahim, I. A. *A Brief Illustrated Guide to Understanding Islam*. Houston: Dar-us-Salam, 1997. 9.

8 Ibid, 32.

9 Ibid, 40.

10 Ibid, 56.

11 *A Summary of the Creed of As-Salaf As-Saalih*. Riyadh: Dar-us-Salam, 2002. 5.

12 Ibid, 14.

13 Ibid, 20–21.

14 Ibid, 24.

15 Ibid, 25.

16 Ibid.

17 Ibid, 26–27.

18 Ibid, 28.

19 Ibid, 29–30.

20 Ibid, 31–32.

21 Ibid, 34–35.

22 Ibid, 33.

23 Ibid, 37.

24 Ibid+.

3

1 Borges, Jorge Luis. "The Aleph." *A Personal Anthology*. New York: Grove Press, 1967. 150.

2 Robinson, Neal. *Discovering the Qur'an: A Contemporary Approach to a Veiled Text*. Washington, D.C.: Georgetown University Press, 2003. 224.

3 Sands, Kristin. *Sufi Commentaries on the Qur'an in Classical Islam*. New York: Routledge, 2006.

4 Hoover, Jon. *Ibn Taymiyya's Theodicy of Perpetual Optimism*. Leiden: Brill, 2007. 54.

5 Zadeh, Travis. *The Vernacular Qur'an: Translation and the Rise of Persian Exegesis*. Oxford: Oxford University Press, 2012. 433–35.

6 Khan, Muhammad Muhsin, and Muhammad Taqi-ud-Din al-Hilali. *Translation of the Meanings of the Noble Qur'an*. Medina: King Fahd Complex for the Printing of the Holy Qur'an, n.d. 1–2.

7 Al-Misawi, Um Abdullah. "The Meaning of 'fi as-samaa' in ayah (67:16) and the Hadith of the Slave Girl (Al-Jariyah). *Beliefs of the Righteous Salaf*. http://as-salaf.com/article.php?aid=62&lang=en.

8 Yahagi, Mohammad Jafar. "An Introduction to Early Persian Qur'anic Translations." *Journal of Qur'anic Studies*. Vol. 4 (Oct 2002). 105–9.

9 Bellos, David. *Is That a Fish in Your Ear?* New York: Faber and Faber, Inc., 2011. 79.

10 Ernst, Carl. *How to Read the Qur'an*. Chapel Hill: University of North Carolina Press, 2011. Robinson, Neal. *Discovering the Qur'an: A Contemporary Approach to a Veiled Text*. Washington, D.C.: Georgetown University Press, 2003.

11 Wild, Stefan. "Why Self-Referentiality?" in Stefan Wilder, ed. *Self-Referentiality in the Qur'ān*. Otto Harrassowitz Verlag, 2006. 1–21.

12 Heisenberg, W. *Physics and Philosophy: The Revolution in Modern Science* (1958). Lectures delivered at University of St. Andrews, Scotland, Winter 1955–56.

13 Graham, William A. *Divine Word and Prophetic Word in Early Islam*. Paris: Mouton & Co., 1977. 36.

14 Ibid, 29–30.

15 Geissinger, Aisha. "The Exegetical Traditions of 'Ā'isha: Notes on their Impact and Significance." *Journal of Qur'anic Studies*. Vol. 6 (Apr 2004). 1–20.

16 Whelan, Estelle. "Forgotten Witness: Evidence for the Early Codification of the Qur'an." *Journal of the American Oriental Society*, Vol. 118 (1998). 1–14.

17 Derrida, Jacques. *Archive Fever: A Freudian Impression*. Chicago: University of Chicago Press, 1998. 2.

18 Khan, Ruqayya Y. "Did a Woman Edit the Qur'ān? Hafṣa and her Famed 'Codex.'" *Journal of the American Academy of Religion*. Vol. 82, No. 1 (March 2014). 174–216.

19 Gilliot, Claude. "Creation of a Fixed Text." In Jane Dammen McAuliffe, ed. *The Cambridge Companion to the Qur'an*. Cambridge: Cambridge University Press, 2008. 41–58.

20 Ibid.

21 Whelan, Estelle. "Forgotten Witness: Evidence for the Early Codification of the Qur'an." *Journal of the American Oriental Society*, Vol. 118 (1998). 1–14.

22 Khan, Ruqayya Y. "Did a Woman Edit the Qur'ān? Hafṣa and her Famed 'Codex.'" *Journal of the American Academy of Religion*. Vol. 82, No. 1 (March 2014). 174–216.

23 Neuwirth, Angelika. "Two Faces of the Qur'ān: Qur'ān and Musḥaf." *Oral Tradition*, 25, 1 (2010). 141–56.

24 Gilliot, Claude. "Creation of a Fixed Text." In Jane Dammen McAuliffe, ed. *The Cambridge Companion to the Qur'an*. Cambridge: Cambridge University Press, 2008. 41–58.

25 Whelan, Estelle. "Forgotten Witness: Evidence for the Early Codification of the Qur'an." *Journal of the American Oriental Society*, Vol. 118 (1998). 1–14.

26 Gilliot, Claude. "Creation of a Fixed Text." In Jane Dammen McAuliffe, ed. *The Cambridge Companion to the Qur'an*. Cambridge: Cambridge University Press, 2008. 41–58.

27 Radscheit, Matthias. "The Qur'ān—Codification and Canonization." In Stefan Wilder, ed. *Self-Referentiality in the Qur'ān*. Otto Harrassowitz Verlag, 2006. 93–115.

28 "Nafs." *Encyclopaedia of Islam, Second Edition*. Edited by: P. Bearman, Th. Bianquis, C.E. Bosworth, E. van Donzel, W.P. Heinrichs. Brill Online, 2014.

29 Bilici, Mucahit. *Finding Mecca in America: How Islam Is Becoming an American Religion*. Chicago: University of Chicago Press, 2012. 87.

30 Morris, James W. "Qur'an Translation and the Challenges of Communication: Towards a 'Literal' Study-Version of the Qur'an." *Journal of Qur'anic Studies*, Vol. 2, Issue 2 (2000). 53–67.

31 Berg, Herbert. *Elijah Muhammad and Islam*. New York: New York University Press, 2009. 60–61.

32 Khan, Mofakhkhar Hussain, "A History of Bengali Translations of the Holy Qur'ān." *Muslim World*, Vol. 72, No. 2 (1982), 129–34.

33 Ernst, Carl. *Following Muhammad: Rethinking Islam in the Contemporary World*. Chapel Hill: University of North Carolina Press, 2003. 63.

34 Jane Dammen McAuliffe, "The Tasks and Traditions of Interpretation." In Jane Dammen McAuliffe, ed. *The Cambridge Companion to the Qur'an*. Cambridge. Cambridge University Press, 2008. 181–210.

35 Hoyland, R. "Physiognomy in Islam." *Jerusalem Studies in Arabic and Islam*, 30 (2005). Jerusalem: the Hebrew University of Jerusalem. 361–402.

36 "Rereading 'Status of Women in Islam' (VII)." *Sober Second Look*. http://sobersecondlook.wordpress.com/2013/02/03/rereading-status-of-woman-in-islam-vii/#more-760.

4

1 Derrida, Jacques. *Archive Fever*. Chicago: University of Chicago Press, 1997. 17.

2 Donner, Fred M. *Narratives of Islamic Origins: The Beginnings of Islamic Historical Writing*. Princeton: Darwin Press, 1998. 40–51.

3 Ibid.

4 Ibid.

5 Motzki, Harald. "The *Muṣannaf* of ʿAbd al-Razzāq al-Ṣanʿānī as a Source of Authentic Aḥādīth of the First Century A.H." *Journal of Near Eastern Studies* 50 (1991). 1–21.

6 Günther, Sebastian. "Modern Literary Theory Applied to Classical Arabic Texts: *Ḥadīth* Revisited." In Verena Klemm and Beatrice Grundler, eds. *Understanding Near Eastern Literatures*. Weisbaden: Harrassowitz, 2000. 171–76. Also "Fictional Narration and Imagination Within an Authoritative Framework: Towards a New Understanding of Ḥadīth." In Stefan Leder, ed. *Story-telling in the Framework of Non-fictional Arab Literature*. Weisbaden: Harrassowitz, 1998. 433–71.

7 Tayyara, A. E. "The Evolution of the Term *Qarn* in Early Islamic Sources." *Journal of Near Eastern Studies*, Vol. 72, Issue 1 (Apr 2013). 99–110.

8 Ibid.

9 Ibid.

10 Ibid.

11 Ibid.

12 Osman, Amr. "*'Adālat al-ṣaḥāba:* The Construction of a Religious Doctrine." *Arabica* 60 (2013). 272–305.

13 Jabali, Fu'ad. *A Study of the Companions of the Prophet: Geographical Distribution and Political Alignment*. Diss. McGill University, 1999. 61–89.

14 Ibid.

15 Ibid.

16 Ibid.

17 Ibid.

18 Baldick, Julian. *Imaginary Muslims: The Uwaysi Mystics of Central Asia*. New York: NYU Press, 1993. 15–39.

19 Siddiqi, Muhammad Zubayr. *Hadith Literature: Its Origins, Development, and Special Features*. Cambridge: The Islamic Texts Society, 1993. 14–18.

20 Geissinger, Aisha. "A'isha bint Abi Bakr and her Contributions to the Formation of the Islamic Tradition." *Religion Compass* 5/1 (2011): 37–49.

21 Myrne, Pernilla. *Narrative, Gender and Authority in 'Abbāsid Literature on Women*. Göteborg: University of Gothenburg, 2010. 185.

22 See Rubin, Uri. *The Eye of the Beholder: The Life of Muḥammad as Viewed by the Early Muslims*. Princeton: Darwin Press, 1995. Also Colby, Frederick S. *Narrating Muhammad's Night Journey: Tracing the Development of the Ibn 'Abbas Ascension Discourse*. Albany: SUNY Press, 2009.

23 Rubin, Uri. *The Eye of the Beholder: The Life of Muḥammad as Viewed by the Early Muslims*. Princeton: Darwin Press, 1995.

24 Nawas, John A. "The Contribution of the *Mawālī* to the Six Sunnite Canonical Ḥadīth Collections." In Sebastian Gunther, ed. *Ideas, Images, and Methods of Portrayal. Insights into Classical Arabic Literature and Islam*. Leiden: Brill, 2005. 141–51.

25 Bulliet, Richard. *Islam: A View from the Edge*. New York: Columbia University Press, 1995.

26 Sayeed, Asma. *Women and the Transmission of Religious Knowledge in Islam*. Cambridge: Cambridge University Press, 2013.

27 Melchert, Christopher. "Sectaries in the Six Books: Evidence for Their Exclusion from the Sunni Community." *Muslim World*. Vol. 82, No. 3–4 (1992). 287–95.

28 Juynboll, G.H.A. *Authenticity of the Tradition Literature*. Leiden: Brill, 1969. 50.

29 Kugle, Scott Siraj al-Haqq. *Homosexuality in Islam*. Oxford: Oxford Publications, 2010. 77.

30 Musa, Aisha. *Ḥadīth as Scripture: Discussions on the Authority of Prophetic Traditions in Islam*. New York: Palgrave Macmillan, 2008. 22–25.

31 A'zami, Muhammad Mustafa. *Studies in Early Hadīth Literature*. Indianapolis: American Trust Publications, 1978.

32 Ibid.

33 Schoeler, Gregor. "Oral Torah and Ḥadīth: Transmission, Prohibition of Writing, Redaction." In Harald Motzki, ed. *Ḥadīth: Origins and Developments*. Aldershot and Burlington: Ashgate/Valorium, 2004.

34 Ibid.

35 Ibid.

36 Ibid.

37 Dutton, Yasin. *The Origins of Islamic Law: The Qur'ān, the Muwatta' and Madinan Amal*. New York: Routledge, 2013. 43–45.

38 Ibid.

39 Lucas, Scott C. *Constructive Critics, Ḥadīth Literature, and the Articulation of Sunnī Islam: The Generation of Ibn Sa'd, Ibn Ma'īn, and Ibn Ḥanbal*. Leiden: Brill, 2004.

40 Brown, Jonathan A. C. *The Canonization of al-Bukhārī and Muslim: The Formation and Function of the Sunnī Ḥadīth Canon*. Leiden: Brill, 2007.

41 Imām Abul Hussain Muslim bin al-Hajjaj. Nasiruddin al-Khattab, trans. Huda Khattab, ed. *English Translation of Sahīh Muslim*. Riyadh: Darussalam, 2007.

42 Maghen, Ze'ev. *Virtues of the Flesh: Passion and Piety in Early Islamic Jurisprudence*. Leiden: Brill, 2004.

43 For an example, see Amirebrahimi, Maryam. "Proactive Women and the Prophet." *Suhaib Webb*. N.p., 17 Jul 2012. Web. 21 Nov 2013. http://www.suhaibwebb.com/relationships/gender-relations/the-female-companions-and-the-prophet-/.

44 "Radical Muslims." Facebook.com.

45 Jackson, Sherman. *Islam and the Problem of Black Suffering*. Oxford: Oxford University Press, 2009. 34–35.

46 Melchert, Christopher. *Ahmad ibn Hanbal*. Oxford: Oneworld, 2013. 92.

47 Brown, Jonathan A. C. *The Canonization of al-Bukhārī and Muslim: The Formation and Function of the Sunnī Ḥadīth Canon*. Leiden: Brill, 2007. 300–34.

48 Martin, Luther H., Huck Gutman, and Patrick H. Hutton, eds. *Technologies of the Self: A Seminar with Michel Foucault*. Amherst: University of Massachusetts Press, 1988. 18.

49 Katz, Marion Holmes. *Body of Text: The Emergence of the Sunnī Law of Ritual Purity*. Albany: SUNY Press, 2002. 1.

5

1 Wiener, Norbert. *God and Golem, Inc: A Comment on Certain Points where Cybernetics Impinges on Religion*. Boston: MIT Press, 1964.

2 Moosa, Ebrahim. *Ghazālī and the Poetics of Imagination*. Chapel Hill: University of North Carolina Press, 2005. 40.

3 Ibid, 41.

4 Ibid.

5 Chakrabarty, Dipesh. *Provincializing Europe: Postcolonial Thought and Historical Difference*. Princeton: Princeton University Press, 2009. 243.

6 Shaikh, Sa'diyya. *Sufi Narratives of Intimacy: Ibn 'Arabi, Gender, and Sexuality*. Chapel Hill: University of North Carolina Press, 2012. 32–33.

7 Ibid.

8 Ibn al-Jawzī. Michael Cooperson, trans. *Virtues of the Imām Aḥmad ibn Ḥanbal*. Vol. 1. New York: NYU Press, 2013. 391.

9 Ibid, 401–403.

10 Ibid, 391.

11 Ibid, 357.

12 Ibid, 411.

13 Ibid, 473.

14 Ibid, 471.

15 Ibid, 469.

16 Ibid, 483.

17 Ibid, 489.

18 Ibid, 327.

19 Ibid, 255.

20 Ibid, 197.

21 Ibid, 261–65.

22 Ibid, 337.

23 Ibid, 93.

24 Ibid, 415.

25 Zaman, Muhammad Qasim. *Religion and Politics Under the Early 'Abbāsids: The Emergence of the Proto-Sunnī Elite*. Leiden: Brill, 1997.

26 Duri, A. A., and Lawrence I. Conrad, trans. *The Rise of Historical Writing Among the Arabs*. Princeton: Princeton University Press, 1983.

27 Hoyland, Robert G. "History, Fiction, and Authorship in the First Centuries of Islam." In Julia Bray, ed. *Writing and Representation in Early Islam*. New York: Routledge, 2006. 16–46.

28 Ibid.

29 Lecker, Michael. "Wāqidī's Account on the Status of the Jews of Medina: A Study of a Combined Report." *Journal of Near Eastern Studies*, Vol. 54, No. 1 (Jan. 1995), 15–32.

30 Ibid.

31 Jackson, Sherman. "Ibn Taymiyyah on Trial in Damascus." *Journal of Semitic Studies* XXXIX/1 (Spring 1994). 41–85.

32 Ibid.

33 Jackson, Sherman. *Islam and the Problem of Black Suffering*. Oxford: Oxford University Press, 2009. 130.

34 Deleuze, Gilles. "I Have Nothing to Admit." *Semiotext(e)*, Vol. 2, No. 3 (1977). 114.

35 Rakim. "The Mystery (Who is God)." *The 18th Letter*. Universal Records, 1997.

36 Williams, Wesley. "Aspects of the Creed of Imam Aḥmad ibn Ḥanbal: A study of Anthropomorphism in Early Islamic Discourse." *International Journal of Middle East Studies*, Vol. 34, Issue 3 (July 2002). 441–63.

37 Melchert, Christopher. "God Created Adam in His Image." *Journal of Qur'anic Studies*, 13.1 (2011). 113–124.

38 Sayeed, Asma. *Women and the Transmission of Religious Knowledge in Islam*. Cambridge: Cambridge University Press, 2013.

39 Melchert, Christopher. "Sectaries in the Six Books: Evidence for Their Exclusion from the Sunni Community." *Muslim World*. Vol. 82, No. 3–4 (1992). 287–95.

40 Knysh, Alexander. *Ibn 'Arabi in the Later Islamic Tradition: The Making of a Polemical Image in Medieval Islam*. Albany: SUNY Press, 1998.

41 Safi, Omid. *Politics of Knowledge in Premodern Islam*. Chapel Hill: University of North Carolina Press, 2006. 156.

42 Melchert, Christopher. "The Ḥanābila and the Early Ṣūfīs." *Arabica*, Vol. 48, Issue 3 (2001). 352–367.

43 Kinberg, Leah. "The Legitimization of the Madhahib Through Dreams." *Arabica*, Tome xxxii, 1985.

44 Cooperson, Michael. "Ibn Ḥanbal and Bishr al-Ḥāfī: A Case Study in Biographical Traditions." *Studia Islamica*, Issue 86 (1/1997). 71–101.

45 Melchert, Christopher. "The Ḥanābila and the Early Ṣūfīs." *Arabica*, Vol. 48, Issue 3 (2001). 352–367.

46 Ibid.

47 Said, Edward W. *Orientalism*. New York: Vintage, 1979. 268–70.

48 Massignon, Louis. H. Mason, trans. *The Passion of al-Hallaj*. Princeton: Princeton University Press, 1994. 136.

49 Gauvain, Richard. *Salafi Ritual Purity*. New York: Routledge, 2012.

6

1 Gramsci, Antonio. *Prison Notebooks*. New York: International Publishers, 1971. 324.

2 Curtis, Edward E. IV. *Black Muslim Religion in the Nation of Islam, 1960–1975*. Chapel Hill: University of North Carolina Press, 2006. 9.

3 Dallal, Ahmed. "The Origins and Objectives of Islamic Revivalist Thought, 1750–1850." *Journal of the American Oriental Society*, 113.3 (1993): 341–59.

4 Jung, Dietrich. *Orientalists, Islamists, and the Global Public Sphere: A Genealogy of the Modern Essentialist Image of Islam*. Sheffield and Oakville: Equinox, 2011. 108.

5 Josephson, Jason Ānanda. *The Invention of Religion in Japan*. Chicago and London: University of Chicago Press, 2012. 109–17.

6 Ibid, 103.

7 Ibid.

8 Ibid.

9 Ibid, 131.

10 Ibid, 8.

11 Ibid, 7.

12 Ibid, 241.

13 Snodgrass, Judith. *Presenting Japanese Buddhism to the West: Orientalism, Occidentalism, and the Columbian Exposition*. Chapel Hill: University of North Carolina Press, 2003. 116–17.

14 Jaffe, R. M. "Seeking Sakyamuni: Travel and the Reconstruction of Japanese Buddhism." *Journal of Japanese Studies*, Vol. 30, Issue 1 (2004). 65–96.

15 Ibid.

16 Snodgrass, Judith. *Presenting Japanese Buddhism to the West: Orientalism, Occidentalism, and the Columbian Exposition*. Chapel Hill: University of North Carolina Press, 2003. 5.

17 McMahen, David L. *The Making of Buddhist Modernism*. Oxford: Oxford University Press, 2008. 96–97.

18 Ibid.

19 Ibid.

20 Ibid, 18.

21 Prothero, Stephen. *White Buddhist: The Asian Odyssey of Henry Steel Olcott*. Indianapolis: Indiana University Press, 2010. 150.

22 Ibid, 151.

23 Ibid.

24 Van der Linden, Bob. *Moral Languages from Colonial Punjab*. Manohar, 2008.

25 Khan, Dominique-Sila. *Crossing the Threshhold: Understanding Religious Identities in South Asia*. London: I. B. Tauris and the Institute of Ismaili Studies, 2004. 71.

26 Ibid, 77.

27 Keddie, Nikki R. *Sayyid Jamal ad-Din "Al-Afghani": A Political Biography* Berkeley and Los Angeles: University of California Press, 1972. 16–18.

28 Ibid, 38.

29 Ibid, 86.

30 Ibid, 141.

31 Ibid, 95.

32 Sedgwick, Mark. *Muhammad 'Abduh (Makers of the Muslim World)*. Oxford: Oneworld Publications, 2009. 41.

33 Keddie, Nikki R. *Sayyid Jamal ad-Din "Al-Afghani": A Political Biography*. Berkeley and Los Angeles: University of California Press, 1972. 192–93.

34 Ibid, 83.

35 Ibid.

36 Sedgwick, Mark. *Muhammad 'Abduh (Makers of the Muslim World)*. Oxford: Oneworld Publications, 2009. 10–11.

37 Keddie, Nikki R. *Sayyid Jamal ad-Din "Al-Afghani": A Political Biography*. Berkeley and Los Angeles: University of California Press, 1972. 84.

38 Sedgwick, Mark. *Muhammad 'Abduh (Makers of the Muslim World)*. Oxford: Oneworld Publications, 2009.

39 Ibid, 86–87.

40 Escovitz, Joseph H. "He Was the Muhammad Abduh of Syria: A Study of Tahir al-Jaza'iri and His Influence." *International Journal of Middle East Studies*. 18.3 (1986): 293–310.

41 Ibid.

42 Weismann, Itzchak. "Between Ṣūfī Reformism and Modernist Rationalism: A Reappraisal of the Origins of the Salafiyya from the Damascene Angle." *Die Welt des Islams*. 41.2 (2001): 206–237.

43 Ibid.

44 Ibid.

45 Escovitz, Joseph H. "He Was the Muhammad Abduh of Syria: A Study of Tahir al-Jaza'iri and His Influence." *International Journal of Middle East Studies*. 18.3 (1986): 293–310.

46 Ibid.

47 Ibid.

48 Commins, David. "Religious Reformers and Arabists in Damascus, 1885–1914." *International Journal of Middle East Studies*. 18.4 (1986): 405–25.

49 Ibid.

50 Escovitz, Joseph H. "He Was the Muhammad Abduh of Syria: A Study of Tahir al-Jaza'iri and His Influence." *International Journal of Middle East Studies*. 18.3 (1986): 293–310.

51 Ibid.

52 Lauzière, Henri. "The Construction of Salafiyya: Reconsidering Salafism from the Perspective of Conceptual History." *International Journal of Middle East Studies*. 42. (2010): 369–89.

53 Weismann, Itzchak. "Between Ṣūfī Reformism and Modernist Rationalism: A Reappraisal of the Origins of the Salafiyya from the Damascene Angle." *Die Welt des Islams*. 41.2 (2001): 206–237.

54 Ibid.

55 Ibid.

56 Commins, David. *Islamic Reform: Politics and Social Change in Late Ottoman Syria*. New York: Oxford University Press, 1990. 130.

57 Ibid, 45.

58 Ibid, 54.

59 Ibid, 55–59.

60 Ibid.

61 Ibid.

62 Kurzman, Charles. *Modernist Islam, 1840–1940: A Sourcebook*. Oxford: Oxford University Press, 2002. 152–57.

63 Ibid.

64 Ibid.

65 Tauber, Eliezer. "Three Approaches, One Idea: Religion and State in the Thought of 'Abd al-Rahman al-Kawakibi, Najib 'Azuri and Rashid Rida." *British Journal of Middle Eastern Studies*. 21.2 (1994): 190–98.

66 Ardic, Nurullah. "Genealogy or Asabiyya? Ibn Khaldun between Arab Nationalism and the Ottoman Caliphate." *Journal of Near Eastern Studies*. 71.2 (2012): 315–24.

67 Ibid.

68 Ibid.

69 Tauber, Eliezer. "Three Approaches, One Idea: Religion and State in the Thought of 'Abd al-Rahman al-Kawakibi, Najib 'Azuri and Rashid Rida." *British Journal of Middle Eastern Studies*. 21.2 (1994): 190–98.

70 Ibid.

71 Commins, David. "Wahhabis, Sufis, and Salafis in Early Twentieth Century Damascus." In Meir Hatina, ed. *Guardians of Faith in Modern Times: 'Ulama' in the Middle East*. Leiden: Brill, 2009. 231–46.

72 Commins, David. *Islamic Reform: Politics and Social Change in Late Ottoman Syria*. New York: Oxford University Press, 1990. 63–64.

73 Ibid.

74 Ibid.

75 Ibid, 109.

76 Commins, David. "Religious Reformers and Arabists in Damascus, 1885–1914." *International Journal of Middle East Studies*. 18.4 (1986): 405–25.

77 Ibid.

78 Ibid.

79 Weismann, Itzchak. "Between Ṣufī Reformism and Modernist Rationalism: A Reappraisal of the Origins of the Salafiyya from the Damascene Angle." *Die Welt des Islams*. 41.2 (2001): 206–37.

80 Commins, David. *Islamic Reform: Politics and Social Change in Late Ottoman Syria*. New York: Oxford University Press, 1990. 130.

81 Tauber, Eliezer. "Three Approaches, One Idea: Religion and State in the Thought of 'Abd al-Rahman al-Kawakibi, Najib 'Azuri and Rashid Rida." *British Journal of Middle Eastern Studies*. 21.2 (1994): 190–98.

82 Escovitz, Joseph H. "Orientalists and Orientalism in the Writings of Muhammad Kurd Ali." *International Journal of Middle East Studies*. 15.1 (1983): 95–109.

83 Commins, David. "Religious Reformers and Arabists in Damascus, 1885–1914." *International Journal of Middle East Studies*. 18.4 (1986): 405–25.

84 Ibid.

85 Lauzière, Henri. "The Construction of Salafiyya: Reconsidering Salafism from the Perspective of Conceptual History." *International Journal of Middle East Studies*. 42 (2010): 369–89.

86 Ibid.

87 Ibid.

88 Ibid.

89 Ibid.

90 Ibid.

91 Ibid.

92 Ibid.

93 Ibid.

94 Ibid.

95 Dallal, Ahmad. "Appropriating the Past: Twentieth-Century Reconstruction of Pre-Modern Islamic Thought." *Islamic Law and Society*. 7.3 (2000): 325–58.

96 Ibid.

97 Kramer, Gudrun. *Hasan al-Banna*. Oxford: Oneworld, 2010. 23–24.

98 Ibid.

99 Ibid, 30.

100 Ibid, 44.

101 Zaman, Muhammad Qasim. *The Ulama in Contemporary Islam: Custodians of Change*. Princeton: Princeton University Press, 2002.

102 Qara'āwī, 30.

103 Cairo University, 141.

104 Lacroix, Stephane. "Between Revolution and Apoliticism: Nasir al-Din al-Albani and his Impact on the Shaping of Contemporary Salafism." In Roel Meijer, ed. *Global Salafism: Islam's New Religious Movement*. New York: Columbia University Press, 2009. 58–80.

105 Marable, Manning. *Malcolm X: A Life of Reinvention*. New York: Viking, 2011. 368.

106 Ibid, 368.

107 Ibid, 369.

108 Wilson, Peter Lamborn. *Sacred Drift: Essays on the Margins of Islam*. San Francisco: City Lights Books, 1993. 15–16.

109 Knight, Michael Muhammad. *Why I Am a Five Percenter*. New York: Tarcher/Penguin, 2011.

110 Elmasry, Shadee. "The Salafis in America: The Rise, Decline and Prospects for a Sunni Muslim Movement among African-Americans." *Journal of Muslim Minority Affairs*, Vol. 30, No. 2 (June 2010). 217–236.

7

1 Bhaba, Homi K. "Unpacking my Library . . . Again." In Iain Chambers and Lidia Curti, eds. *The Postcolonial Question: Common Skies, Divided Horizons*. New York: Routledge, 2002. 199–211.

2 McLuhan, Marshall. "Address at Vision 65," *The American Scholar*. Vol. 35, No. 2 (spring 1966). 196–205.

3 X, Malcolm, and Alex Haley. *The Autobiography of Malcolm X*. New York: Ballantine, 1989.

4 Lewis Lord, Jeannye Thornton, and Alejandro Bodipo-Memba, "The Legacy of Malcolm X." *U.S. News and World Report*, November 15, 1992.

5 X, Malcolm, and Alex Haley. *The Autobiography of Malcolm X*. New York: Ballantine, 1989. 177–78.

6 Ibid, 184–85.

7 Ibid, 183.

8 Ibid, 306.

9 Ibid, 350.

10 Durant, Will. *Our Oriental Heritage*. New York: Simon and Schuster, 1935.

11 Ali, Abdullah Yusuf. *The Meanings of the Holy Qur'ān*. Amana Publications, 1989.

12 Ibid, 9:31 n.1287.

13 Ibid, n.675 (4:171).

14 Ibid, 413 [appendix V].

15 Ibid, note 457.

16 Abdalati, Hammudah. *Islam in Focus*. World Assembly of Muslim Youth (WAMY), Riyadh.

17 Ibid, back cover.

18 Ibid, xv.

19 Ibid, 113.

20 Ibid, 107.

21 Ibid, 108.

22 Ibid, 19.

23 Ibid, 25.

24 Ibid, 54.

25 Ibid, 112.

26 Ibid, 109.

27 Ibid, 116.

28 Ibid, 184.

29 Ibid, 111.

30 Ibid, 64.

31 Ibid, 56.

32 Ibid.

33 Ibid, 61.

34 Smith, Huston. *The Religions of Man*. New York: HarperCollins, 1965.

35 Ibid, 209.

36 Ibid, 220.

37 Ibid.

38 Khomeini, Ayatollah Ruhollah. *Islamic Government*. Manor Books, 1979.

39 Ibid.

40 Ibid, back cover.

41 Ibid, 6.

42 Ibid, 8.

43 Ibid, 5.

44 Ibid, 11.

45 Ibid, 8.

46 X, Malcolm, and Alex Haley. *The Autobiography of Malcolm X*. New York: Ballantine, 1989. 165.

47 M. Tariq Quraishi, ed. *Some Aspects of Prophet Muhammad's Life*. Indianapolis: American Trust Publications, 1983.

48 M. Tariq Quraishi, "The First Word." In M. Tariq Quraishi, ed. *Some Aspects of Prophet Muhammad's Life*. Indianapolis: American Trust Publications, 1983. 7–10.

49 Ibid.

50 Mustapha al-Azami, "The Authenticity of the Sunnah." Ibid, 26–33.

51 Ibid.

52 Ibid.

53 Ahmed Elkadi, "Muhammad as Family Man." Ibid, 59–71.

54 Ibid.

55 Ibid.

56 Ghulam Sarwar, *Islam: Beliefs and Teachings*. Islamabad: Dawah Academy, International Islamic University, 1992.

57 Ibid, 13–14.

58 Ibid, 73.

59 Ibid, 74.

60 Ibid, 75.

61 Ibid, 173.

62 Ibid, 177.

63 Ibid, 166.

64 Ibid, 167.

65 Ibid.

66 Ibid, 168.

67 Ibid, 169.

68 Ibid.

69 Ibid, 172.

70 Ibid, 203.

71 Ibid.

72 Ibid.

73 Muhammed Shafiq, *Growth of Islamic Thought in North America: Focus on Isma'il Raji al-Faruqi*. Brentwood: Amana Publications, 1994.

74 Ibid, 9–10.

75 Ibid, 72–83.

76 Ibid, 87.

77 Ibid, 109.

78 David Westerlund, "Ahmed Deedat's Theory of Religion: Apologetics Through Polemics," *Journal of Religion in Africa*, Vol. 33, Fasc. 3 (Aug 2003), 263–78.

79 Hart, Michael. *The 100: A Ranking of the Most Influential Persons in History*. Hart Publishing Company, 1978. 3.

80 Larkin, Brian. "Ahmed Deedat and the Form of Islamic Evangelism." *Social Text 96*, Vol. 26, No. 3 (Fall 2008), 101–21.

81 Qutb, Sayyid. *In the Shade of the Qur'an*. Riyadh: World Assembly of Muslim Youth, 1985.

82 Ibid, xi.

83 Ibid, xii.

84 Ibid.

85 Ibid, xiii.

86 Ibid, 3.

87 Ibid.

88 Ibid.

89 Ibid, 123.

90 Ibid, 125.

91 Ibid.

92 Ibid, 126.

93 Ibid, 126–27.

94 Ibid, 360.

8

1 Derrida, Jacques. Barbara Johnson, trans. *Dissemination*. Chicago: University of Chicago Press, 1983. 143.

2 Qasmi, Ali Usman. *Questioning the Authority of the Past: The Ahl al-Qur'an Movements in the Punjab*. Oxford: Oxford University Press, 2012. 72.

3 Ibid, 71.

4 Ibid, 67.

5 Ibid, 62.

6 Brown, Daniel W. *Rethinking Tradition in Modern Islamic Thought*. Cambridge: Cambridge University Press, 1999. 32–36.

7 Schimmel, Annemarie. *And Muhammad Is His Messenger: The Veneration of the Prophet in Islamic Piety*. Chapel Hill: University of North Carolina Press, 1985. 230–31.

8 Ibid, 232.

9 Qasmi, Ali Usman. *Questioning the Authority of the Past: The Ahl al-Qur'an Movements in the Punjab*. Oxford: Oxford University Press, 2012. 116.

10 Ibid, 114.

11 Ibid, 121.

12 Ibid, 157.

13 Kurzman, Charles. *Modernist Islam, 1840–1940: A Sourcebook*. Oxford: Oxford University Press, 2002. 277–90.

14 Ibid.

15 Ibid.

16 Qasmi, Ali Usman. *Questioning the Authority of the Past: The Ahl al-Qur'an Movements in the Punjab*. Oxford: Oxford University Press, 2012. 133.

17 Ibid, 168.

18 Ibid, 176.

19 Jung, Dietrich. *Orientalists, Islamists, and the Global Public Sphere: A Genealogy of the Modern Essentialist Image of Islam*. Sheffield and Oakville: Equinox, 2011. 180.

20 Ibid, 159.

21 Brown, Daniel W. *Rethinking Tradition in Modern Islamic Thought*. Cambridge: Cambridge University Press, 1999. 37.

22 Ibid.

23 Ibid, 40–41.

24 Musa, Aisha. *Ḥadīth as Scripture: Discussions on the Authority of Prophetic Traditions in Islam*. New York: Palgrave Macmillan, 2008. 87.

25 Ibid, 86–87.

26 Kurzman, Charles. *Modernist Islam, 1840–1940: A Sourcebook*. Oxford: Oxford University Press, 2002. 152–57.

27 Musa, Aisha. *Ḥadīth as Scripture: Discussions on the Authority of Prophetic Traditions in Islam*. New York: Palgrave Macmillan, 2008. 84–85.

28 Ibid, 86.

29 Ibid, 80.

30 Mattson, Ingrid. *The Story of the Qur'an: Its History and Place in Muslim Life*. Oxford: Wiley-Blackwell, 2007. 126–27.

31 "The *Muṣḥaf al-Madīna* and the King Fahd Holy Qur'an Printing Complex." *Journal of Qur'anic Studies*, Vol. 1, No. 1 (1999). 155–58.

32 Mir, Mustansir. "The Sūra as a Unity: A Twentieth Century Development in Qur'ān Exegesis." In G. R. Hawting and A. K. A. Shareef, eds. *Approaches to the Qur'ān* New York: Routledge, 1993. 211–24.

33 Rahman, Fazlur (Ebrahim Moosa, ed.) *Revival and Reform in Islam*. Oxford: Oneworld Publications, 2000. 257.

34 Moosa, Ebrahim. "Introduction." Ibid. *Revival and Reform in Islam*. Oxford: Oneworld Publications, 2000.

35 Ibid.

36 Rahman, Fazlur. *Major Themes of the Qur'an*. Chicago: University of Chicago Press, 2009. 2nd ed. 48.

37 Hammer, Juliane. *American Muslim Women, Religious Authority, and Activism: More Than a Prayer*. Austin: University of Texas Press, 2013. 69.

38 Spellberg, D.A. *Politics, Gender, and the Islamic Past: the Legacy of 'A'isha bint Abi Bakr*. New York: Columbia University Press, 1994.

39 Moosa, Ebrahim. "The Debts and Burdens of Critical Islam." In Omid Safi, ed. *Progressive Muslims: On Justice, Gender, and Pluralism*. Oxford: Oneworld, 2003. 111–27.

40 Wadud, Amina. *Inside the Gender Jihad*. Oxford: Oneworld Publications, 2006.

41 Mahmood, Sabah. "Secularism, Hermeneutics, and Empire: The Politics of Islamic Reformation." *Public Culture*, Vol. 18, No. 2 (2006). 323–47.

42 Ibid.

43 Ibid.

44 McCarthy, R. J. *Freedom and Fulfillment: Al-Ghazali's Munqidh min al-Dalal*. Boston: Twayne, 1980. 185.

45 Wadud, Amina. *Inside the Gender Jihad*. Oxford: Oneworld Publications, 2006. 200.

46 Ibid, 204.

47 Chaudhry, Ayesha. *Domestic Violence and the Islamic Tradition*. Oxford: Oxford University Press, 2014.

48 Hidayatullah, Aysha. *Feminist Edges of the Qur'an*. Oxford: Oxford University Press, 2014. 178.

49 Berg, Herbert. *Elijah Muhammad and Islam*. New York: New York University Press, 2009. 124.

50 Eagleton, Terry. *Literary Theory: An Introduction*. Minneapolis: University of Minnesota Press, 2008. 74.

51 Wadud, Amina. *Inside the Gender Jihad*. Oxford: Oneworld Publications, 2006. 201.

52 Sands, Kristin. *Sufi Commentaries on the Qur'ān in Classical Islam*. London: Routledge, 2006. 48.

53 Shaikh, Sa'diyya. *Sufi Narratives of Intimacy: Ibn 'Arabi, Gender, and Sexuality*. Chapel Hill: University of North Carolina Press, 2012. 2.

54 Gumbrecht, Hans Ulrich. *Production of Presence: What Meaning Cannot Convey*. Stanford: Stanford University Press, 2004. 109.

55 Kittler, Friedrich. *Optical Media*. Cambridge: Polity Press, 2010. 35.

56 Douglas, Susan J. *Listening In: Radio and the American Imagination*. Minneapolis: University of Minnesota Press, 2004. 7.

57 Kermani, Navid. "Revelation in its Aesthetic Dimension: Some Notes about Apostles and Artists in Islamic and Christian Culture." In Stefan Wild, ed. *The Qur'ān as Text*. Leiden: Brill, 1995. 213–224.

58 Guo, Li. *Commerce, Culture, and Community in a Red Sea Port in the Thirteenth Century: The Arabic Documents from Quseir*. Leiden: Brill, 2004. 75.

9

1 Butler, Octavia. *Parable of the Sower*. Grand Central Publishing, 2000.

2 Brown, Jonathan A. C. "How We Know Early Ḥadīth Critics Did *Matn* Criticism and Why It's so Hard to Find." *Islamic Law and Society* 15:2 (2008), 143–84.

3 Dickinson, Eerik. *The Development of Early Sunnite Ḥadīth Criticism: The Taqdima of Ibn Abī ḥātim al-Rāzī (240/854-327/938)*. Leiden: Brill, 2001.

4 Bürger, Christa. "The Reality of 'Machines': Notes on the Rhizome-Thinking of Deleuze and Guattari." *Telos* 64 (1985), 33–44.

5 Deleuze, Gilles, and Felix Guattari. Brian Massumi, trans. *A Thousand Plateaus: Capitalism and Schizophrenia*. Minneapolis: University of Minnesota Press, 1987. 3–25.

6 Ibid.

7 Ibid.

8 Zaheer Ali's presentation on his "Malcolm X Mixtape Project" at the Duke-UNC "Legacy of Malcolm X" conference, February 20, 2015.

9 Dannin, Robert. *Black Pilgrimage to Islam*. Oxford: Oxford University Press, 2005. 39.

10 Nance, Susan. "Respectability and Representation: The Moorish Science Temple, Morocco, and Black Public Culture in 1920s Chicago." *American Quarterly*, Vol. 54, No. 4 (December 2002). 623–59.

11 Dannin, Robert. *Black Pilgrimage to Islam*. Oxford: Oxford University Press, 2005. 39.

12 Ibid.

13 Hakim, Jameela A. *History of the First Muslim Mosque of Pittsburgh, Pennsylvania*. Pittsburgh: Igram Press, 1979.

14 Bowen, Patrick D. "Notes on the MSTA Schisms in Detroit and Pittsburgh, 1928–29." Printed for the East Coast Moorish Men's Brotherhood Summit, Baltimore, MD. March 29–31, 2013.

15 Ibid.

16 Dannin, Robert. *Black Pilgrimage to Islam*. Oxford: Oxford University Press, 2005. 39, 99.

17 Hakim, Jameela A. *History of the First Muslim Mosque of Pittsburgh, Pennsylvania*. Pittsburgh: Igram Press, 1979.

18 Dannin, Robert. *Black Pilgrimage to Islam*. Oxford: Oxford University Press, 2005. 34.

19 Nash, M. Naeem. "Ezaldeen, Muhammad." In Curtis, Edward E., IV, ed. *Encyclopedia of Muslim-American History*. New York: Facts On File, Inc., 2010. *American History Online*. Facts On File, Inc. http://www.fofweb.com/activelink2.

asp?ItemID=WE52&iPin=EMAH0092&SingleRecord=True (accessed June 19, 2014).

20 Dannin, Robert. *Black Pilgrimage to Islam*. Oxford: Oxford University Press, 2005. 34.

21 http://www.firstmuslimmosque.com/about.html.

22 Abd-Allah, Umar F. *A Muslim in Victorian America*. Oxford: Oxford University Press, 2006. 274.

23 Halevi, Leor. *Muhammad's Grave: Death Rites and the Making of Islamic Society*. New York: Columbia University, 2007. 192–95.

24 Maag, Christopher. "Young Muslims Build a Subculture on an Underground Book." *New York Times*. December 22, 2008.

25 Hidayatullah, Ayesha, and Taymiya Zaman, "Speaking for Ourselves: Muslim Women's Confessional Writings and the Problem of Alterity." *Journal for Islamic Studies*, Vol. 33 (2013).

26 Ibid.

27 "I've Been a Muslim for 3 Years Today." http://whitemansturban.wordpress.com. June 10, 2014.

28 Wilson, Jeff. *Mindful America: The Mutual Transformation of Buddhist Meditation and American Culture*. Oxford: Oxford University Press, 2014.

ACKNOWLEDGMENTS

FIRST AND ALWAYS, gratitude to my mom and to Sadaf.

I cannot express the appreciation that I have for a place like Counterpoint where I can do this kind of work. Peace and thanks to Rolph Blythe, Matthew Hoover, Claire Shalinksy, and everyone at Counterpoint who made this book possible. With respect for the incredible cover art, please explore the work of the FADED ART LORD, Rob Regis.

Again, endless thanks to Allison Cohen at Gersh Agency for her insight and advocacy.

Peace to my mentors, colleagues, and conversation partners at UNC Chapel Hill. Give them some credit if I have shown any growth since coming here, and don't blame them for moments when the punk reappears. And peace to the UNC Muslim Students Association for so much more than simply providing a place to pray after drug trips. Our encounters in the past year have been personally and professionally transformative for how I see myself in relation both to Muslim communities and academic institutions. Thank you.

INDEX